The Fixers

The Fixers

Local News Workers and the Underground Labor of International Reporting

LINDSAY PALMER

OXFORD
UNIVERSITY PRESS

OXFORD
UNIVERSITY PRESS

Oxford University Press is a department of the University of Oxford. It furthers
the University's objective of excellence in research, scholarship, and education
by publishing worldwide. Oxford is a registered trade mark of Oxford University
Press in the UK and certain other countries.

Published in the United States of America by Oxford University Press
198 Madison Avenue, New York, NY 10016, United States of America.

© Oxford University Press 2019

Library of Congress Cataloging-in-Publication Data
Names: Palmer, Lindsay, author.
Title: The fixers : local news workers and the underground labor of
international reporting / Lindsay Palmer.
Description: New York, NY : Oxford University Press, [2019] |
Includes bibliographical references.
Identifiers: LCCN 2018053719 | ISBN 9780190680824 (hardcover : alk. paper) |
ISBN 9780190680831 (Universal PDF) | ISBN 9780190680848 (electronic publication) |
ISBN 9780190680855 (Oxford Scholarship Online)
Subjects: LCSH: Foreign news. | Reporters and reporting. |
Translating and interpreting.
Classification: LCC PN4784.F6 P38 2019 | DDC 070.4/

1 3 5 7 9 8 6 4 2

Printed by Sheridan Books, Inc., United States of America

Contents

Acknowledgments

THIS BOOK COULD not have been written without the help and encouragement of so many people. But first, I have to thank the people who took the time to share their opinions and experiences with me: the news "fixers." Though their time was limited and valuable, these media professionals still chose to set some of this time aside to answer my questions and to recommend other journalists and locally based news staff for me to interview. For this, I would like to thank them.

Next, I have to thank my incredibly supportive colleagues in the School of Journalism and Mass Communication at the University of Wisconsin-Madison: Hemant Shah, Mike Wagner, Dhavan Shah, Hernando Rojas, Sue Robinson, Karyn Riddle, Doug McLeod, Kathryn McGarr, Young Mie Kim, Lucas Graves, Lew Friedland, Greg Downey, Katy Culver, Kate Christy, and Chris Cascio. I also need to thank my UW-Madison colleague Jennifer Gaddis, for countless "writing dates" and for some much-needed moral support! I am very lucky to have colleagues like these, and I have greatly benefited from their advice, feedback, and general encouragement throughout the process of writing this book.

A number of other amazing scholars have also offered their feedback and support as I worked on this research project. In this spirit, I'd especially like to thank Jad Melki, Lisa Hajjar, Lisa Parks, Danny Grinberg, Herman Wasserman, Howard Tumber, Chris Paterson, Mel Bunce, Soomin Seo, Kenneth Andresen, Colleen Murrell, Saumava Mitra, Kate Wright, Matthew Powers, Nikki Usher, Bhaskar Sarkar, Michael Curtin, Linda Steiner, and Barbie Zelizer.

The graduate students who took my 2015 research seminar on war and journalism provided valuable insights throughout the class, but most particularly in the weeks when we discussed news fixers and local producers. Through that class, along with other graduate seminars I taught in following years, I was lucky enough to hire some remarkable graduate student researchers: Alicia Wright, Lisa Speckhard, and Shezad Baloch. Thanks to each of you for transcribing all that material and for sharing your thoughts on the broader project!

Special thanks to my original editor on the project, Hallie Stebbins, and also to Holly Mitchell who took up the project when Hallie took a new position. You were both very patient with me, and I can't tell you how much I appreciate it!

Finally, I would like to thank my family for their tireless enthusiasm about my work. Yonnie Palmer, John Palmer, Katie Palmer, Josh Palmer, Pat Palmer, and Teresa Williams: I affirm you! Thanks for affirming me, throughout all these years. And to Jeff Shaffer, the love of my life, I give the most thanks of all. You and our precious sons, Cade and Cameron, have made my life so much more meaningful than it ever would have been without you.

Author's note: Some of the material in this book builds off of insights first formulated in the following publications: Palmer and Melki, "Shape Shifting in the Conflict Zone," *Journalism Studies*, 2016; Palmer, "Being the Bridge," *Journalism*, 2016; Palmer, *Becoming the Story: War Correspondents Since 9/11*, Champaign: U of Illinois P, 2018.

1

Introduction

DEFINING THE LABOR: WHAT DO NEWS FIXERS DO?

WHEN BARACK OBAMA visited Kenya in the summer of 2015, his internationally recognizable face lit up television and smartphone screens around the world. News organizations as diverse as Al Jazeera, China Central Television, Russia Today, the *Guardian*, the *New York Times*, CNN, and the BBC all ran stories about Obama's journey to his "ancestral home," transforming a diplomatic excursion into a media spectacle. As news audiences in a multitude of geopolitical regions were deluged with the sparkling photographs and videos of Obama smiling kindly into the crowds and publicly embracing his sister Auma, a much more harried process unfolded off-screen. Newsrooms on multiple continents buzzed with ringing phones, clacking keyboards, and editors issuing commands to people located thousands of miles away. On the other end of the editors' phone calls, journalists scribbled notes, listening to their bosses with one ear and to Obama's speech with the other. In the July air of Kenya's "cool season," they worked to capture Obama's words and transform those words into a global story.

Just off to the side, stood the journalists' "fixers." These locally based media workers helped the reporters arrange interviews, interpret unfamiliar languages, and navigate challenging geographical and cultural terrain. Most of the people watching Obama address Kenya's citizens likely did not even know that fixers existed, let alone that they were vital to the coverage they were seeing on their screens. But despite their relative invisibility, media workers, like Immanuel Muasya, held this global story on their shoulders. During Obama's visit, Muasya spent his days arranging logistics for the slew of different dignitaries who would appear in the journalists' news coverage, even finding a light source for an angry technician when the power suddenly went out (Muasya, pers. comm., May 2016). If the visiting journalists had questions about how to get around Nairobi or the best (and safest) places to shoot video, Muasya was the one to ask. Without media employees like Muasya, many visiting journalists would not have been able to adequately cover Obama's visit to Kenya, especially since some of these correspondents had only just "parachuted" into Nairobi a few days before. In this sense, the global story of Obama's visit to Kenya was shadowed by another set of stories—those of the news fixers who make foreign reporting possible.

This book is about these resourceful media workers who are vital to the profession of international journalism. The term "fixer" refers to the locally based interpreters and guides who journalists hire to help them cover international news. Some of these media employees embrace the term "fixer," taking pride in their role in "fixing" tough problems. Others dislike the term because of its association with unskilled labor, and because of the industrial tendency to subtly or not so subtly separate the foreign correspondents' ostensibly more "professional" role from that of their purportedly less-professional fixers. I will retain the term "fixer" throughout this book because of its international recognizability. The word has come to signify a liminal figure, one who stands at the crossroads between regional ways of life and "foreign" news agendas. However, I use the term cautiously and critically because of the fact that fixers have traditionally been rendered invisible by professional news industries— often due to the very assignation of that term.

When I say that news fixers have been rendered invisible, I seek to illuminate the fact that these important media employees rarely receive official credit for their work. They have historically struggled to get bylines or even contributing credits in print news coverage, and their faces do not typically appear in the video news reports that they help create. Instead, news audiences are invited to focus more on the foreign correspondents whose faces appear onscreen and whose names adorn the text-based stories associated with major newspapers. Though this problem has slowly been changing, news fixers suggest that their work is still mostly relegated to the shadows of the international news industry.

What is more, news fixers are rarely discussed in the academic research on international journalism. There does exist a rich and robust scholarly literature on international news and, especially, on foreign correspondence. This literature has outlined the broader structures of the international news industries (Boyd-Barrett 1980; Boyd-Barrett and Rantanen 1998; Paterson and Sreberny 2004; Williams 2011), the history of foreign reporting (Knightley 2004; Hamilton 2011; Broussard 2013), the coverage produced by war reporters (Hallin 1986; Kellner 1992, 2003), the daily routines and longer term working practices of international journalists (Pedelty 1995; Hannerz 2004), the unique challenges of local photojournalists working with international news brands (Mitra 2017), and the various challenges faced by international correspondents in the 21st century (Zelizer and Allan 2002; Allan and Zelizer 2004; Tumber and Webster 2006; Matheson and Allan 2009; Paterson 2014; Cottle, Sambrook, and Mosdell 2016; Armoudian 2017; Palmer 2018). Without this research, there would be no foundation on which to build a much-needed scholarly discussion of news fixers' labor.

Yet, only a handful of studies have directly addressed news fixers. Some of the scholarship on foreign reporting has certainly referenced the existence of the "foreign nationals" who are "another increasingly relied upon means to cover events overseas" (Hamilton and Jenner 2004, 313). Other research has shown that there is an industrial hierarchy in professions like war reporting, with Mark Pedelty most directly pointing out the hierarchical distinction between foreign correspondents and local freelance journalists or stringers who worked together in El Salvador at the end of the 20th century (1995). More recent research has done the important work of illuminating this same hierarchical relationship between international correspondents and local hires who collaborate at the bureaus of major news agencies (Bunce 2010, 2011; Dell'Orto 2016; Seo 2016). These studies focus on particular news organizations or on particular regions, aiming for a deeper, rather than a broader approach to the question of the "local hire," and include local journalists, freelancers, and stringers in that category.

But the work of news "fixing" is not quite the same thing as the work of being a local stringer or staff reporter. Though the same person can (and often does) play the role of "journalist," "stringer," or "fixer" depending on the assignment, when that person wears a fixer's hat, he or she typically does not write or visually appear in the final news story. Unlike stringers (that is, freelancers who do tend to write stories or sometimes appear in video reports), fixers are overwhelmingly expected to do everything except this final task. And because they are almost never perceived as having written the story, they also rarely receive a byline or an on-camera mention. For this reason, I contend that the work of news fixing deserves its own extended scholarly study.

Some research on international reporting has compellingly mentioned the specific logistical tasks that fixers complete, the dangers they face in the field, or fixers' roles in constructing the journalist's understanding of a particular news event (Hannerz 2004; Tumber and Webster 2006; Paterson, Andresen, and Hoxha 2011; Cottle, Sambrook, and Mosdell 2016; Armoudian 2017).

This scholarship is crucial, in that it brings attention to news fixers and takes the time to outline a few of the things that fixers actually do. However, this research does not focus solely on the figure of the fixer but instead examines a number of factors involved in the broader profession of international reporting. There is a much shorter list of groundbreaking academic studies that do take the role of the fixer as their central object of focus. While these studies are essential reading for anyone who wants to learn more about fixers, it should be noted that they tend to foreground the perspectives of international journalists rather than the perspectives of fixers (Palmer and Fontan 2007; Murrell 2010, 2013, 2015).

My book is indebted to this prior research. I hope to contribute to this productive conversation by focusing on news fixers' perspectives on the work that they do. Following the call of critical media scholars who argue that academics and communications industry practitioners based most especially in the Anglophone West need to engage with more diverse cultural perspectives and participate in more productive and egalitarian cross-cultural dialogue (Shome and Hegde 2002; Wasserman 2011; Rao and Wasserman 2015), this book seeks to examine some perspectives that have long been ignored. Drawing upon in-depth, qualitative interviews with 75 news fixers working in 39 different countries, I hope to show that fixers from diverse regions of the world have some important viewpoints in common. They also have some very different stories to tell than perhaps we are used to hearing.

The concept of "story" will surface throughout this book, not only in terms of the news story itself, but also in terms of fixers' stories about their professions. I am inspired by the critical film and media scholar John Caldwell's observation that media workers' professional narratives are creative constructions of particular realities, constructions that can illuminate the contradictions entangled within the broader media industries (2008). Indeed, the scholarship found in the field of critical-cultural media production studies has deeply influenced my approach to studying news fixers' perspectives on their work. This is because the field of critical production studies "examines specific sites and fabrics of media production as distinct interpretative communities" as well as emphasizes the "tension between individuals' agency and the social conditions within which agency is embedded" (Banks, Conor, and Mayer 2016, x). By focusing on news fixers as members of "distinct interpretive communities," I follow critical production scholars in their efforts at investigating "the goals of producers, in their own words," while also taking care to consider the broader economic, industrial, and cultural constraints that help to shape these words in the first place (2016, xi).

My intention in this book is to maintain an analytical, interpretive stance, while at the same time, ensuring that scholars, students, and journalists get the chance to hear a set of perspectives that have long been ignored. This is not an easy strategy, and it will certainly result in an interpretation of news fixers' stories that sometimes diverges from those fixers' own interpretations. At other times, this strategy might result in an interpretation that diverges unsettlingly from the more familiar understandings of journalistic practice found in the field of journalism studies—perhaps most especially where the concepts of objectivity and safety are concerned. But in taking this approach, I echo the strategies of critical production scholars who want to "challenge the 'overdetermined cultural mystique' that assigns media industries such authority over their own processes" (Banks, Conor, and Mayer 2016, xiv). I believe that one way of challenging this mystique is "to build bridges with other workers, whether deemed 'creative' or not, 'artistic' or not, 'professional' or not" (Banks, Conor, and Mayer 2016, xiv.).

I explore news fixers' production narratives in hopes of gaining a more nuanced perspective on the news reporting that crosses geopolitical borders. In order to properly analyze these production narratives, I also draw upon the interrelated theoretical frameworks found in postcolonial theory, critical global studies, and global media ethics. Postcolonial theory has long explored the complex cultural performances in which colonized peoples have engaged in order to destabilize the dominance of the world's various colonizers (Bhabha 1994; Spoturno 2014). Yet, at the same time, postcolonial criticism has also worked to highlight the deep structural constraints that continue to limit the agency of people living in postcolonial states (Said 1978; Spivak 1999). News fixers working in former colonial regions certainly face this fluctuation between agency and constraint. They constantly draw upon cultural performances in order to navigate the structural constraints of the news outlets that hire them. They also negotiate the perpetual imposition of certain (reductive) identities upon themselves.

Postcolonial theory is most helpful to my analysis of news fixers who work in postcolonial states and who collaborate with journalists based in places like Britain or Western Europe. Many of the fixers with whom I have spoken allude to the insidious ways in which the logic of colonialism continues to haunt their lives in the 21st century, especially in their dealings with white, "Western" journalists or with news sources, both of whom might try to dominate or dismiss the fixers along ethnic or racialized lines. But it is important to note that fixers also work in places like the United States or in regions of the world where British or Western European colonialism may not have made such an obvious mark. Fixers also do not always work with British, Western European, or—with an eye toward the "neocolonialism" of the 21st century (Shome and Hegde 2002; Nayar 2016)—US journalists. And even those news fixers working in regions that were formerly colonized by European or British powers might be "foreigners" in those regions, expatriates from the places where their clients are based. As this book will show, fixers destabilize the self-evidence of cultural identity by virtue of their liminal positions. Because of this, it is necessary to move past simplistic notions of "East" vs. "West," and "colonizer" vs. "colonized," when examining the labor of news fixing in the 21st century.

There is a sense in some scholarship that postcolonial studies has moved past these binaries and into "an emphasis on exchanges, links, hybridities" (Nayar 2016, 2). This is something that more recent postcolonial scholarship arguably has in common with critical global studies, though the field of global studies is still often understood as addressing the present more than the imperial past (Krishnaswamy 2008). Though there is some truth to this claim, critical global scholars also assert that their work "acknowledge[s] the historical specificity of existing social arrangements," which in turn "acknowledge[s] that the society in which we live is only one possible form of society" (Robinson 2005, 11). For these scholars, the existing global order is not only the result of European colonialism but also of US neocolonialism. What is more, in regions like China, Russia, and Turkey there are very different systems of power than those that are most often critiqued in postcolonial studies (Appelbaum and Robinson 2005; Burbank and Cooper 2014). Rather than dividing the world into "East" and "West," the goal is to understand today's globalized world in all its complexity, "viewing [globalization] from many cultural perspectives" (Juergensmeyer 2014, xvi).

But alongside the effort at better understanding today's globalized world, the field of critical global studies also aspires to achieve social justice, however impossible or utopic such an achievement may seem (Appelbaum and Robinson 2005). Scholars working in this field are not interested in the "neutrality" of the researcher but instead believe that the world is divided by the inegalitarian distribution of resources, capital, and power. I also take this view, as well as sharing critical global studies' dedication to social justice. As my interviewees' narratives will show, news organizations enjoy varying degrees of power and influence depending on where they are based in the world. What is more, the practice of international reporting is profoundly hierarchical, despite the fact that it is also, by definition, profoundly collaborative. This book seeks to illuminate the productive moments of collaboration that inform the profession of international reporting, while simultaneously exposing the inequalities that plague the profession as well.

It may come as no surprise, then, that this book is also influenced by the theoretical frameworks found in the field of global media ethics—a subfield of communication studies that not only seeks the "best practices" for media production in a global era (Ward 2013), but that also hopes to inspire more nuanced cross-cultural dialogue among media industry practitioners, students, and scholars (Wasserman 2011; Couldry 2013; Rao and Wasserman 2015). As Shakuntala Rao and Herman Wasserman explain, "Global media ethics are a response to the dilemmas of globalization and the need to address injustices that span national jurisdictions and spheres of influence" (2015, 6). Yet, they assert, "Discussions that connect media globalization to concerns of ethics and justice have remained marginal," despite their belief that "all global interactions between peoples, nations, states, and cultures must be understood in ethical terms" (2015, 4).

This is because, as Nick Couldry has observed, "A global scale implies a space of irreducible moral disagreement and diversity" (2013, 17). Despite the long-standing contention that the most powerful media organizations are homogenizing culture in a globalized world, Couldry believes that "media do not reduce or resolve such disagreement: On the contrary, they bring it into view" (2013, 17). The question for Couldry, as well as for other global media ethicists, is what do we *do* with this difference and disagreement? How do we live with it? And, more important for my purposes here, how do scholars and media producers simultaneously live under the weight of this difference while sometimes still trying to erase it or, worse, demonize it?

This leads me to the first argument I advance in this book: Scholars, students, and journalists have much to gain from carefully considering news fixers' diverse perspectives, because through these stories, a more complex picture of international reporting emerges: one that can tell us a great deal about the complexity—and slipperiness—of cultural difference in an era when international media practices and products are often understood to be more and more homogenous. Indeed, news fixers' narratives suggest that these media workers play a complicated role in bolstering some forms of cultural homogeneity while destabilizing others. In order to remain marketable, for instance, some fixers might contribute to simplistic news narratives that draw upon stock characters. Others might try to show their clients something different than their audiences have ever seen before. We need to understand fixers' perspectives, not simply because they "diversify" the field of international journalism (sometimes they do not), but instead because their professional narratives reveal the tensions between the homogenizing thrust of the capitalist system that deeply informs international news reporting in the 21st century and the stubbornness and creativeness of cultural difference that simultaneously complicates the practice of international journalism.

Fixers' cultural identities also confound any effort at drawing upon simplistic "self-other" dichotomies. These important media employees work all over the world. Their existence is not simply a product of "Western" journalists traveling to "non-Western" and, specifically, "developing" nations. Though there is undeniably a vexed history to the use of so-called native guides and interpreters in postcolonial regions (Pratt [1992] 2007; Karttunen 2000), and though some of my interviewees suggest that the racialized and ethnicized hierarchies of colonialism sometimes still resonate in the fixer-journalist relationship, news fixers cannot usually be placed into one coherent culture. Indeed, they remind us that culture is permeable and fluid rather than made up of a homogenous whole (Hall 1990; Bhabha 1994).

Some of my interviewees work in Sweden, France, Italy, and the United States, for example, and even fixers based in places that have long been "othered" in Anglophone scholarship and popular culture destabilize the pejorative stereotype of the "exotic," "native" guide—a stereotype that has all too often imposed a problematic notion of "authenticity" onto people living in the places to which journalists travel (Griffiths [1994] 2006). Most of my interviewees have received some form of higher education, have lived or traveled outside the region where they work, and have encountered different perspectives from the ones with which they were originally raised. These figures cannot be simplistically homogenized or exoticized as being fundamentally "native" or "local."

This is important to understand, especially because, at first glance, news fixers' professional narratives might seem to bolster a simplistic binary opposition between the "global" and the "local." These media workers are, after all, drawing upon regional knowledge in order to help visiting correspondents do their job. Yet, critical global studies scholars have productively complicated such simplistic binaries (Robertson [1995] 2006; Darian-Smith and McCarty 2017). As Eve Darian-Smith and Philip C. McCarty suggest, "The local and global are mutually constitutive, creating and recreating each other across conceptual fields in a constant dynamic" (2017, 4). While the nation continues to be a powerful structure in the contemporary moment, the "global" operates even at the most microcosmic levels, suggesting that the two concepts are not polar opposites (2017, 4). The labor of news fixing especially highlights the messy collision of global processes and specific cultural differences that continually impact the profession of international news reporting.

Thus, this book examines the *locally based* media workers who (1) may or may not be "native" to the places where they work but, either way, are more reflective of the permeability, rather than the unified coherence of culture, and (2) are constantly negotiating between the specificities of the region the journalists visit—specificities that are always articulated within the framework of the global—and the agendas of news organizations that are based in myriad other parts of the world. For these reasons, it is not the contention of this book that fixers should be understood as simplistically "local." Instead, I emphasize that news fixers' knowledge is often *regionally specific*, in that it is relevant to the regions where they are currently working. Even so, news fixers also work to gain knowledge of news cultures and industries that might be located at a geopolitical distance from them but that are still connected to them through the imperatives of globalization.

Just as news fixers' stories reveal that fixers are not simplistically "local," so too do their narratives suggest that neither can their clients' very different news organizations be lumped into a single "global" news industry. It is easy to confuse the promise—or the threat—of globalization with the messy reality of what globalization looks like on the ground. Over the past few decades, some scholars have suggested that journalism in general is now a global practice (Löffelholz and Weaver 2008; Berglez 2013; Ward 2013). Other scholars have instead noted that certain news organizations based in the Anglophone West are attempting to dominate and homogenize news production and content for the rest of the world (Boyd-Barrett and Rantanen 1998; Herman and McChesney 2001; Thussu 2007; Williams 2011).

It is impossible to deny that the practice of news reporting does indeed cross geopolitical borders more and more easily. It is also impossible to deny that some—mostly US or British—news organizations are more powerful than others. My interviewees' narratives indeed point to an unlevel playing field in this regard. Almost every one of my interviewees reported that they worked with one of these major "global" (but, actually, US or British) news brands at one point or another. Yet, my interviewees also rather paradoxically noted that there are thousands of news organizations telling stories at the present moment. Some of these organizations are regional, some are national, and some are transnational. While news production and consumption does increasingly cross national borders, news fixers suggest that this does not necessarily mean that all journalists now see world events from a single perspective, nor does it mean that disparate news audiences will have the same reaction to what they see on their screens.

The diverse journalists who work for these various organizations also come from particular places with specific histories, histories that affect how they understand the places they feature in their stories. What these journalists usually have in common is the fact that, due to their status as "outsiders," they need the regionally specific knowledge of a locally based fixer in order to get the job done. For this reason, I have chosen not to entirely jettison the term "foreign correspondent" in this book, despite the growing sense in some media scholarship that "foreign journalists" should now be seen as "global journalists." My interviewees suggest that cultural difference—indeed, a very real sense of "foreignness"—continues to impact many of the journalists who work internationally, however permeable and fluid culture might be (Bhabha [1988] 2006). This is one of the main reasons why the profession of news "fixing" exists.

Rather than asserting the existence of a "global" news profession, I find it more useful to think in terms of a transnationally interconnected set of news *markets,* where certain players undoubtedly possess more capital, infrastructure, and influence than others. In this economic milieu, news outlets with disparate goals and priorities might still compete for potential news audiences who watch Al Jazeera online, CNN on satellite, or a Facebook video produced by a freelance journalist in Hong Kong. Even news outlets that identify as "national" in scope may find themselves competing with international news organizations or citizen journalists for the attention of news audiences located within their own state borders. Fixers offer valuable services to news organizations based in these competing but interconnected markets, sometimes contributing to a homogenous pool of news narratives while at other times leading their clients to more nuanced angles on international news events. Both the news fixers and their clients are haphazardly bound up in the interplay between specific—and unevenly powerful—articulations of cultural identity, on the one hand, and the imperatives of an increasingly interconnected and competitive *set* of sometimes very different news markets, on the other hand.

Because of this, it is critical that scholars, students, and journalists take fixers' professional narratives seriously. These narratives reveal that the practice of international news reporting remains a site of cultural contestation, no matter how technologically, socially, and politically interconnected the world now sometimes appears. Fixers' stories also complicate the notion of culture itself in the age of globalization. This leads me to the second argument

I advance in this book: news fixers do not represent their work as being merely logistical, despite news organizations' tendency to think of fixers as passive logistical support—as the people who simply "fix" problems (Murrell 2015; Palmer 2017). Fixers also do not stop at a representation of their labor as being "editorial" in nature, despite Colleen Murrell's ground-breaking assertion that news fixers do sometimes impact the editorial elements of the story (2015). This book instead points to something else: fixers' professional narratives overwhelmingly foreground the *performative* nature of their labor, representing each task as an active effort at cultural mediation between different lived experiences of race, ethnicity, gender, sexuality, religion, politics, community, and nation.

I should take a moment to explain what I mean by "cultural mediation." News fixers are hardly the first to engage in this process. Though an exhaustive history of cultural mediation is outside the scope of this book, it should be said that for centuries, people with the proper linguistic and social skills have acted as interpreters and guides. For instance, interpreters were present throughout China's long imperial history (Lung 2011), though their foreign language skills were at different historical moments highly distrusted by Chinese rulers (Roland 1999). Interpreters were also central to the various European conquests of the "new" world (Pratt [1992] 2008; Luna 2014; Langford 2014), though many of these interpreters were forced into their labor, and their survival rates were appallingly low (Karttunen 2000).

Mary Louise Pratt has suggested that these figures were part of the construction of the imperial "contact zone," a "space in which people geographically and historically separated come into contact with each other and establish ongoing relations, usually involving conditions of coercion, radical inequality, and intractable conflict" ([1992] 2008, 8). Doña Marina, or "La Malinche" as she came to be called, is one notable example of an interpreter who contributed to the construction of a colonial contact zone (Figure I.1 and I.2).

She is remembered by historians as a woman who served as the chief interpreter for the conquistador Hernán Cortés, and—according to some accounts—as the "traitor" who actively *mis*communicated with the king of the Aztecs in order to facilitate the Aztecs' downfall at the hands of the Spanish (Castillo and Schweitzer 2001). Other scholars have emphasized Doña Marina's active agency (Moraga 1983; Cisneros 1991; Spoturno 2014)— "her possibility of assuming various identities in different contexts of interaction, definitely one of her major assets as an interpreter, but also of her

FIGURE I.I A plaque on a house in Mexico City, traditionally viewed as once being the home of "La Malinche," or Doña Marina. Photo by the author.

condition as an intercultural subject, emerging in a context of constant negotiation and conflict and reciprocal borrowing" (Spoturno 2014, 123).

This interplay between connection and disconnection, between communication and miscommunication, is central to my understanding of cultural mediation. Such mediation is an inherently tricky thing, especially when considering Stuart Hall's now famous argument that cultural identity is itself a "production" rather than a static and coherent entity, a process of "becoming" as much as a state of "being" ([1990] 2003, 234, 236). Though, as Hall asserts, identity *exists* and has a material impact—as the "foreignness" of

FIGURE I.2 "La Conchita" Church in Mexico City. The conquistador Hernán Cortés built this church, and, according to tradition, his interpreter Doña Marina went to this church to pray. Photo by the author.

the journalists who seek out fixers surely reveals—for Hall, cultural identity is always in flux (1990] 2003). It is just as much about the future as it is about a shared past (1990] 2003). Following Hall, news fixers' cultural mediation involves the ability to navigate an array of differences while also "assum[ing] various identities" of your own (Spoturno 2014, 123) in order to stage an encounter between people or groups who do not understand each other, and whose own identities are more dynamic and malleable than even they might realize.

Yet, even the fluidity and permeability of cultural identity can run up against the imposition of certain identifications from the "outside." An international correspondent might be read as a "foreigner," in other words, whether or not she actively accentuates this cultural role. And a news fixer might be read as an "authentic" "native," even if such a reading is inaccurate. This is why cultural mediation must be understood as a "constant negotiation," (Spoturno 2014, 123). This is also why the labor of cultural mediation will inevitably be fraught with tension and marked by moments of communicative failure—intentional or otherwise. In the case of colonial interpreters, it is necessary to remember that their own cultural mediation occurred against the broader horizon of material conquest and coercion, unfolding on a landscape of drastically unequal systems of power. Perhaps this is part of the reason why the figure of the interpreter is still sometimes regarded with suspicion. In the context of colonialism, these individuals often had to engage in their work against their will or to ensure their own survival. Because of this, it was difficult for colonizers to tell where their interpreters' loyalties might actually lie. There was also undoubtedly a great deal of anxiety around the fact that the very need for "native" guides revealed the instability of the colonial system's purported identificatory coherence (Langford 2014). Thus, the labor of cultural mediation was vexed—and transgressive—even in these early centuries, pointing to the potential for disconnection and miscommunication that sat uneasily alongside the promise of bridging cultural divides.

The European (and later, North American) suspicion of "native" guides continued into the 18th and 19th centuries, when white travelers would hire "dragomen," or "local" tour guides, to take them on weeks-long tours of "exotic" places in the Middle East and to translate for them along the way (Mairs and Muratov 2015). In these cases, the distribution of power was different from that of the conquistadors and their interpreters. Dragomen guided their charges for a living and were paid for their skills. Yet, they were also at certain points in their history regarded with distrust or as being "inferior" to the mostly white people who depended on them so heavily (Mairs and Muratov 2015). Rachel Mairs and Maya Muratov define the figure of the dragoman as "a guide and translator, engaged by foreign travelers to facilitate their journey" (2015, 1). In this sense, the dragoman was in charge of logistics as well as the travelers' safety. But "on the other hand, his role was to interpret the Orient for travelers whose lack of Arabic or Turkish language skills would otherwise have made it impossible for them to interact with and understand their surroundings" (2015, 1). This labor required that the dragoman "assum[e] various identities" and make the "Orient" legible to the white travelers who often arrived with a number of preconceived notions (Spoturno 2014, 123). Sometimes these cultural performances worked, while at other times, tourists complained of the vast disconnections between themselves and their guides.

There are some stark differences between news fixers and the interpreters and tour guides of past centuries, especially because fixers tend to work specifically with journalists and other media employees in order to produce media texts meant to be consumed by a broader public. Yet, the interpreters and guides of bygone centuries also worked with journalists at times, playing much the same role that news fixers play today. For example, *New York Herald* correspondent Henry Morton Stanley enlisted the help of an interpreter and guide when he went on his 1869–1871 journey through central Africa, searching for the missing missionary and explorer David Livingstone (Fernández-Ocampo 2014). Stanley's interpreter was known as "Selim," and he even made an appearance in a photograph that was later published in the British newspaper *The Graphic* (Fernández-Ocampo 2014). Selim serves as only one example of the many locally based interpreters and guides who have historically helped international journalists in the field. His story reveals that even in the more specific profession of international news reporting, news fixers are not a particularly new phenomenon.

This book does not argue that news fixers' cultural mediation has emerged suddenly out of a cultural void. Instead, I offer some new perspectives on this cultural labor: the perspectives of the mediators themselves. One thing that news fixers suggest they have in common with interpreters and guides of the past is the potential for connection and disconnection, communication and miscommunication. In some cases, the news fixer might veer in favor of the visiting journalist. For instance, some fixers might take more pride in getting the story the international correspondent wants than in giving the correspondent a more nuanced picture of the region. In these cases, the fixer is still mediating culture by helping the journalist achieve his or her goals while operating in an unfamiliar environment.

Yet, in other cases, the fixer might veer in favor of the people who live in the region. For example, the fixer might translate a journalist's very direct questions in a way that is more palatable to the interviewee. Similarly, the fixer might not share everything that the interviewee has said with the journalist who cannot understand the language the interviewee is using. The very same news fixer could, in certain moments, identify more with the journalist, and, in other moments, identify more with the people on the ground. On top of this, the fixer might have to tell the client "no," either because the logistics will not allow for the pursuit of the story or because the fixer firmly disagrees with the journalist's views. In these instances, the work of news fixing is informed more by disconnection than connection.

Another thing that news fixers have in common with cultural mediators of the past is the multifaceted nature of their labor. Dragomen were in charge of everything from interpreting to safety to managing logistics—so, too, are fixers. When they describe the work they do, news fixers tend to focus on five key tasks: 1) conceptualizing the story, 2) navigating the logistics, 3) networking with sources, 4) interpreting unfamiliar languages, and 5) safeguarding the journalist. In each of these cases, the news fixer must "assum[e] various identities" and negotiate between competing agendas (Spoturno 2014). For instance, news fixers like Muasya must interpret Nairobi's languages and traditions for his clients. Yet, Muasya might also have to interpret his clients' behavior for the people on the ground, smoothing thorny interactions with people unhappy to see the journalists in their communities and convincing people to do on-the-record interviews. To secure the trust of the various people living in Nairobi, Muasya might have to emphasize certain aspects of his cultural identity—his nationality, his race, or his status as a resident of Nairobi. To safeguard his clients, Muasya might have to speak to local authorities on their behalf or vouch for his clients' trustworthiness. Even the labor of navigating the logistics depends heavily on Muasya's ability to pilot his clients through competing cultural notions of time and space.

Entangled within both the microcosm and macrocosm of international news reporting are an array of shifting sociocultural identifications that the fixer must become an expert at navigating. A performance of cultural identity that might work one day might not work the next day. Thus, it is crucial to understand that though cultural identity can be fluid, permeable, and performative, difference still matters—and it can be imposed from the "outside" as well as performed from the "inside." The labor of news fixing highlights this phenomenon, as well as exposing how the purportedly "global" news organizations are profoundly impacted by highly specific types of cultural mediation that occur at the most microcosmic of levels. Because of this, news organizations based in a variety of different regions depend heavily on outsourcing the labor of cultural mediation to someone with more knowledge of the specific cultural performances that must be deployed.

Popular knowledge would have people believe that it is the foreign correspondent who ostensibly guides news audiences through landscapes they do not know and through conversations with people who speak different languages than they do. The correspondent in the field is the person who has, for the past few centuries, served as the authoritative "eyewitness" (Zelizer 2007), translating raw experience into a story for the people "back home," and more literally translating cultural difference in a way that makes certain parts of the world legible to news readers and viewers. Much of the foreign correspondent's authority arguably rests on this important role as cultural mediator, fully realized in the figure of the intrepid reporter who travels to distant lands and tells "the" story of what is happening there. Yet, Matt Carlson productively argues that the notion of journalistic authority in general needs to be understood in less mythological terms, requiring that we seek "a broader vision of journalistic practices, news forms, underlying technologies, organizational structures, and the wider context in which news is produced and consumed" (2017, 5).

A broader vision of international reporting shows that, in many cases, international journalists outsource the labor of cultural mediation, without always crediting the people who do much of this work for them. Thus, rather than conceptualizing international journalism in terms of its mythological ideals or in terms of its major players, we need instead to investigate the news work of the profession's "rank and file" (Hardt and Brennen 1995)—most especially those whose labor is hidden from view. This leads me to the final argument I advance in this book. News fixers represent their work as part of an uneven and inegalitarian underground economy upon which the various international news industries heavily depend. My interviewees suggest—sometimes directly, sometimes indirectly—that each element of their labor involves the completion of a number of tasks, *without which*, the majority of their clients would not be able to tell their stories at all.

This representation especially makes sense in the context of the parachute journalists who land in one region, cover a disaster on a quick deadline, and then turn around and fly to another region to do the same thing all over again. In the era of closing foreign news bureaus and slashed news budgets, parachute journalism is becoming all the more common (Williams 2011; Sambrook 2010; Cottle, Sambrook, and Mosdell 2016). Parachute journalists overwhelmingly rely on the assistance of news fixers, especially when they do not speak any of the regional languages. When parachute journalists hire fixers, they usually hire them on a freelance basis. According to my interviewees, these journalists almost never provide fixers with insurance or hazardous environment training, largely because fixers' labor is considered to unfold "underground"—informally, and outside the purview of existing newsroom policies.

On top of this, my interviewees' testimonies reveal a remarkable level of unpredictability in what is considered to be the "market rate" for news fixers' labor. News fixers might receive more—or less—money based on their level of experience, the "riskiness" of the story, how wealthy the news organization is, or the region of the world in which the fixer works. Though most of the news fixers I interviewed express satisfaction with the money they make, their accounts also illuminate the fact that fixers working in Africa tend to be paid significantly less than those working in the Middle East, while fixers working in the Middle East tend to make less than fixers working in Europe and North America. One former news editor for the *Washington Post* told me that this is because of the perceived "inexpensiveness" of living in some parts of the world over others (Hoffman, pers. comm., February 2015). This editors' statement situates the underground labor of news fixing within the broader context of the inegalitarian distribution of the world's resources in the age of globalization.

This editor also argues that locally based fixers and stringers working more regularly with foreign bureaus are paid substantially less than correspondents because they are not engaging in the same level of "skilled" labor as the reporters (Hoffman, pers. comm., February 2015). Such an assertion points to a troubling hierarchy that many of my interviewees also outlined: their labor, vital though it may be, is still not always valued as highly as that of the foreign correspondent—even though the correspondent needs the fixer in order to do the job. One of my interviewees, who works with the *New York Times* bureau in Beirut, suggests that the foreign correspondents at her bureau make more money because they're American citizens (Saad, pers. comm., June 2015). Some also indicate that the foreign journalists at their bureaus make more money and receive benefits because of their titles, because of their mythical status as "foreign correspondents," a phenomenon that other research on foreign bureaus has also illuminated (Seo 2016).

As these accounts suggest, it is not only parachute journalists who rely on news fixers; international news bureaus also depend heavily upon locally based media workers. These media employees are brought onto the staff of a particular bureau to help with translation, networking, and cultural literacy. In these cases, the fixers work mostly with a single news organization, though they are typically allowed to do freelance fixing work for non-competitors. Their title is usually "news assistant," and though they do substantial work on major stories for the bureau, they do not tend to receive benefits such as health insurance. They are paid less than the correspondents based at the bureau, and they are never guaranteed a byline or even the more unobtrusive credit of "contributor," though they sometimes do receive these things. Like the parachute journalists who draw upon freelance news fixers, the correspondents working at international news bureaus do not systematically make their dependence on their news assistants explicit to their news audiences, though news assistants are much more likely to receive a contributing credit than their freelance counterparts.

Because of these various issues, I understand news fixers' (and news assistants') work as *underground* labor. The term "underground" is not meant to imply news fixers' complete distrust of their clients or fixers' displeasure with the work they do. As the next section of this introduction will show, some news fixers thoroughly enjoy their work. Instead, the term "underground" refers to the fact that this labor is informal and relegated to the shadows. In the best-case scenarios, when journalists convey their admiration and respect for the work that fixers do, they still do not tend to give these media employees any official credit for their role in reporting the story, and they also do not tend to offer fixers significant protection for the often dangerous labor of working with foreigners. In the worst-case scenarios, fixers say that they are viewed as "unskilled" laborers who cannot be considered "real" journalists, and this categorization is then used to justify the mistreatment of news fixers in the field, or their omission from the reporting process. Thus, the very last task that news fixers describe in their professional narratives—"relinquishing the story"—is less an act of cultural mediation than a moment of ambivalent acquiescence to the erasure of that mediation, to the separation of news fixers from the products of their labor.

This book hopes to bring this underground economy more firmly into the light, destabilizing the understanding of international correspondents as the sole experts who interpret cultural difference for their broader publics. News fixers' professional narratives complicate this notion, as well as painting a more nuanced picture of how international reporting actually works. Before I defend these arguments in more depth, I first provide more information on who these media employees are and how they started working as news fixers in the first place.

The Interviewees

Although this book does engage with the testimonies of 60 international correspondents and news editors, testimonies which sometimes diverge and sometimes overlap with those of news fixers (see appendix 3), the book most importantly foregrounds the production narratives of news fixers themselves (see appendix 2). These news fixers have currently or formerly worked with text-based journalists, photographers, and television journalists, as well as with feature-length documentarians and, in a few cases, with the human rights NGOs whose own media production has increasingly begun to operate in a feedback loop with that of professional news organizations (Powers 2018; Wright 2018). Though I largely refer to these media workers as "news" fixers, my interviewees suggest that it is not at all uncommon for a fixer to spend one week working with journalists, another week working with documentarians whose films may air cinematically or on television, and another week working with an advertising agency or a fiction film crew.

For the purposes of this book, I am most interested in fixers who have worked with professional journalists or documentarians at some point in their career. I have tried to steer away from discussions of advertising or fiction film production, since the risks and challenges that fixers face are very different in entertainment and advertising than those they face in news production. For instance, fiction film crews tend to be much larger than news teams, and thus, even more difficult to manage logistically (Carbajal, pers. comm., March 2017). They also have a different concept of what a "story" actually is and what it is supposed to accomplish.

However, I have learned that there is some overlap between fixing for journalists and fixing for documentarians, especially since many of the documentaries that my interviewees mention in their testimonies have aired on television networks that also produce news content (Al Jazeera is a case in point). Like journalists, documentarians are trying to tell stories that have some sort of "truth value," though they may take more creative liberty with the way that "truth" is foregrounded in their films and videos. What is more, the "nonfiction," "realistic" nature of documentary production can, like that of news production, place fixers in tension with locally based people who may not want certain information to emerge. For these reasons, I include the testimonies of fixers who have worked with documentary crews as well as with journalists. Still, the vast majority of my interviewees' testimonies are specifically geared toward their work with foreign correspondents.

My interviewees have worked in 39 different countries: Lebanon, Palestine, Israel, Turkey, Pakistan, Egypt, Iran, Iraq, China, Indonesia, India, Nepal, Japan, Kenya, Somalia, Nigeria, Ghana, South Africa, El Salvador, Colombia, Brazil, Guatemala, Mexico, Serbia, Croatia, Hungary, Bosnia and Herzegovina, Ukraine, Russia, Sweden, Greece, Austria, Germany, the UK, France, Belgium, Italy, Spain, and the United States (see appendix 1). As figure A.1 shows, the majority of the people I interviewed are (or were previously) working in Lebanon, Russia, or Mexico. This is because I traveled in person to Beirut, Moscow, and Mexico City in hopes of conducting longer, face-to-face interviews with fixers based in three very different but internationally significant news hubs. The rest of the interviews were conducted via Skype, WhatsApp, or phone. I provide more detail on my research methods in the appendix to this book.

Forty-seven of my interviewees are men and 28 are women. The vast majority of the people I interviewed say they have acquired at least some university-level education, and many of them have completed undergraduate or graduate-level degrees. Some of my interviewees have studied journalism in college, and many—though not all—of them say that they have obtained some other type of professional media experience outside their work as news fixers. Some of my interviewees have also worked for local or national news outlets in their own regions. Others have quite a bit of skill with a camera or with writing, but they have not been able to break into their regions' local news industries. Still others have never worked in the media outside their role as fixers or news assistants.

"Breaking into" the work of news fixing is a process that also needs more elaboration. One way that fixers get hired is simply by word of mouth. This is especially the case for people with prior experience working in the news industries. For instance, a British fixer working in Italy says that he had previously worked for ABC. One of his former ABC colleagues contacted him when he moved to Italy, "where I had vainly hoped to find work as a freelance producer in local news. He [the ABC colleague] was working at BBC Television Features in Bristol, which at the time was preparing a six-part TV documentary history of hour-long films on the CIA, for BBC 1." This soon-to-be news fixer (who asked to remain anonymous) says that he was told "to identify a local investigative journalist prepared to help work on the project" and also "to find local CIA agents prepared to talk on camera about their experience in the postwar period. In the end, that journalist was me, and I found the people the director was looking for" (pers. comm., September 2016).

Other fixers get hired because they are actively working as professional journalists in their own regions, a rather baffling phenomenon since even fixers who work locally as journalists are typically not conceptualized as journalists when they are working as fixers for foreign correspondents. In these cases, foreign journalists might go to the local newspapers and TV stations to seek fixers out, despite the fact that they will then expect their new hire to relinquish the role of "journalist" for the duration of the assignment. Freelance journalist and sometimes-news fixer Alasdair Baverstock says that for a journalist who needs a fixer, the local newspaper is an important place to look (pers. comm., March 2017). And Salman Siddiqui, who worked as both a stringer and fixer in Karachi, Pakistan, says that he was originally sought out by foreign journalists because he worked at the best local paper in the city (pers. comm., April 2013).

Though many news fixers already have professional journalism experience, some of them get their first job despite the fact that they do not—and have never— specifically worked in journalism. For example, Renato Miller, a Chilean fixer working in Mexico City, says that after studying journalism in college, he had no luck becoming a reporter in the region. Instead, he

ended up working for a Mexican television talk show, before becoming disen-
chanted. Then, things turned around:

> I know this British journalist working in Mexico, his name is Rodrigo.
> And he works drugs, he works drug trafficking stories. And I got to
> know him by chance in a protest. And he got to know my work, we
> became friends and then, he kind of asked me to shoot a picture for
> his book, like a picture of the author, the one on the back cover. Not
> the good stuff in the middle, but the back-cover picture. And through
> him I kind of got connected. . . . My first story was a story for CNN, it
> was in Mexico state and it turned out great, and they were really happy
> with me. Then it kind of snowballed. So, it was basically through
> connections, through friends. (Pers. comm., March 2017)

Miller's story is very common, in that it reflects the importance of
recommendations, friendship, and "word of mouth" in the process of breaking
into the news-fixing business.

But some of my interviewees note that the "word of mouth" hire does not
only apply to people who have worked in some kind of media industry or who
have studied journalism at a university. Abd Nova, a Syrian refugee who had
trained to become a doctor before he fled the Syrian Civil War, was living in
Beirut when a friend asked him if he wanted to do some translating for a television journalist she knew:

> I said sure. And I went along—I worked with them for three
> days . . . and she [Nova's friend] told me, "This is another stage. You
> can start fixing and stringing. Just take the contacts, and you can
> call and set up interviews. Whenever a journalist asks you for a cer-
> tain interview, he needs this, he's covering this story, he needs what-
> ever story he's looking for. You can find it for him." (Pers. comm.,
> June 2015)

After Nova completed this first fixing job, he quickly found more work
due to the connections he made and the recommendations he received from
journalists. This is one of the most typical ways in which news fixers turn a
first-time job into a fixing career—through the "snowballing effect." For instance, a Somalian fixer who wishes to remain anonymous says that after his
first fixing job, his client told him: " 'I trusted you, and you worked with me.
I'm going to make you a great fixer. I'm going to connect you to the rest of the

world, so that you have so many friends and so many colleagues.' That's how I started as a fixer in Mogadishu" (pers. comm., May 2016). The same thing happened to Haidar Adbalhabi, an Iraqi fixer who won the trust of a Danish journalist; according to Adbalhabi, anytime someone asks the journalist who they should hire in Baghdad, the journalist now says, "Okay, go work with Haidar" (pers. comm., May 2016).

The small amount of scholarly research that has been conducted on news fixers also shows that visiting journalists like to hire their fixers by word of mouth, at least in the context of covering news in Iraq (Palmer and Fontan 2007; Murrell 2013). Yet, these studies argue something else as well: the journalists working in Iraq during the US occupation sometimes instead tended to hire fixers through "serendipity" or "coincidence" (Palmer and Fontan 2007; Murrell 2013), running into potential fixers by accident and quickly bringing them aboard the news team. Interestingly, my interviewees do not foreground the notion of coincidence, though some of the journalists with whom they work could easily interpret things this way. Instead, my interviewees understand the hiring process more in terms of "connected-ness"—of friends and colleagues linking them to potential employers, even if the connection is made very suddenly.

This notion of connectedness only intensifies in the internet age. Mostafa Sheshtawy, who worked as a fixer in Cairo during the post-Mubarak uprisings, says that

> to get a job, you have to be on the map in a way. So, you have to be ac-tive and making news and breaking news, and also you have to have a lot of connections, and at that time. . . . I was very active online and on the social media, especially Twitter back then was the big thing. (Pers. comm., July 2015)

Social media sites like Twitter can be especially important in the context of covering international activist movements, and they can indeed con-tribute to the "coincidental" or "serendipitous" encounters with fixers that journalists working in Iraq also described (Palmer and Fontan 2007; Murrell 2013). Yet, Sheshtawy's account focuses less on serendipity and more on the active effort on the part of the would-be news fixer. To get a job, Sheshtawy says, "you have to be active" and to "have a lot of connections" (pers. comm., July 2015).

This statement also seems to resonate for the myriad fixers who now ad-vertise their services on websites like World Fixer and Hack Pack, both of

FIGURE I.3 The World Fixer home page. Screenshot by the author.

which launched in 2015 (see figure I.3). These websites provide a space for current or would-be fixers to share their contact information with journalists who will soon be visiting their regions. Fixers can list their prior experience, their media skills, and their skills with specific languages. Crucially, they can also reach out to former clients who have the option of "reviewing" the fixers' work on the website. These journalists can leave testimonials discussing the individual fixer's work ethic and innovativeness in the field. In this sense, the "word of mouth" recommendation remains a powerful thing even in the digital age. On top of this, the World Fixer website tries to verify that news fixers are who they say they are and that they have actually worked on the projects they list on their profiles. The verification function is meant to assuage the anxiety of journalists who need that extra measure of trust (Garrod, pers. comm., 2016).

Some of the media employees who have worked as news fixers have, over the years, formed production companies of their own, which journalists and documentarians might seek out instead of looking for freelance fixers (see figure I.4). These companies might provide visiting journalists and documentarians with camera equipment, with locally based video crews, with guides who accompany the foreigners into the field, and with translators. Some of the people who work with these companies do not prefer to use the word "fixer" but rather "local producer," since they feel that their work might take them past news "fixing" and into video production. Others continue to use the word "fixer," since these companies provide all of the same services that freelance news fixers provide.

FIGURE I.4 A studio at Newsgate, a production company based in Beirut. Photo by the author.

Perhaps the biggest difference is that these companies have the reputation—and thus, the capital—needed to protect their fixers both professionally and physically. In this sense, the labor that these companies provide can be viewed as the least "underground" of all such labor, though it still unfolds behind the scenes. For instance, these companies are able to negotiate more aggressively for their staff members' day rates, and they can also more aggressively ensure that their staff members do indeed get paid for their work. Similarly, these companies provide their staff members with insurance and safety equipment, as well as demanding that the journalists and documentarians who work with them wear safety equipment. These companies' established presence in the field is expected to inspire the trust of the client, though sometimes, clients still do not listen very carefully to the advice they receive from these employees.

Because trust is so important to the fixer-journalist relationship, a number of my interviewees say that they continue to be hired the old-fashioned way—through verbal recommendations rather than through websites like World Fixer. On the flip side, my interviewees suggest that trust is the necessary ingredient in determining which journalists make the best clients. A prevalent theme in my interviewees' testimony is the notion of professional autonomy—the fact that news fixers *decide* whether to work with someone and decide whether to *continue* working with them. The news fixers can refuse to collaborate with particular journalists in the future if they feel they were mistreated; they can also inform other fixers in their network that a certain journalist is untrustworthy and should be avoided.

In extreme cases, the news fixers might discontinue the working relationship in the middle of the story—provided that they do not desperately need the money, which sometimes they do. Though the playing field is rarely even, and though the distribution of power depends heavily on the fixer's experience level, professional connections, and financial stability, my interviewees represent themselves as still having some measure of autonomy in the fixer-journalist relationship. This is critical to note because it helps explain why these important media employees decide to work as fixers at all. If this kind of labor were only negative and always exploitative, then the figure of the fixer would simply not exist. But in truth, there are a number of positive aspects to doing this work, and these aspects also need to be explored.

One of the most obvious "pros" that draws people to news fixing is the "good money." The process of negotiating payment usually happens before the fixer's actual work begins, and the general sense among journalists and news editors—at least, in the Anglophone world—is that news fixers are expensive (Palmer 2017). News fixers' production narratives do not necessarily go that far, but they do reflect a general sense of satisfaction with the amount that they get paid. News fixers' day rates seem to vary drastically by world region (one fixer working in Ghana accepts USD$50 a day, while another fixer in Moscow accepts USD$200, and a third fixer working in the United States is more accustomed to $400–$500 daily). These rates also vary drastically *within* world regions (fixers in Mexico might make anywhere from USD$100 a day to USD$400 a day, depending on their level of experience, the type of news organization hiring them, and the types of stories they cover). Despite these differences, news fixers' production narratives largely suggest that they tend to make better money working as fixers than they do working as reporters for locally based news organizations or working in other regionally based industries.

For example, Siddiqui says that in Pakistan, "fixers can make in three days [an amount that] would be equal to as much as a month's salary at the [local] paper" (pers. comm., April 2013). Another fixer working in India says, "when I was in a job, my salary for a whole month was approximately seventy-five [US] dollars. . . . And the moment I started freelance [fixing], that was my daily rate" (Gupta, pers. comm., June 2016). And Swedish fixer and producer Niclas Peyron charges

> twenty to twenty-five thousand Swedish krona [USD$350–$430] a day, [for] which most American [clients] say, "Oh!" And then I tell them, "Yeah, but that's the way it is." . . . If you look at the costs of

which is the most expensive country in the world, well, Sweden is one of the five top, you know. So, it does cost. And then some people say, "Oh, but we can't pay that!" And then I usually say, "Well, then you shouldn't come." (Pers. comm., September 2016)

Though, as later chapters of this book will show, there are certainly some news fixers who do not feel that they are paid enough money to justify the risks they take or the general level of work they do, and while other fixers do not feel that they are paid in a timely manner, many of my interviewees suggest that the money is still one of the most positive elements of news fixing.

But fixers do not only do this work for the money. There are many other reasons why they find value in their work. An anonymous Russian fixer and documentary filmmaker in his own right says that without fixing "I wouldn't have seen that much of Russia" (pers. comm., January 2017). One of this person's favorite fixing jobs not only provided him with good money very quickly—it also gave him the opportunity to travel and see parts of the country that he had never seen before.

Another fixer working in Mexico City cites a different reason: "I love the fixing mainly because . . . I love learning. I was never good at school, but I had to learn. And I think this is a job that allows you to learn new things constantly" (Carbajal, pers. comm., March 2017). And Samuel Okocha, a fixer based in Nigeria, says that working with foreign journalists is a great way for a fixer to strengthen his or her own journalism skills: "I respect international journalists a lot, especially those I find quite knowledgeable as far as the craft of journalism is concerned. Because I am always willing and ready to learn and tap the knowledge of more experienced journalists" (pers. comm., May 2016).

News fixers like Sharad Chirag Adhikaree identify advantages to working with foreigners specifically:

I've worked for certain beats in the capital of Nepal, in Kathmandu. Because I had some limitations. Some reports I could not write, I could not publish in local media. But as a fixer I could travel with foreigners, with foreign journalists to remote areas, or conflict areas, and then I could [publish the story]." (Pers. comm., August 2016)

Because of political tensions underscoring the coverage of certain stories in Nepal, Adhikaree sometimes finds it liberating to work with foreign journalists, whose editors might not be as cagey about publishing stories on certain political issues.

These more positive aspects of news fixing are vital to understanding the creative work in which fixers engage, work that results in the construction of the stories through which people understand the world. The "pros" to news fixing sit ambivalently alongside the "cons," revealing the need for a cautious and nuanced approach to understanding news fixers' labor. Before I turn to a more detailed outline of this book's organization, in hopes of signaling the multifaceted nature of news fixers' work, I will first take a moment to discuss the concept of "story" itself, especially as it pertains to international news reporting. Since my interviewees assert their deep involvement in conceptualizing the story, and since their production narratives also reveal the expectation that fixers eventually "relinquish" the story and move on to new assignments, it is important that I explain precisely what I mean by this compelling but rather vague term.

What Is the "Story?"

Though numerous scholars across the social sciences and humanities have productively discussed the news "story" as an entity unto itself, usually by conducting content or textual analyses of particular news reports, this book conceptualizes "story" in terms of its close connection to news work. There is a long scholarly tradition of investigating the labor of journalists. Some of this scholarship reevaluates the teleological and overly celebratory histories of journalism (Hardt 1990; Hardt and Brennen 1995; Nerone and Barnhurst 2003), while other research conducts ethnographic studies of news reporting processes (Gans 1979; Tuchman 1980; Pedelty 1995; Hannerz 2004; Boczkowski 2010; Usher 2014, 2016). Both strands of scholarly literature inform my understanding of how news "stories" are connected to the labor that produces them.

As the sociologist Herbert Gans suggests in his 1979 classic, *Deciding What's News,* the journalistic story is not only the final product that people read in the paper or watch on television. It is also something that has to be "selected" for the journalist's pursuit, out of a number of other possible stories. This selection happens at an earlier point in time than the act of writing the story or reading the story. The journalist—or often, the editor—must select and then assign the "story" as something to chase, to investigate, to "get." Gans notes that part of this selection process is determining the story's "suitability," or its value to particular news outlets' audiences (1979). As chapter 1 of this book will show, fixers feel that they contribute a great deal to helping journalists determine this suitability in the international context.

Once this selection has been made and the story has been assigned, the journalist then begins the labor of "getting," or pursuing, the story. At this point in the news-reporting process, the term "story" is used to describe a wide variety of things. "Getting the story" might mean securing interviews with important sources, capturing video footage of relevant people or events, or witnessing an occurrence of central importance to the journalist's assignment. Thus, at this stage, correspondents (as well as their fixers) tend to refer to any element that might comprise the final report as "the story." News fixers' production narratives paint a picture of an international reporting practice in which the fixers play a vital role, helping their clients secure interviews, to get the best footage, and even to navigate the logistical challenges that are entangled within the events that journalists try to narrativize.

After the correspondent has gathered all the elements central to the assignment, he or she must then "write" the story. In other words, the journalist must construct the final product that news audiences will see or read, depending on the medium being used. This is the stage in the journalistic process from which news fixers say they are most often excluded, either because they personally do not wish to construct the final product themselves or because the client will not allow them to do so. From fixers' perspectives, journalists and editors become rather territorial when it comes to the construction of the final product. Indeed, journalists and editors tend to refer back to whoever was most involved in this final construction if and when the question of who should be credited arises. Sometimes, this question does not arise at all. Instead, the correspondent takes the byline or the on-camera standup without even thinking about it, and the fixer's contribution is basically erased from the public eye.

When fixers discuss the imperative to "relinquish the story," this is partly what they mean. By virtue of their status as fixers—and not "actual" journalists—they are not traditionally allowed to take any sort of professional ownership of the final news product. In this sense, news fixers can be seen as working at the boundaries of journalistic practice (Carlson and Lewis 2015) or, at least, the boundaries that some professional journalists and news editors anxiously try to reassert each time they use a fixer's services. The very need for fixers to "relinquish the story" points to the ambivalence that professional news outlets show toward fixers' specific "boundary work" in international journalism (Carlson and Lewis 2015).

But there is another meaning to the phrase "relinquishing the story," which illuminates a different way in which the term "story" gets used. In relinquishing the story, news fixers are also supposed to ultimately acquiesce to the correspondents' particular angle on what it is that has happened. Though the fixer may find it necessary to help the journalist understand the complex sociopolitical context of the events in question, and though the fixer may personally see a very different angle on the story than the correspondent sees, at the end of the day, the fixer is supposed to go along with the correspondents' view. Thus, even if the fixer believes that the correspondent might be "packaging terrorism," for example, in an effort to create a sensationalizing and simplistic narrative (Moeller 2009), this critique may not ultimately impact the way the story is told. Yet, the fixers' sometimes very different perspectives on the angle of the story destabilizes the notion of one immutable "truth" that the story ostensibly tells, suggesting the validity of Hall et al.'s famous argument that news stories are socially constructed and ideologically inflected ([1978] 2013).

These overlapping, and, sometimes, competing definitions of the news "story" inform the different ways in which "story" is discussed in this book. The news story can be anything from a story idea, to a story assignment, to an important interview, to the final product. As if things were not already complicated, the term "story" can also refer to the sociopolitical angle that the journalist might take that the fixer is expected to support. Finally, there are the narratives that news fixers tell about pursuing and "getting" the news story. Each of these definitions points to the fact that, on one level, I am investigating the pursuit and construction of the news story itself. Yet, on another level, I am also investigating the behind-the-scenes stories that news fixers tell about the international reporting process.

Organization of the Book

This book is organized according to the primary elements of news fixers' labor, elements that my interviewees have themselves identified as being central to the work that they do: "conceptualizing the story," "navigating the logistics," "networking with sources," "interpreting unfamiliar languages," "safeguarding the journalist," and "relinquishing the story." Each chapter looks at one of these tasks, examining how each task requires the fixer to serve as an active cultural mediator on behalf of the visiting journalist or documentarian. Each chapter also considers the different ways in which the news fixers' professional narratives outline a flexible, informal, and hidden economy upon which the various international news industries heavily depend. Finally, each chapter closes with a discussion of the ethical implications of the news fixers' representations of their labor, asking how scholars and industry practitioners might benefit from more carefully listening to the stories that fixers tell about their work.

Chapter 1 focuses specifically on the labor of "conceptualizing the story." When news fixers describe this element of their work, they tend to emphasize three things: (1) their role in anticipating and successfully "getting" the story that the journalist originally wants, (2) their role in suggesting new story ideas to journalists who either do not know which events to cover or whose story ideas have not panned out, and (3) their role in educating visiting journalists on the political, social, and historical background knowledge that they sometimes sorely lack. While some might argue that this element of news fixers' labor points to their dubious efforts at slanting the story in a "biased" direction, chapter 1 argues that news fixers' narratives about conceptualizing the story instead illuminate the fact that there is rarely one, immutable story to be found. From fixers' perspectives, the journalistic "story" is an effort at lending coherence to a much more complex reality, one defined by competing angles and experiences. Chapter 1 also shows that without the news fixers' more extensive background knowledge, visiting journalists run the risk of grossly misrepresenting the people and places being covered.

Chapter 2 examines the labor of "navigating the logistics." A central tenet of this chapter is news fixers' suggestion that logistical labor is "skilled" labor; this type of work requires creativity and cultural savvy. The work of navigating the logistics requires the fixer to guide journalists through challenging sociopolitical environments, helping clients meet their deadlines while also keeping the local authorities satisfied that they are following regional laws. Sometimes visiting journalists and documentarians try to enter a country without the proper permits for their equipment or without the proper work visa. In these cases, news fixers try to find creative ways to smooth things over and gain access for their clients, despite the fact that their clients have not respected the laws of the spaces they are trying to enter. Time and space are revealed to be relative, depending on who has the most power in a given situation. In the process of helping their clients navigate the logistics, then, news fixers are ultimately helping them navigate competing cultural notions of time and space.

Chapter 3 investigates the labor of "networking with sources." News fixers indicate that their networks of potential interviewees are perhaps the most lucrative thing they can offer a visiting reporter. Because of this, they spend years cultivating trust with a variety of contacts, some of whom are dangerous people to displease. Parachute journalists might try to "buy" fixers' local contacts, showing little regard for the years of emotional labor that have led the fixers to build trust with people who might pose a threat to both the journalist and the fixer. Once the journalist arrives and the news fixer draws upon his or her contact list, another problem emerges: the fixer must ensure that the client does not upset the valuable contact by showing cultural ignorance or insensitivity. This can become a complicated dance of "playing to both sides," something that many fixers say is necessary to keep the contact for future jobs, while also helping the journalist get the interviews needed to tell the story.

Chapter 4 looks at the labor of "interpreting unfamiliar languages." Fixers place great emphasis on their role as translators, but they echo much of the recent scholarship on translation by indicating that the task of translating and interpreting is not a passive process. The very act of standing at the crossroads between two (or more) languages places news fixers in the role of cultural mediator, demanding that they live simultaneously within more than one linguistic expression of culture. Though some news fixers certainly conceptualize translation and interpreting as the process of "building a bridge," they also suggest that the act of translation is fraught with moments of disconnection and miscommunication. Sometimes, the fixer might choose to translate a journalist's question differently than the journalist intended, for instance, in order to assuage the anxiety of a source or an authority figure. Sometimes the fixer might leave some of the source's response out of the translation or paraphrase instead of translating word for word. Throughout the entire process of interpreting unfamiliar languages, the news fixer makes active decisions about what to say and how to say it. These decisions are typically guided by the fixer's understanding of both the source's cultural identification and the journalist's. From news fixers' perspectives, interpreting is much more than translating words—it is also a process of actively and creatively interpreting "culture," however complex culture may be.

Chapter 5 explores the labor of "safeguarding the journalist." Fixers represent themselves as playing a vital role in keeping foreign reporters out of harm's way, most especially when these reporters' status as racial, national, and even gendered "others" might put them at risk. Sometimes the fixer must speak on behalf of the journalist, smoothing things over with a suspicious police officer or an angry crowd. Other times, the fixer might give the journalist advice on how to safely navigate the complex sociocultural landscape, for example, imploring female journalists to dress conservatively in certain areas or recognizing certain neighborhoods that no foreign reporter should visit alone. For these reasons, news outlets tend to conceptualize fixers as a key element of the security measures they must take to keep their journalists safe in the field (Palmer 2017). Yet, chapter 5 closes by showing the flip side of this labor—the possibility that the news fixers themselves will be injured or killed. Notwithstanding this danger, news organizations rarely provide their fixers with safety equipment, hazardous-environment training, or medical insurance.

The conclusion to this book examines the labor of "relinquishing the story." Despite their active role in conceptualizing the story at its beginning and assisting with the construction of the story at every turn, fixers say that they are denied ownership of the final product in any significant sense. Sometimes, the journalist or news organization will invoke the fact that the fixer is getting paid in order to justify the separation of the fixer from the final product of his or her labor. Some of my interviewees suggest that this especially seems to happen when a fixer takes issue with the journalist's interpretation of what is "true" or what is most newsworthy. Once the story is finished, news fixers rarely receive substantial credit for their role in reporting the story. Some of my interviewees say that this does not bother them, while others assert that the inability to get a byline hurts their chances for upward mobility in the international reporting industries. Still, very few news fixers appear to feel comfortable with actively contesting this problem. Thus, the conclusion of this book argues that the labor of relinquishing the story is also the moment in which the fixer—sometimes willingly and sometimes unwillingly—acquiesces to his or her own erasure from the practice of international news reporting.

Ultimately, this book hopes to reverse some of this erasure by engaging with the narratives that news fixers construct in order to understand their thoughts on the production of international news. I do not pretend to be "giving voice to the voiceless"—fixers are *not* voiceless, as their diverse stories reveal. I also do not pretend to be offering some privileged glimpse into a set of "authentic" cultures that are necessarily "foreign" to Anglophone academics, journalists, and students. Many of my interviewees have much in common with the people who will be reading about them, and thus, cannot be relegated to the "local" or, even more simplistically, to the "authentically native." Instead, this book aims to open up a space for more egalitarian dialogue between these figures whose liminal labor requires the strategic performance of multiple cultural identifications, and the people who either study or practice the work of international reporting. By encouraging this dialogue, I hope to offer a more nuanced understanding of the complex and contested nature of international reporting in the contemporary age.

I

Conceptualizing the Story

I got asked last week if I wouldn't mind doing a Zika story related to prostitution, and it's like, "Oh, that old chestnut again."

—INGRID LE VAN, fixer in Rio de Janeiro

INGRID LE VAN is a French citizen of German and Vietnamese descent, working as a news fixer in Brazil. She says she traveled to Brazil for a holiday in 2010, and she has been there ever since. Le Van asserts that her status as a foreigner contributes to her deep level of interest in the events that unfold in her new country: "You choose to be here, so the engine that guides you is you really like the country. You consciously decide to be here, and to take an interest in anything around you, whether it's political life, social, economic" (Le Van, pers. comm., August 2016). Le Van's fascination with the multitude of stories to be found in Brazil, along with her knowledge of various languages, eventually led her to become a fixer. "I usually get involved with a lot of foreigners who come to Brazil, and who need this type of bridge to understand things . . . to understand how some of the stories locally work" (pers. comm., August 2016).

But for Le Van, the question of the "story" itself can be a sticky one, especially because many visiting journalists tend to see Brazil through a very specific lens:

> When you have journalists coming here, they're full of clichés. All the stories that people want to do now are basically all [about] Zika. . . . Brazil's not all about Zika. First of all, it's not the rainy season, all the mosquitos have died, because it's cold and this is not the rainy season. Second, there's still no one hundred percent evidence about some of the factors, you know, some of the things that you hear on the news. And third, if you want to find a mosquito disease that really is dangerous, that's Dengue and not Zika. So, the misinformation of some of

the journalists, and the clichéd stories they want to do, sometimes really annoys me. You're trying not to let it show, but sometimes you just think, "Could you talk about something that hasn't been done over and over again?... Don't you want to talk about something that's new and interesting, that no one's covered?" (Pers. comm., August 2016)

Le Van's statement points to a problem that lies at the heart of international news reporting: the tendency for journalists and media workers from differing regions or sociocultural backgrounds to disagree on which events and issues should be covered in the first place. Of course, journalists disagree about what should be covered all the time, even when they are not covering stories that take them outside their own regions. Always elusive, the concept of "the story" can drastically change, depending on who is doing the reporting and who has the authority to make the final editorial decisions. But my interviewees suggest that the layers of negotiation involved in identifying and pursuing the most "legitimate" stories only multiply in the context of international news reporting, especially because news editors are located at a physical and intellectual distance from the places they send their reporters. What may seem like an urgent (and marketable) story to a foreign desk editor may seem equally unimportant—even reductive—to a locally based news fixer.

Because of this, there is potentially a great deal of tension involved in the very first task for which a visiting journalist or documentarian might hire a fixer: conceptualizing the story. As Le Van's testament implies, this tension does not solely lie with the fixers considered "native" to the geopolitical region being covered. Le Van was not born in Brazil, nor did she grow up speaking Portuguese or participating in regional traditions. Yet, even with her "foreigner" status, Le Van finds that she sometimes disagrees with what she views as many visiting journalists' limited understanding of the myriad stories that Brazil has to offer. Her goal is to give her clients more access to what she calls "the real Brazil," something she feels the more properly "local" news fixers also seem to avoid:

Brazilian fixers tend to think that clients just want to see the stuff that is high class, and they don't understand that as a gringo, sometimes you want the opposite; you want to see something that you don't have at home. You don't care, you don't want to see another Sheraton, because you've got that home. You want to see a samba on the street, because you don't get that at home. And even if it is dirty, and it could be a bit shocking and filthy, it's a tiny little bit of the country. (Pers. comm., August 2016)

Le Van's assertion points to a number of issues. First, Le Van suggests that fixers must anticipate which stories will interest their clients—even if the clients do not directly ask for these types of stories when they first contact the fixer. While journalists and other media producers might hire a fixer to help them tell a Zika story, Le Van says that the fixer should also make suggestions about other stories that will entice the client precisely because of the stories' unfamiliarity. As a part of this process, the fixer can then educate the clients about the nuances of the place they are visiting.

Second, Le Van suggests that Brazilian fixers might not be able to anticipate the international clients' needs as well as a "gringa" like Le Van herself could. The implication is that so-called (non-white) natives will fail to anticipate what the foreigner might *want* to see, as well as what the foreigner might *need* to see. While this part of Le Van's statement undoubtedly reflects some of her reductive sociocultural interpretations of "native Brazilians"—a problematic mindset to which fixers are certainly not immune—it also points to another issue. Le Van suggests that fixers must anticipate the story that the journalist or documentarian initially wants while simultaneously helping the client gain a more complex perspective on the people and places being covered.

At the earliest stages of the news fixer's labor, he or she must engage in the active process of cultural mediation, even when this process requires the fixer to negate or to elaborate upon a journalist's idea for a story. The foreign journalist does not always understand the vital details, for example, nor does he or she always comprehend the obstacles that stand in the way of securing a particular angle on a story. Besides helping their clients "get" the story, fixers often have to tell the journalist or documentarian that certain stories are impossible to pursue because of various sociocultural circumstances that the visiting client did not foresee. At times, fixers must also help journalists understand the story by filling in the blanks in their background knowledge. On a more insidious level, fixers are, in extreme cases, forced to grapple with the preconceived notions that certain clients bring to the field.

News fixers' production narratives suggest that conceptualizing the story is a crucial element of the underground economy of international reporting. Even when the journalist gives the fixer a very specific request at the beginning of an assignment, the labor of chasing that particular story is fraught with contingency, necessitating the fixer's resourcefulness. Without this resourcefulness, the foreign journalist would not be able to tell the story at all, no matter how legitimate he or she has determined the story to be. Thus, in many respects, news organizations outsource the labor of conceptualizing the story to the news employees who are relegated to the shadows.

This is especially the case in the era of shrinking news budgets and the closure of foreign bureaus (Paterson and Sreberny 2004; Sambrook 2010; Williams 2011). In an undeniably unstable economic milieu, more and more journalists "parachute" into regions that they may have never visited before, necessitating the employment of fixers to help them get the story. In turn, the story must be "marketable" for the journalist, something that will be interesting to specific news audiences. The need for marketability sits in tension with the need for nuance and caution, a tension that different fixers might negotiate in different ways. Some fixers pride themselves on their ability to strategically think from their clients' perspectives, making suggestions that they know will attract their clients' target audiences. Other fixers might contest a client's conceptualization of the story, trying instead to make new suggestions. Some foreign journalists are happy to receive input from their fixers, while others expect their fixers to simply do what they are told.

For this reason, scholars, students, and journalists need to more carefully consider fixers' accounts of their role in conceptualizing the story. News fixers' testimonies complicate the authority of the visiting journalist's perspective on what the story actually *is*. When the fixer holds an alternative perspective to that of the client, this perspective can illuminate the particularity of the foreign journalist's perspective. In other words, fixers' testimonies about conceptualizing international news stories suggest that these stories are made up of partial truths, rather than complete truths, and particular perspectives, rather than universal ones. Following this, chapter 1 will first explore news fixers' accounts of what it takes to "get" the story the journalist wants. The chapter will then turn to the narratives that outline the tense process of contesting the journalist's story idea, revealing the tension over matters of "truth" and "reality" that inform the process of international reporting.

Getting the Story the Journalist Wants

For fixers, the question of perspective haunts the tasks they must complete in the process of conceptualizing the story. And though plenty of journalists and news editors—especially those operating in "Western" contexts—have suggested that fixers might try to skew the otherwise "balanced" portrayal of a global or international event (Palmer and Fontan 2007; Murrell 2015; Palmer 2017), my interviewees reveal that the process of conceptualizing the story is far more complex than that accusation suggests. Some fixers will help their clients cover whatever topic they wish, simply because they feel it's their job. Even so, these same fixers may feel that their clients' perspective is contrived or reductive. Other fixers take pride in suggesting new story topics, in hopes of complementing the preliminary work the journalists and editors have done. Still others try to educate their clients on what they feel is a serious lack of background knowledge about the people and places being covered. News fixers' testimonies illuminate the fact that international media stories consist of competing perspectives that can be presented in different ways to different ends.

These narratives also advance the notion that the fixer plays an active, creative role in conceptualizing the story at its outset, even when he or she tries to be as hands-off as possible. For instance, an anonymous Russian fixer and news assistant says that her job requires that she constantly "adjust[s] to reporters' or editors' needs" (pers. comm., January 2017). Rami Aysha, a news fixer and freelance journalist working in Lebanon, similarly says that fixers "should be the eyes and ears of the journalists" (pers. comm., June 2015). Both comments point to the active role that that the fixer must play in the process of helping foreign journalists to get the story. The first statement illuminates the fact that the news fixer needs to be adaptable, "adjusting" to the imperatives of the editors and journalists who have already determined what they think the story should be. Yet, this adjustment still requires that the anonymous news assistant does some thinking on her own, that she interacts with the people and events unfolding in Moscow in order to transform the correspondents' "wish list" into a real story.

Aysha's statement also implies that the fixer sometimes has to act as the journalist's surrogate in the field, and that this is also a creative and active process. In these instances, the fixer "stands in" for the journalist, getting important interviews and video that the journalist cannot get on his or her own. One Lebanese-American news assistant and fixer working in Beirut has this anecdote to tell:

> There was a story on a Syrian girl. She was thirteen years old, and she got a prize for photography. There was [a report on how people had] distributed cameras to refugee children in one of the camps. And they made a competition. They took pictures. And [the journalists] were looking for this girl. This television network, it was actually a Turkish network, she contacted me, and she said, "We want to look for Hiba." I said, "Who's Hiba?" [She replied] "Hiba is a thirteen-year-old in one

of the refugee camps. We want this photography contact. And we want to make a story of her." Well, I have to fine Hiba! (Haidamous, pers. comm., June 2015)

For fixers like Suzan Haidamous, getting the story the journalist wants requires a great deal of cultural savvy. If the story centers on a specific person, then the fixer must find this person, no matter how difficult this task might be. Haidamous says that to achieve her goal of finding Hiba, she had to search the Syrian refugee camps proliferating in Lebanon in the wake of the Syrian Civil War, all to locate one 13-year-old among many. She then had to convince the girl to do the interview, which was another challenge, because the girl had a wedding to attend and did not feel that the reporters' deadline was particularly urgent (Haidamous, pers. comm., June 2015). For a young Syrian girl living in a refugee camp, a Turkish news network's shooting schedule did not register as a thing of great importance. Thus, Haidamous had to prove to the girl that the Turkish journalists were worth her time, while also securing the girl's testimony for the journalists in a way that the girl found acceptable. In the process of getting the story the journalists wanted, Haidamous had to bring two disparate—but interconnected—worlds together at the moment of the story's conceptualization.

Whatever Haidamous might have thought of this particular story idea, she put her best effort into finding Hiba and convincing her to talk, because responding to her clients' specific request was a central part of her job (pers. comm., June 2015). This is an element of the job that makes many fixers very proud—achieving the impossible and "fixing" the problem that the journalist cannot solve alone. Yet, according to my interviewees, visiting journalists and documentarians vary a great deal on how thoroughly they develop their story ideas before contacting a fixer. Sometimes—as in Haidamous's anecdote— they might contact the fixer with specific instructions. In other cases, the client might not be clear at all.

One anonymous Russian fixer who works with television news and documentary crews says:

There can be a producer calling you out of the blue, and then saying, "So we're coming in a week. We don't have the visas yet." And then the next day [they] pitch a story. [And they say], "There's so many empty blanks that we will want [you] to fill in with something, so we are open for suggestions." And so, this is the worst. . . . You just start throwing things, like ideas, at them. [Then they'll say,] "That's fine. That doesn't suck. That's fine." . . . The news productions, of course, they don't have as much time as feature documentaries, and so they're just pretty much trying to get anything out of pretty much nothing. Or trying to get everything from something. So, it's kind of tricky. (Pers. comm., January 2017)

This individual's statement first points to the fact that journalists and documentarians might go into an international assignment without a clear concept of what the "story" actually "is," destabilizing the notion of the story as an objective and external truth that the fixer must help the journalist capture and transmit to expectant audiences. What is more, this fixer suggests that it is quite challenging to grapple with a client's lack of precision. The difficulty lies partly in the amount of time that the client can spend in the field: news crews have shorter windows of time, and, thus, they are more likely to rush a story and try to "get anything out of pretty much nothing."

Compellingly, this fixer's story points to the imperatives of the world's increasingly interconnected news markets. More and more, this interconnection might demand that journalists from very particular locations rush through their foreign news assignments in order to meet their deadlines and beat the competition. Significantly, journalists might dash into the field without a clear concept of what the story actually is, yet this does not necessarily mean that the client will be more cautious about telling the story in a thorough and nuanced way. According to this anonymous fixer in Russia, the journalist's open-endedness does not always translate into his or her active engagement with the nuances of sociocultural difference. Instead, the intense competition among the increasingly interconnected news markets around the world can hamper the foreign journalist's ability to thoroughly engage with the complexity of the story, a problem that highlights the systemic challenges that face journalists in the field. News fixers are ambivalently caught within this intensely competitive milieu, laboring "underground" in order to help journalists define what stories they should pursue.

Some news fixers say that they spend a great deal of energy trying to decode their clients' open-endedness from the outset, attempting to anticipate what it is that the visiting journalists or documentarians desire. The fixer must "stand in the client's shoes," so to speak, to forecast and then truly comprehend the "type" of story that a client might want. For instance, one fixer and media production manager working in Israel says:

The most challenging thing is to "get" what they want: to understand exactly what they want to get, how they want to film it, and what is their wish list. Once we know that— and it is not always easy, given the distance, the fact that we don't always talk to the persons who will eventually come to Israel and many other factors—we can make sure they get what they want. (Shalev, pers. comm., June 2016)

For Noam Shalev, getting the story the journalist wants is not just a passive process of playing "fetch"—instead, Shalev argues, the fixer has to "get," or comprehend, what the client wants before anything else can happen. The fixer must bridge the physical and cultural distance among the journalists, the news editors back at headquarters, and the people who live in the region the journalist is covering. In the process of conceptualizing the story, the fixer must find a common ground from which to help the client gain a clearer picture of what he or she is trying to accomplish in the field.

One way to get, or comprehend, what the journalist wants is to make suggestions on potential story topics. Genny Masterman, a fixer who works in both Austria and Germany, says that sometimes the clients are

not very clear about it, and then you have to try to read what they are trying to do. Either that, or you ask them more specific questions, and if they say, "Well, we don't know that yet," then you just have to supply them with your ideas and say, "Here are some suggestions." You just give it to them and see what comes out and whether they like it or not. (Pers. comm., September 2016)

Significantly, Masterman alludes to the fact that news fixers try to "read" or interpret what types of stories their clients hope to cover. One way fixers might try to engage in this interpretation is to make suggestions themselves, listing potential topics until their clients recognize one of these suggestions as desirable.

Some journalists like it very much when their fixers make suggestions, as Haidar Adbalhabi, a fixer working in Iraq asserts: "[The journalist] asked me 'Haidar, what do you think will be the next story for us?' I told him, 'trafficking.' I told him that some people sell their own kidneys to live. And he said, 'What the hell?' And I said, 'I got this story from the ground!'" (pers. comm., May 2016). As Adbalhabi says, some clients seek their fixers' suggestions about story ideas because they feel that their fixers might be closer "to the ground" than foreign correspondents and, thus, able to suggest ideas the journalists would never have known about. In these instances, the journalists treat their fixers as "local experts" who can guide them toward more "authentic" stories. Though many news fixers represent their own identities as being far more complex than this, some are still willing to perform the role of the local expert to help their clients achieve their goals in the field.

While some journalists are willing to hear their news fixers' suggestions, fixers say that other clients are not so thrilled to receive their input on potential story ideas. Lamprini Thoma, a fixer working in Greece, remarks that she has to assess each of her clients to ascertain

> if they will see [my suggestions] as a good thing or bad thing. If they will see it as a personal insult. "Who are you? I'm paying you." So, you don't talk, if they do that, you don't talk from there on. But if someone gets the suggestions and consideration, then you have the possibility of building something more with them. And I see that the people that will take suggestions are those that make the greatest stories. (Pers. comm., September 2016)

For Thoma, the "greatest stories" are those that result from a more collaborative relationship between the journalist and the fixer. If she is allowed to engage in cultural mediation in a way that encourages connection and communication, she feels that the client will ultimately end up with a better product—a story made up of multiple perspectives. Yet, sometimes the act of conceptualizing the story is riddled with disconnection and miscommunication. As Thoma also notes, cultural difference can influence the client's interest in the news fixers' suggestions, illuminating the lack of common ground between the fixer, the journalist, and the journalist's readers and viewers:

> You're the local, and it's very easy, especially if [your clients are] nice people, [for you] to think that you will have the first say in everything. But you never know. You know more about your land, but you don't know how much they know about their people and how much their people know about your land and what's happening in your land. So, you have to be very careful and try to see from the way they work, what they really want, and not look like you're taking over. (Pers. comm., September 2016)

Here, Thoma points to the moments when the news fixer's knowledge is not considered an important element of the story the journalist is trying to tell. In these cases, the news fixer must attempt to see a story through different eyes, figure out how to get the story the journalist wants, and—especially when the journalist is suspicious of the fixer—try to "not look like you're taking over."

Thoma's production narrative signals that some news fixers might display the tendency to feel a certain ownership of the story being told, especially when the story is linked to an environment with which the fixer feels deeply familiar. Yet, Thoma also suggests that the fixer's regionally specific knowledge will not necessarily result in the satisfaction of the client, since the client might be trying to please an audience that is foreign to the fixer. This assertion points to the stubbornness of the cultural difference that globalization is often said to have homogenized, implying that there are still journalists and documentarians who perceive themselves as addressing discrete audiences rather than truly "global" publics. For these journalists, the story must be both relevant and marketable to a particular set of people, who are imagined as sharing a certain set of characteristics—and the fixer's perspective can be read as a threat to this marketability.

Thoma also suggests that she feels challenged by her work specifically because of the cultural difference that can cause tension with clients. Because of this difference, Thoma must simultaneously provide her clients with knowledge specific to the region while also "not look[ing] like you're taking over." In other words, she must navigate her knowledge of the events unfolding on the ground, as well as navigating her clients' perceptions of their own cultural authority. Though Thoma implies that her clients do not always have a truly authoritative grasp of what is happening in a specific region, she also feels that she cannot appear to be challenging their authority as eyewitnesses and experts. Avoiding the appearance of "taking over" is an important part of her job.

The fear of the fixer taking over the news story has certainly been invoked by journalists and editors who hire fixers (Palmer and Fontan 2007; Murrell 2015; Palmer 2017), especially by those who believe wholeheartedly that the story is an objective truth that can be coherently transmitted to an expectant news audience. In these cases, the fixer looms large as an inevitably biased individual who has to be treated with caution. Yet, news fixers see things a bit differently. Their production narratives show that fixers agree more with the perspectives of some journalists than with others. This is because they work with so many different kinds of clients, from so many different places, that the journalists' perspectives become more visible *as such*—as particular perspectives, rather than as universal truths.

For instance, a Serbian fixer working in Serbia, Croatia, and Hungary remarks:

> I've worked with Western media that are close to my mindset, you know. I think that's the different approach between East and West. That's very obvious, that's very obvious. You can totally see if a journalist is coming from a democratic country and [if] he's free to work. Or if he's coming from Russia, where everything is controlled. It's very obvious. . . . For example, some Hungarian journalists who covered the refugee crisis. You know, Hungary is not very, they are really keen against refugees. And I said, "You have here some people from a Western European aid organization, if you are interested." [They said] "No, no, no, we are not interested in that." So, you know, you see that the level of democracy in countries is most obvious in the media. That's my opinion. And you can see what kind of approach they have. (Inic, pers. comm., August 2016)

In this story, Inic overtly outlines her own sociopolitical stance, and she also directly flags the fact that she tends to agree more with what she calls Western journalists than Eastern journalists. She also suggests that, having worked with journalists from a variety of different backgrounds, she is aware that all of her clients do indeed have particular sets of perspectives. Rather than arguing that Western clients are more objective, she says that these journalists share her perspectives.

Other fixers celebrate the possibility of learning more from the journalists whose perspectives differ from their own. Though, as the next section of this chapter will show, some news fixers do have to tell their clients "no" when conceptualizing the story, it is by no means a given that news fixers will stubbornly refuse to consider their clients' views. Rather than categorically railing against the perspectives of their clients, some news fixers enjoy the different cultural perspectives that their clients provide. For instance, a fixer and journalist working in Nepal says:

> This is very interesting for me, as a local journalist [in Nepal]. Because some issues I have always seen as not important, or I have a different perspective as a local. . . . Some issues I have seen all the time, and I never thought that it is that important. So, this is amazing for me, because I get to know the perspectives of the people from other worlds. Like another corner of the world, or some Western world, they are

interested in such a story. Some angles of a story. So that is new to learn. (Adhikaree, pers. comm., August 2016)

Similarly, a fixer working in Beirut remarks:

I have a Lebanese mentality and [foreign] journalism sometimes doesn't make sense to me—why would you want to dive into that detail? They were just clashes in the street—why are you asking about this guy's family, or where does he come from, or how did he learn to hold guns? Shouldn't we cover the clashes? And then it would be different. Their [the foreign journalists'] angle would be the background of the people, for example, holding their guns and going through the clashes. How did they get here? Why are they doing this? And I've come to think about it later, it's much more interesting than just covering clashes. It's knowing who are these personalities clashing with each other. How did they get to this point? (Safwan, pers. comm., June 2015)

Both Adhikaree and Safwan believe that the story itself will be different for journalists from disparate sociocultural backgrounds. Adhikaree and Safwan realize that their clients will see a very different story in a particular event than the fixers do. Yet, in these fixers' opinions, this different angle on the story is not a problem. Instead, both Adhikaree and Safwan feel that they can learn a great deal from the distinct ways their clients understand and construct the story. Indeed, they can learn more about their journalistic craft by encountering new interpretations of what the story might be. This mindset complicates the notion of the news fixer as an inevitably biased individual who might try to derail the "correct" interpretation of the story.

Still, it is not always easy for fixers to celebrate or go along with the client's interpretation of the story, especially when they feel the client is approaching an event too carelessly. For example, Anna Nekrasova, a fixer working in Ukraine, remarks that in 2014, journalists began parachuting into the region to cover the conflict with Russia. Nekrasova felt that these reporters' philosophy was to "make the news, go back to their countries, and go into other countries that have other problems" (pers. comm., August 2016). From Nekrasova's perspective, the foreign journalists' idea of the story was a quick and easy play-by-play of the war. She implies that Ukraine was just the latest flavor of the month for parachute journalists who were suddenly and superficially engaging with the country.

Alongside the sense of urgency that arises in the context of conflict or crisis, my interviewees suggest that some of their clients flock to certain places for a different reason: they believe that these places offer a perpetual, predictable story of danger or violence. For instance, an anonymous Russian fixer who works with television crews says that, for a period of time, when journalists and other media workers would come to Russia, "they would be doing stories about gay rights, and corruption, and about HIV. Those were the three stories that they were doing." In turn, this anonymous fixer remarks, "we do have a big problem here with [those things]." Yet, he says that foreign journalists and documentarians focus on "so very, very few positive things, I guess" (pers. comm., January 2017), suggesting that many of his clients have failed to take a truly balanced approach when covering stories in Russia.

For Guatemalan fixer Carlos Duarte, the journalists' stories "mostly would be immigration, poverty, violence and insecurity, human trafficking. War, the long-lost war (pers. comm., August 2016). Yet, Duarte argues that there are other possible perspectives on Guatemala than one that emphasizes violence:

> Guatemala has a lot of things to offer. We have beautiful landscapes, we have beautiful volcanos, we have a lot of tourist attractions. We have a lot of diversity in our culture, our ethnicity. We have great tourist spots that nobody knows; we have a great deal of tourist activities to be done here. Not just your typical tourism, but extreme tourism and adventure. I do believe that it is important that we tell the stories about drugs or human trafficking, violence, human immigration, because it is important to know that not everything out here is perfect or is beautiful. We have a lot of problems that can traverse borders and frontiers and even affect conflicts like with the US. It is important that we tell these stories, but maybe we could focus also on the good stories Guatemala has to offer. (Pers. comm., August 2016)

In Duarte's view, Guatemala is too complex a place to justify the continued journalistic obsession with violence. While some journalists and editors might suggest that Duarte is simply biased in favor of his country, it is crucial to note that Duarte says he often helps his clients cover the stories of violence that they associate with Guatemala. He does not stand in their way, because he feels that it is his job to help these journalists get their story (pers. comm., August 2016). But he does lament the fact that there are many more layers to Guatemala than the typical foreign news reporter tends to pursue. In this sense, the news fixer can inhabit two sociocultural registers at once: disagreeing with the journalist's perspective on a particular event or region, while at the same time helping the journalist tell the story from that very perspective.

News fixers who inhabit these dual registers tend to describe their work in terms of the broader set of world news markets. They often assert that this is not, at the end of the day, their own story, but someone else's story—and this story needs to be marketable for the client. Duarte is far from naive about why it is that foreign reporters tend to portray the story of Guatemala as a violent one. He feels that this type of story "attract[s] audiences. People really are attracted to drug dealers and guns and money and that kind of thing. People are attracted to that, and that's why these stories get so much attention" (pers. comm., August 2016). Some of my other interviewees also make this argument. One anonymous fixer and photographer working in Istanbul says that international photographers working for major agencies "always shoot the same stuff" (pers. comm., July 2015). Seeing a similar pattern of repetition in the work of the journalists who cover Lebanon, a fixer based in Beirut says that this "pattern shows me that there's literally a market for news. Like [there's] a market for anything else. And so, there's an item that everybody wants to buy. And so, in news, there's few stories and items, that everybody wants to write about. And ironically, major news outlets want to cover it as well" (Nayel, pers. comm., June 2015). Nayel especially notes this tendency

FIGURE 1.1 Graffiti on a wall in Beirut, June 2015. News fixers working in the area suggest that the conflict in Syria is a difficult story to "conceptualize" due to its complexity and its proximity. Photo by the author.

with news organizations flocking to Beirut to cover the Syrian Civil War, a conflict that fixers in Beirut suggest is intensely complicated (see figure 1.1).

In Nayel's view, the lack of diversity in international news stories is related to the fact that international reporters tend to echo the foreign policies of their governments in their reports (pers. comm., June 2015), which in turn attracts patriotic readers. This very critical statement invokes what some scholars have identified as the underbelly of globalization: the homogenization of media messages (Thussu 2007; Paterson 2010), and the imposition of particular ideological stances—specifically, that of the US-led "war on terror"—onto diverse regions of the world (Thussu and Friedman 2003; Kellner 2003; Miller 2007). In a sense, these statements point to the contradictions embedded within globalization: the potential dominance of more powerful sociocultural perspectives, even as the world's deep disjunctures and divides become all the more visible. The proliferation of certain news narratives across various world news markets not only leads to a limited set of stories—it also potentially leads to a dire misrepresentation of disparate ways of life.

While not all of my interviewees see things from such a bleak perspective, many of them do assert that there are instances in which their clients' version of the story cannot be allowed to stand. Sometimes this is because the client's wishes are culturally or logistically impossible to fulfill. At other times, it is because the journalists do not adequately understand the complicated sociohistorical background of the place they are visiting. And at other times, the clients might reveal such a limited set of preconceived notions about the people and places being covered that the fixer will either try to directly correct the journalist or stop working with the client altogether. News fixers are paid to work with their clients, and they also retain the right to refuse certain assignments that go against their ethics. In these circumstances, the process of cultural mediation is marked with moments of disconnection rather than connection.

Contesting the Story the Journalist Wants

When the news fixer contests or even refuses to conceptualize a story from the client's perspective, working relationships can quickly become riddled with distrust. From the journalist's perspective, the fixer might be trying to control the story at its earliest stage because he or she might not understand or care about journalistic objectivity or balance (Palmer and Fontan 2007; Murrell 2015). This fear is not always unfounded. For instance, Finnish journalist Ida Tikka says that she was working with a fixer in Crimea, shortly after the 2014 conflict (pers. comm., January 2017). Tikka's goal was to discuss how the Crimean education system was being revamped to display a more "Russian" mindset. But to her dismay, her fixer instead found her a school that still used a "Ukrainian" curriculum, despite the fact that the majority of the schools in the area had already switched over. From Tikka's perspective, it was very clear that her fixer was trying to push a specific political agenda:

> After that I was kind of against using fixers. . . . If you choose a fixer as randomly as I did, it's the worst way to go, because then you can choose a fixer who is pushing you to places. And then you end up seeing what the fixer wants you to see. I mean if it's not trustworthy, then it's of course kind of problematic. (Pers. comm., January 2017)

Evgeni Balamutenko, a Russian television news reporter who has used news fixers on assignment in Yemen, voices a similar complaint. He says that during his assignment, he struggled to cover any official story without a fixer assigned by the Ministry of Information: "He had all the papers, information, and [through him], we spoke to some army generals. . . . [The fixer also] translated. He didn't bring us any big exclusives. No. But as for officially—well, you need to have some official interviews from the army, from politicians, stuff like that" (pers. comm., January 2017). Balamutenko says that he and his crew had to sneak off with a different, "secret" fixer in order to get some of the "big exclusives" for which they were searching, exclusives that involved rather different perspectives than those of Yemen's Ministry of Information.

Though some news fixers are undoubtedly assigned by local governments to keep an eye on the foreign press—most especially in Syria during the early years of the civil war, as well as in Iran at least as early as the 1990s and continuing into the 21st century—this arrangement is usually something journalists know ahead of time. In these cases, the journalists can anticipate their fixer's limitations and make plans to work around these obstacles, as Balamutenko did. Yet, there are a vast number of fixers working across the world, and they do this work for a number of reasons. All but one of the fixers I interviewed assert that they work on an entirely freelance basis, or that they were hired by foreign bureaus to work with their correspondents. One out of my 75 interviewees says that she had previously been recruited by the government of Iran to report back to Iranian officials on what foreign journalists were doing. Even so, this fixer enjoyed a long relationship with the *New York Times*, among other international news organizations, before eventually moving to Canada in 2009 (Fathi, pers. comm., July 2015; Chira, pers. comm., 2016).

Rather than conceptualizing a story along directly "official" lines, in most cases, news fixers might contest a journalist's version of the story for other reasons—some of them professional, and some of them cultural. For instance, freelance journalist Alasdair Baverstock tells this anecdote about a time his fixers in Venezuela refused his version of the story:

> I'd been sent in by the newspaper to do a story on how disastrous the situation in Venezuela was. So, I was very focused on that story. We go take pictures, and we're going to find examples of the most extreme cases that you could find in Venezuela. And the fixer and camerawoman team said that this wasn't ethical "because you're not telling the whole truth." So that was a relationship that broke down slightly. . . . I was saying, "I've been sent down here to do a very specific story on how disastrous the situation in Venezuela was and how the people are suffering." So, we would go to certain places like schools and I would find examples of people—you know, a kid who hadn't eaten all day. And I would say, "Right, well, we need a picture of this kid because he hasn't eaten today," but they would say, "Oh well, what about his twenty-four other classmates?" And I would say, "Well, it's true, they are here, but that doesn't affect his situation. Just because his twenty-five other classmates have eaten doesn't mean he's any less hungry." So, we came to a sort of a crossroads there, and they said, "We've decided not to continue," and that's that. (Pers. comm., March 2017)

In Baverstock's case, the news fixer fundamentally disagreed with the ethics of Baverstock's angle on the story. As Baverstock mentions, he had been sent to Venezuela "to do a very specific story on how disastrous the situation" was. Disaster *was* the story as far as Baverstock's editors were concerned. Yet, Baverstock's fixer and locally based camerawoman did not see disaster in the same places where Baverstock was looking. Baverstock saw one child who was starving, and his fixer and camerawoman saw 24 children who were not starving. Because Baverstock's locally based team felt that he was foregrounding hunger in a situation where there was far more evidence of children being fed, his team decided to discontinue the working relationship altogether. According to Baverstock, the fixer and camerawoman said that this was a problem of ethics—they felt that Baverstock was twisting the evidence to fit a predetermined angle. Significantly, the professional ethics of Baverstock's team differed from his professional ethics—a fear that is often invoked by journalists when they discuss their relationships with news fixers

(Palmer and Fontan 2007; Murrell 2015; Palmer 2017). Yet, this did not cause Baverstock to end the relationship. Instead, things happened the other way around.

Baverstock's case illuminates the moments of disconnection that sometimes arise in the process of conceptualizing the story. Though the news fixer's job is to help the journalist get the story, there are times when the fixer's efforts may veer more in favor of the regional cultures, rather than in favor of the journalist's agenda. This can take the shape of total disconnection, when a news fixer discontinues the working relationship. It can also take the shape of the news fixer staying with the client but actively contesting the story the journalist wants to do. This contestation might come as a result of irreconcilable disagreement over the perspective the story should take. It might also come as a result of the correspondent's misunderstanding of what type of story is feasible in the environment he or she is visiting.

One of the first ways in which news fixers might contest the story at its moment of conceptualization is by saying that the story simply cannot be done, for logistical or cultural reasons. For example, Balamutenko—who, besides working as a journalist, also works as a fixer for foreign journalists visiting Moscow—says that because he knows the Moscow elite very well, he can tell a journalist from the outset whether it makes sense to try to build a story around a particular person. "You have to have some reasons," Balamutenko explains, "some sense, and then, [the journalists will say] 'OK, we trust you. We're not meeting him'" (pers. comm., January 2017). In Balamutenko's case, presenting the clients with good reasons for redirecting their conceptualization of the story can convince the journalists to consider his advice.

Still, news fixers sometimes receive what they consider to be highly problematic suggestions from potential clients. One anonymous news fixer and production company owner in Mexico City, gives this example:

> I once got a request from a crazy correspondent who wanted to do an interview with a drug lord. In two days. Just go in and do it and come back. And I told him that this was not possible, that time needed to be invested, to achieve this. Time needed to be invested so we could nail it, and we have nailed it before for another client. And then the reporter was like, "Oh, tell them that my name is this and that," and—you know what? They don't really care. They don't really care who you are. (Pers. comm., March 2017)

In this individual's case, the client was so out of touch with the way things worked in Mexico that he simply assumed he could parachute into the country, interview a powerful cartel member, and then leave without a problem. What is more, the journalist felt that his professional reputation should gain him quicker and easier access to this individual. Thus, this fixer had to bring the correspondent back to reality, informing him that such a story idea—combined with such a tight deadline—simply could not be executed. The realities of the story were bigger and messier than the correspondent understood.

Nabih Bulos, a former news assistant working in Lebanon, tells a similar story: "This was a request that I received from someone: 'Can you take me to the Hezbollah opium fields?' Right? Hezbollah doesn't have opium fields, for one. And, even if they did, it's not like they're going to sit there and take anyone there. I mean the level of idiocy" (pers. comm., June 2015). For Bulos, the "idiocy" of such impossible requests stems from what he views as many visiting correspondents' profound lack of background knowledge on the people and places they are trying to represent in their stories: "The fact of the matter is, when you go into a new place, you can and should do proper research beforehand" (pers. comm., June 2015).

In some cases, a journalist's lack of knowledge might inspire the fixer to object to the story from the outset. For instance, Nayel tells this anecdote about a time when he escorted a visiting journalist to a Palestinian refugee camp in Lebanon:

> We got to the camp and I was like, "We are at the camp now." And she literally, with a straight face said, "Oh really? Where are the tents?" And I thought she was joking, and I told her, "Look, this is not a joke. It's been about sixty-seven years these people have been living as refugees in these shanty towns." She said, "No, when you said, 'camps,' I imagined 'camps.'" So, I asked her, "Do you know, do you know about the Palestinian refugees, and since when they have been kicked out of their country?" And so, when I realized she didn't know much about it, I said, "We need to go back home. I don't think we can do the story now." And I prevented her from doing the story. (Pers. comm., June 2015)

In Nayel's case, the visiting journalist's lack of background knowledge on the Palestinian refugee camps in Lebanon was so disturbing that he actively convinced her not to do the story at all. Because he felt that she had not engaged enough with the history of the place on which she was reporting, Nayel felt that the best course of action was to refuse the story altogether.

Nayel's case is one of the more extreme examples my interviewees have shared with me. More typically, a news fixer will try to fill in the gaps in a visiting journalist's knowledge. This is an element of the news fixer's labor that makes some fixers very proud. For instance, Larisa Inic says that it is her job

> to provide information, not just translating, but to research, to prepare your journalist for the story, to make it properly. I think it's a very responsible job. You have some kind of responsibility because it's up to you how that story will be published. If you do your research well, your journalist will have a good story. (Pers. comm., August 2016)

For Dzmitry Halko, a fixer working in Ukraine, the fixer must help the correspondent "separate the wheat from the chaff, [the] facts from bullshit" (pers. comm., August 2016). And for an anonymous French fixer, a big part of the fixer's job is "giving the general context" (pers. comm., September 2016). In each of these cases, the implication is that journalists hire fixers to help them learn more about the places they are visiting. This is a task that some fixers embrace, taking delight in the opportunity to share their knowledge about a particular place with their clients and, by extension, with their clients' audiences.

Yet, some fixers also imply that their clients' lack of background knowledge is rather staggering. Colombian fixer Catalina Hernández says that one visiting reporter "mostly wanted to know about how Colombia works, how Bogota works, how Colombian society works, all that stuff. And then about displaced people" (pers. comm., August 2016). Hernández's words suggest that this reporter knew next to nothing about Colombia on entry. And Leena Saidi, a very well-known fixer who has long been based in Beirut, asserts: "Sometimes, their knowledge of the country is very, very limited. You really have to sort of open their eyes to things. You have to explain history, things like that. . . . I'm not saying that happens all the time, but sometimes it does" (Pers. comm., May 2013).

Crucially, Saidi says that some journalists *have* done their homework ahead of the assignment: "Other times you're really surprised when people come in and they've really done their research, and they've really read, and they come back. And sometimes they surprise me by telling me something that I didn't know. You know, it can work both ways." Palestinian fixer Abeer Ayyoub echoes Saidi's observation, declaring that the journalists with whom she has worked "know Gaza by meter" (pers. comm., September 2014).

Ayyoub says that she has learned professionalism from these journalists who sometimes seem to know her city as well or better than she does.

But despite these more positive assessments of foreign correspondents' knowledge of the places they cover, most of my interviewees suggest that it is not necessarily uncommon for foreign correspondents to go on assignment without enough background knowledge to do the story alone. Instead, the journalists must hire fixers to help them fill in the blanks, pointing to the remarkable dependence of the various international news industries on the labor of locally based support staff. Though fixers imply that this dependence on regionally specific knowledge undeniably contributes to the fixer's income, they also sometimes feel that the level of ignorance that journalists tend to display is too high: "Sometimes I got shocked," says Lebanese news assistant Hwaida Saad, of her former days as a freelance fixer. "They [journalists] don't know the area. At the same time, they want to come and cover it. And most of the time, we sit with our friends and we complain, 'If you want to come to the area, you should know the area'" (pers. comm., June 2015).

Saad is aware that journalists hire fixers for this very reason—to inform them of the crucial details they are missing. Yet, the short deadlines so typical of the world's competitive news industries make it difficult for fixers to help in the more extreme situations where correspondents display far too much ignorance about their own news story:

> What can you do? You can do the best to clarify, make things much clearer, but at the same time, if he doesn't have the background, what can you do? . . . He will be here for a couple of days. What can you do? And he wants to do this assignment, so you don't have much time to tell him, "you should do this, this, and this." (Saad, pers. comm., June 2015)

An anonymous British fixer working in Italy puts Saad's concerns even more bluntly: "Deadlines make for errors galore" (pers. comm., September 2016). Fixers can help journalists avoid these errors—if the journalists are willing to listen. As Kenyan fixer Immanuel Muasya asserts: "I take care of how the story gets done, how the story gets said. Because most people who come here, they've never been to Kenya, and they don't know much about Kenya, and they mostly know about Kenyans [from] what they see on the media, or what they see online" (pers. comm., May 2016).

In Muasya's experience, many journalists come to Kenya with preconceived notions that they ostensibly learned by watching TV or reading stories on the internet. In fixer Daniel Saneo's experience, these preconceived notions come straight from the correspondents' editors. Of the many journalists who Saneo has worked with in the Balkans since the 1990s, he says: "They usually came with prepared lines, sort of instructions from the editors . . . and not knowing the history, when the history is a pretty slippery place" (pers. comm., August 2016). Both Muasya's and Saneo's remarks point to a more insidious problem than a mere lack of background knowledge. They argue that, sometimes, journalists come to a place with an astonishing level of false knowledge about the region or the people. This differs slightly from the lack of background knowledge, in that it signals a set of assumptions that are often one-sided, but that sometimes masquerade as the whole "truth."

Inic feels that this is a problem that has intensified over time:

> The approach of journalists changed. You know, that's what I've found strange, even some media that are not boulevard media or tabloids. Even some serious media have that approach: searching for, you know, they call it a personal angle, but I'm very sensitive when it comes to professionalism in journalism. Because it's a really, really thin line between that personal approach and digging into something that would hurt someone. I think that's the line you can't cross as a journalist: to hurt someone. (Pers. comm., August 2016).

Crucially, Inic points to the ethical problem with pursuing predetermined news angles, especially those that focus on sensationalism over nuance. In carelessly pursuing a predetermined angle on a story, the journalist potentially hurts someone—either individually or on a larger social level. The obsession with chasing a particular angle on a story can lead to coverage that relies heavily on sociopolitical stereotypes.

For instance, one fixer in Beirut who wishes to remain anonymous says that when reporters were coming into the region to cover the early years of the Syrian Civil War, they were seeking a very distinct angle on that incredibly complicated story: "So I understand that the policy or the concept in general is supportive to the rebels in Syria and the anti-Islam regime or whatever. OK. Sometimes, sometimes they [the journalists] try to focus on how good are the rebels" (pers. comm., June 2015). Yet, even in its earliest stages, the civil war in Syria was far more complicated than the "good guys versus bad guys" narrative suggested; a narrative that was markedly popular in US news coverage of the story (Palmer 2018). As the rise of the Islamic State of Iraq and the Levant (ISIL) has shown, the monolithically termed "rebels" were made up of competing groups with different agendas. Because of that, my interviewee found some of her clients' preconceived notions on the story too reductive.

A former fixer and stringer for a wire service in Pakistan sees a connection between some news organizations' competitive angles on the story and the damaging stereotypes that can be propagated as a result:

> International wire services, they look for a particular angle in a story. They have that mindset already. Like, for example, Karachi is, according to them, without being there on the ground, they would say that it's a hotbed of terrorism and militancy. But on the ground, it's not like that at all, you know? It's not like that at all. But they would push for that angle because that's how I know they are able to sell the story worldwide. It's their compulsion, it's the commercial value that they make there. You see terrorism these days has become a keyword to sell stories. (Siddiqui, pers. comm., April 2013)

In this statement, Siddiqui is specifically addressing the international news services that have long furnished many of the world's news organizations with stories (Paterson 2010). In the wake of the September 11 attacks on the World Trade Center, and the resulting US-led "war on terror," Siddiqui argues that news agencies increasingly pursued the "terrorism" angle—at the expense of the far more nuanced situation unfolding on the ground.

It is important to note that preconceived notions are not a failing only on the part of Western journalists. Alexander Bratersky, a Russian fixer who has also worked as a foreign correspondent in the United States, says:

> A lot of Russian journalists also have stereotypes about America, when they come over. When I was a foreign correspondent, I remember that people were calling me from Moscow and asking me all these stupid questions for the Pentagon. And I said, "I wouldn't be allowed into the Pentagon if I would ask those questions, people would think that I'm crazy." (Pers. comm., January 2017)

In Bratersky's assessment, stereotypes plague journalists from all sociocultural backgrounds. Rather than pointing to a "West" versus "the rest" flow of media production and narrativization, Bratersky illuminates the increasingly interconnected media sphere, where misconceptions about social and political difference can move in multiple directions.

Because of these misconceptions, some of my interviewees feel it is part of their job to try to balance their clients' preconceived notions rather than disconnecting with them. And in certain cases, their clients do consider what the fixers have said. According to Alyona Pimanova, a Russian fixer and production company owner, and Daniel Smith, Pimanova's British partner who also works in Moscow, journalists and other media workers

> come here with a preconception that it's going to be not safe. Or, that Russians are really serious and unhappy. And then at some point, they see the difference. Depending also on the location, we know the spaces that we can show [the region] from a different angle. So, it's just also interesting to them. (Smith, Pers. comm., January 2017)

For Smith and Pimanova, encountering a client with preconceived notions about Russia is a typical part of the job. In turn, they suggest that it is also their job to draw upon their regionally specific knowledge to show their clients some "different angle[s]." Through the act of showing the visiting journalists or documentarians some alternatives to their preconceptions, Smith and Pimanova play an active role in mediating the cultural misunderstandings that plague the practice of international news reporting.

Nitzan Almog, a fixer working in Israel, agrees that a proactive approach is best:

> The crews that I work with, when they come here, they usually have some kind of opinion from things that they were exposed to in the news about Israel, about the conflict, about everything. And for me, I think it's important, valuable at the end, when they leave, that I helped them to understand both sides. (Pers. comm., May 2016)

And Benjamin Zagzag, a French news fixer whose parents are Jewish Tunisians, gives a more specific example of how this type of mediation might occur:

> Regarding the way French people see the Muslim population: like in Paris, for instance, people were OK after the [2015 terrorist] attack. The [foreign] journalists were like, "Oh the Muslim people were not afraid something was going to happen or of being attacked?" And we were like, "No, no, no, that's not the way we react in France. You know,

it's not because of a terrorist attack that we're going to blame all the
Muslim population." (Pers. comm., September 2016)

In each of the above testimonies, my interviewees express their conviction
that they can help their clients see the story from a more nuanced angle.
Rather than disconnecting from their clients, as some fixers choose to do,
other news fixers decide to engage with their clients' preconceived notions
and show them some alternative perspectives. While some journalists and
news editors might argue that in these instances news fixers are trying to
skew an otherwise "objective" story (Palmer and Fontan 2007; Murrell
2015), there is a different way of reading these scenarios. One could also
argue that in the process of helping their clients conceptualize the story,
news fixers are revealing the complexity of the story itself, illuminating the
need for more cross-cultural dialogue between the news organizations who
send correspondents to disparate geopolitical regions and the locally based
fixers who mediate between the always interconnected articulations of the
"global" and the "local."

Conclusion

Media ethicist Nick Couldry says that "our formulations of a specific ethics
of media must be shaped by the distinctive human needs that media can fulfill and the distinctive harms that media can cause: respectively, the need for
information and the harm of misrecognition, or lack of recognition" (2013,
17). The need for information can all too easily give way to the tendency toward misrecognition, a problem that postcolonial media scholars associate
with the "politics of communication" (Shome and Hegde 2002, 261). For
these scholars, the daring act of directly critiquing the politics of communication "will lead eventually to the production of a more just and equitable
knowledge base about the third world, the other, and the 'rest' of the world"
(2002, 261).

Whether or not they see themselves as being based in the "third world,"
news fixers' production narratives arguably reveal a similar concern with the
problem of international journalists sometimes misrepresenting—or indeed,
misrecognizing—the people and places they cover in their stories. In turn,
fixers suggest that this misrecognition can happen quite early in the reporting
process—at the very moment of conceptualizing the story. But for news fixers
making a living in the field, critiquing the politics of communication is not

always easy, and, sometimes, it is simply unfeasible. Because of the increasingly interconnected set of news markets in the age of globalization, certain news narratives are currently more marketable than others. These narratives might be riddled with (mis)representations; yet, some news fixers might feel the need to bolster these narratives anyway in order to make a living. In other instances, news fixers might steer their clients away from these narratives and toward a different understanding of what the story should be about.

Clearly, the labor of conceptualizing the story is highly complicated for news fixers. On one level, fixers might receive a specific request from a potential client—a request that may or may not be realistic. Though plenty of fixers take pride in their ability to make such requests come true, no matter how challenging, there are other fixers who occasionally have to say "no." When fixers and their clients do successfully proceed into a working relationship in the field, even more complications can arise. While fixers sometimes receive very specific story requests, at other times, they might receive only the vaguest description of a story idea from the journalist or documentarian, a problem that can be even more challenging than receiving an impossible request. In these cases, the fixer must strike the balance between "getting," or understanding, what the journalist wants and making new suggestions without appearing to take over.

In the best cases, journalists and other media workers who hire fixers do listen to the varying perspectives their fixers provide—most especially when those clients lack the necessary historical and political background knowledge on the events being covered. These are occasions where locally based fixers can serve as active collaborators in the story's conceptualization, helping to clarify the nuances that need to be properly represented. Though not all fixers are perfect, and not all fixers are experts, my interviewees each argue that they have much to offer a foreign journalist or media worker visiting their region. Clients can learn from their fixers in the same way that fixers can learn from their clients.

In the worst cases, though, news fixers suggest that some reporters and documentarians travel to certain regions with a particular angle in mind, and this angle might be informed by preconceived notions that could lead to a misrepresentation of the people or places being covered. These are the cases that most profoundly illuminate the need for scholars, students, and industry practitioners to pay more heed to news fixers' professional narratives. Listening to news fixers' accounts of conceptualizing the story can help both scholars and practitioners to be more capable of "tak[ing] global cultural diversity seriously rather than incorporate[ing] it as epistemological exotica," as well as "avoid[ing] treating whole regions and traditions as homogenous and internally uncontested" (Wasserman 2011, 793).

News fixers' professional narratives paint a more complicated picture of the places, people, and events that foreign correspondents cover. They also illuminate the cultural mediation that occurs in the earliest stages of the international reporting process. Though foreign journalists have long been understood as the authoritative eyewitnesses who see the "truth" firsthand and then transmit it to their audiences (Zelizer 2007), news fixers' testimonies complicate that idea. Their accounts instead point to the central role that locally based media employees play in identifying, fine-tuning, and capturing the story.

The labor of conceptualizing the story largely unfolds "underground," and it is a complicated dance of connection and disconnection, communication and silence. Another aspect of the news fixer's labor also operates in this way. Chapter 2 discusses the work of navigating the logistics of an international news assignment, a job that at first glance seems deceptively simple. Journalists and editors often suggest that a fixer's job is mostly just to handle the logistics (Murrell 2015; Palmer 2017). Yet, as chapter 2 will show, even the "logistical" elements of the fixer's labor require the fixer to play an active role, helping the journalist navigate the culturally specific red tape and the geographically specific terrain that can make the difference between a journalist's success or failure in filing a report from the field.

2

Navigating the Logistics

*As a fixer, you're a tool. No more than a tool. . . .It's like if
you have a Swiss Army knife, you might have the tool set
[with which] you can do more than fifty things.*

—Anonymous photojournalist and fixer in Istanbul

*The fixer is not only a guide that is fixing things for you,
arranging things for you. . . . if you don't know where you're
going, then you can end up in some very difficult situations.*

—JAIME VELAZQUEZ, journalist and fixer in South Africa

A MAJOR POINT of discussion among news fixers and the media professionals
who hire them is the question of whether fixing is "skilled labor." In journalism, as well as in other types of media production, skilled labor is linked
with the active and the creative—with purposefully crafting a compelling
newspaper article or editing the moving images of "real" people and places
into an impactful visual narrative. Some media professionals invoke this notion of the active and the creative when describing the difference between the
skilled labor of the journalist or documentarian and the ostensibly "unskilled"
labor of the fixer. For instance, the photojournalist quoted in the epigraph
to this chapter says, "as a fixer, you're a tool. No more than a tool. So, I don't
prefer to do fixing too much, that's why I keep my prices going up" (pers.
comm., July 2015).

As his statement suggests, this photojournalist sees fixing as a passive en-
terprise, one in which the fixer is used by someone else. Because he believes
the fixer is passively used for another's purposes, this photojournalist implies
that fixers cannot be viewed as journalists at all. Other foreign reporters echo
this observation: "They [the fixers] are not the journalist," says freelance correspondent Sulome Anderson. "I'm the journalist. I do the work myself."
Clarifying what the "work" actually is, Anderson adds: "I have the story, I ask

the questions. It's not like [my fixer] is doing my job for me" (pers. comm., June 2015).

Some journalists and documentarians feel that correspondents' jobs are simply different from fixers' jobs. For instance, they suggest that fixers "are the ones to get you things" (anonymous camerawoman, pers. comm., December 2012) or that fixers are the people who pick journalists up when they arrive at the airport (Pool-Eckert, pers. comm., February 2015). Even some fixers appear to agree with this perception: for instance, Nabih Bulos, a former news assistant for the *Los Angeles Times* in Beirut, says that fixing involves "just showing [the journalists] around, helping them arrange for drivers, you know, logistics." Bulos also says that during his tenure with the *LA Times*, he tried not to "act like a fixer" and that he wants "to remove any notion of the word 'fixer' from anything I do in the future" (pers. comm., June 2015). This is because Bulos's ultimate goal was to work as a full-fledged news correspondent—something he later achieved. For Bulos, as with the anonymous photojournalist and fixer in Turkey, the logistical role of the fixer was precisely the thing that foreclosed his ability to take ownership of the story, and, by extension, to be a true journalist.

Few fixers would disagree that navigating the logistics of foreign news assignments is a central element of their labor. These media employees do tend to retrieve journalists from the airport, drive them around the city, or hire drivers for trickier excursions. They also deal with the bureaucracy inherent to each country, helping the correspondent to secure the necessary visas for entry, as well as obtaining the permissions required to bring their media equipment into the region or to shoot video in certain areas. Alongside these more concrete logistical tasks, fixers say they help journalists "get" a diverse array of relevant and irrelevant things—from camel's milk (Kaloki, pers. comm., June 2016) to power generators (Duarte, pers. comm., August 2016), to drugs and women (anonymous fixer in Mexico, pers. comm., March 2017).

Yet, in the cases where visiting journalists cannot hire a news fixer—usually because they cannot afford one—the correspondents complete these tasks. The young freelancers who do not have the budget for a news fixer will likely find their own hotels, hire their own drivers, and take care of their own visas. Even so, they are still considered journalists. Thus, it is difficult to relegate news fixers to the realm of "unskilled labor" simply because—on top of all the other roles they play—they often play a logistical role.

It is also necessary to realize that the notion of the "logistical" is far more complicated in international news reporting than some journalists and documentarians might admit. The labor of arranging, procuring, and navigating is highly active and resourceful, something that requires cultural know-how and collaborative skill. "You get really tight deadlines, you get really fucked-up requests, and you've got to achieve all of that. And so, you have to be extremely creative," says one anonymous fixer and production company owner in Mexico City (pers. comm., March 2017). Another fixer working in Mexico City similarly argues that news fixers should not be called "fixers" at all but rather "local producers"—"because 'fixer' is a word that fixes something that doesn't have a word" (Miller, pers. comm., March 2017). As Miller suggests, the "fixing" element of his labor addresses something more ineffable, more fluid, than travel arrangements and visas. In a similar line, Israeli news fixer and local producer Oren Rosenfeld bluntly states: "We don't 'fix' things. We arrange things, we produce things" (pers. comm., May 2016).

This chapter will look more closely at the task of navigating the logistics, arguing that although news fixers' logistical work might seem like the most uncreative and passive element of their labor, fixers' production narratives represent this task as a creative cultural process. This is because navigating the logistics requires the fixer to negotiate with differing temporalities and spatialities. In a quite material fashion, fixers help international journalists come to terms with sometimes vastly different articulations of both space and time. The fixer must rush to meet the journalists' deadlines, hurtling across terrain that is sometimes bewildering to the foreign correspondent. Often, the correspondent's work schedule differs drastically from regional understandings of time. The fixer must in turn grapple with locally based articulations of space, which may be elusive of (or hostile to) the journalists' desire to go to particular places. In this sense, the fixer must truly navigate the client through competing temporalities and spatialities.

But the effort at navigation is not always successful. The stubbornness of cultural difference looms large in news fixers' stories about navigating the logistics, pointing to the fact that this task is riven with moments of disconnection as well as connection, with miscommunication as well as with communication. In some cases, fixers simply cannot help their clients overcome certain laws about bringing camera equipment into a given nation-state. In other cases, the specificities of the space itself might confound the client's schedule. For instance, the tendency for certain roads to close very suddenly or for gunfire to break out in particular hot zones might lead the fixer to tell the client "no" rather than to magically fix the problem. Finally, regionally specific notions of cultural identity—of nation, of ethnicity, of gender—might inhibit the fixer from accompanying a journalist to a particular area, no matter how hard the fixer might try to "assume various identities in different contexts" (Sporturno 2014, 123).

These moments of disconnection are a reality of cultural mediation, and they sit uneasily alongside the expansive imperatives of the world's increasingly interconnected news markets. News fixers' accounts of "navigating the logistics" say a great deal about the precarious economy of international news reporting in the 21st century. In the era of shrinking news budgets and foreign-bureau closures (Paterson and Sreberny 2004; Williams 2011), correspondents move quickly to different sites around the world. This quick movement from one site to the next results in journalists' lack of familiarity with the places they visit, causing them to rely heavily on the regionally specific knowledge of their fixers.

What is more, the intensifying interconnection of disparate media markets, platforms, and technologies contributes to the staunch international competitiveness that leads correspondents from diverse regions to pursue tighter and tighter deadlines. This industrial precariousness surfaces in news fixers' stories about their work, most especially when they describe instances in which their clients become anxious about visiting the most compelling—and often, the most dangerous—places in the timeliest, yet safest, manner. Fixers describe these moments with both pride and frustration. They are proud of their ability to sometimes reconcile competing temporalities and spatialities, yet, they are also frustrated by the correspondents' or news editors' occasional inability to be temporally and spatially flexible.

In order to discuss these points in more detail, this chapter first examines the nature of the word "logistics," thinking carefully about the word's connection to the skilled labor to successfully navigate competing cultural articulations of both time and space. I will then show that the task of navigating the logistics requires that news fixers inhabit more than one temporality and spatiality at the same time. This phenomenon plays out in the process of making travel arrangements, obtaining photography permissions, and securing visas. It also informs the fixer's role in guiding foreign correspondents across unfamiliar geographical terrain. The very need for a news fixer in the first place reveals that news organizations' understandings of time and space are particular, rather than universal, and that they are influenced by the imperatives of the world's increasingly interconnected global news markets—imperatives that do not always take disparate lived experiences of time and space into account.

Logistics in Time and Space

The *Oxford English Dictionary* defines the term "logistics" as follows: "The organization of supplies, stores, quarters, etc., necessary for the support of troop movements, expeditions" (2017). According to the *OED*, this is the current definition of the word, and it certainly seems relevant to news fixers. For instance, this definition places an emphasis on organization, on the ability to juggle a number of different tasks all at once. This definition also uses the word "support," another term that tends to surface in both fixers' and journalists' discussions of the work that fixers do. Finally, this definition suggests the carefully orchestrated navigation of both time and space: "organization" is "necessary" to facilitate the movement of large groups of people across space in a specific allotment of time.

The *OED*'s examination of the term's historical usage is even more telling. First, there is an example of logistics being viewed as an "art"—"the art of moving and quartering troops" (1898 cited in *OED* 2017). The concept of logistics has also been defined as a "science"—"the science of moving and supplying troops" (Burne 1944, cited in *OED* 2017). Conceptualizing this term as an art and a science suggests that the people who historically managed logistics were viewed as skilled laborers. This becomes all the more evident when examining one of the obsolete definitions of the word in its adjective form: "pertaining to reasoning; logical." Since reason and logic have long been viewed as the accomplishments of scholars and philosophers in the English-speaking world, the word's history suggests a certain mastery that requires a high level of skill. The term's etymology also invokes something much loftier than "support" or even basic "organization." The *OED* shows that a precursor to the adjective "logistic" is the related word, "logos." This ancient Greek term has become associated over time with the creative concept of language, writing, and even the divinity of the Christian messiah, who is understood by practitioners of Christianity to have embodied the divine word of God in human form.

Following this etymological trail, the history of the English-language term "logistics" suggests that the tendency for media professionals to conceptually separate the labor of logistics from the ostensibly more skilled labor of writing and producing is misguided. Even if the concept of logistics did not retain traces of the headier notions of creativity, reason, and metaphysics, the 1944 use of the word suggests that logistical tacticians possess a special sort of knowledge that sets them apart: "knowledge of the material conditions" (Burne 1944, cited in *OED* 2017). Without this knowledge, the military endeavors and large-scale expeditions mentioned in the *OED*'s definition would not be possible. This is because such knowledge ideally informs the broader negotiation that unfolds between a person or group with a specific set of goals and the material conditions that potentially challenge these goals.

Compellingly, the *OED*'s various definitions of the term "logistics" also subtly point to something else: the collision between competing cultural articulations of time and space. For instance, while the leader of an expedition might have a very particular set of goals for navigating time and space, the material conditions on the ground might actively inhibit the realization of these goals. It is the task of the logician to translate these material conditions for the leader of the expedition, and, in so doing, the logician must be able to comprehend—and, ideally, bring into harmony—very different approaches to the temporal and the spatial. If we look at news outlets' efforts at covering international stories as a type of modern-day "expedition," the connections become clear. Journalists and documentarians hire fixers because they assume that these locally based media employees will know the material conditions "on the ground." This does not mean, however, that journalists—and especially, their editors back at headquarters—will always accept the material conditions at face value. Instead, the news fixer must actively grapple with both the regional and the distant understandings of particular times and spaces.

But in many cases, this complicated task gets recoded as something more vulgar or, at best, as something entirely different from the work that a journalist or documentarian does. For instance, Evgeni Balamutenko, a Russian journalist who occasionally works as a fixer in Moscow, says: "As far as I understand, the fixer's job is to arrange the work of the group. I mean to make appointments, make some arrangements, travel arranging. A travel agent! Yes. The travel agent" (pers. comm., January 2017). An Armenian journalist, Artem Galustyan, says that the fixer serves as the journalist's "city guide" (pers. comm., January 2017), while the Lebanese fixer Moe Ali Nayel remarks that the fixer is often little more than a "tour guide" (pers. comm., June 2015). Reducing the fixer to a tour guide or travel agent serves to rhetorically separate the fixer from the construction of the story, belying the possibility of the fixer's collaboration in the production of international news.

Yet, even tour guides play an active rather than a passive role in constructing the experiences of the people who visit certain places (Holloway 1981; Cohen 1985; Salazar 2006). These individuals grapple with a number of different factors to move people across disparate spaces in a specified time. They also help their visitors make sense of different places, interpreting these places for the tourists who have chosen to travel there. In this sense, the logistical role of the tour guide is no more "unskilled" than that of the news fixer. The difference is that the news fixer is guiding a client who is typically not visiting for leisure but for work, with the specific goal of narrativizing certain elements of the journey for a geographically or culturally distant public.

Since the client is expected to focus on creating this narrative, the labor of navigating the logistics is outsourced to the fixer. Nitzan Almog, a fixer and producer working in Israel, explains this logistical labor in the following manner:

> There's a lot of things going on. It's the crew, production assistants, vehicles, getting to locations, making sure the locations are ready for you to arrive, all the permits for going to the location, hotels where the people are staying, transportation, food, all these things. You know, the fixer needs to—if he's good at what he's doing, he's thinking all the time a step ahead, looking at the big picture. Making the whole picture work. I think that's a description of what we do. (Pers. comm., May 2016)

Almog's statement points to the fixer's crucial organizational skills. On one level, Almog says that the fixer must juggle the needs of the many clients who are visiting the region—a task that is even more daunting with the sometimes larger documentary crews than with the smaller news crews, according to another of my interviewees (Carbajal, pers. comm., March 2017). But perhaps most importantly, Almog notes that the fixer's job is to remain "a step ahead" and to always be "looking at the big picture" (pers. comm., May 2016). This means that the fixer has to stand at the nexus of the client's sense of time, and the temporality of the places and people being covered. If the fixer were not aware of both temporalities, he or she could not remain "a step ahead."

Almog's discussion of temporality cannot be neatly separated from notions of spatiality—even figuratively, the phrase "a step ahead" refers to both time and space. The fixer's need to think logistically, in the *OED*'s sense of the word—in a manner "pertaining to reasoning or logic" but also "pertaining to reckoning or calculation"—necessitates that the fixer grapple with temporalities and spatialities that are constantly colliding, overlapping, and diverging (*OED* 2017).

For instance, Kenyan news fixer Immanuel Muasya says, "you're constantly talking online. 'Is there something that has happened along the way there?' Maybe the road is broken, or there are lines on the road, and you guys are heading straight on to it. So, you have to be doing a lot of calculation, especially when you're doing daily shows" (pers. comm., May 2016).

Muasya's assertion flags both the temporal and spatial elements of navigating the logistics. If a road is damaged or blocked, for example, then this incident can tamper with the clients' ability to meet deadlines. The space may present obstacles that require the client to move within a different temporality than that of the news editors back at headquarters. Muasya says this is especially the case if "you're doing daily [TV] shows," which require both the correspondent and the fixer to think in terms of live shots often scheduled for audiences living in different time zones. But the live-shot schedule may be hindered by road closures on the way to the scene. This risk is a reality of international news reporting, something that news fixers are expected to help their clients navigate as smoothly as possible.

It is not always easy to help clients navigate these challenges, especially when news reporters and editors remain "stuck" in a different temporality. One anonymous fixer working in Moscow struggles with

the timing in their [the clients'] heads, because that is the biggest problem. Now and then people say, "Oh we should go there, there, there, and in one day." And I say, "We just won't be able to do that physically, because it would take us hours to get there, and then a traffic jam, but we can do it by subway, switching things around." (Pers. comm., January 2017)

According to this news fixer, it can be especially difficult when an editor or administrator back at the client's headquarters is planning the schedule: "There was a draw for this soccer championship, in December [2016], and I had to go to four cities which hosted the games, and the travel itinerary was put together by the person in Miami, and it was not done in the most efficient way" (pers. comm., January 2017). In this fixer's estimation, it makes much more sense to leave the logistical planning to the people who know the material conditions on the ground. Planning the itinerary at a distance is inefficient because such planning does not consider or engage with the cultural differences that might result in very different realities unfolding in the field.

Muasya also finds it problematic when editors and even correspondents try to manage the logistics from a distance:

The other day we were working with a crew from America. . . . And she was a very good producer; she was one of the best producers I've ever worked with. But when she was planning the trip, she was planning the trip from Google Maps. And so, when [her news crew] came down to Kenya, we had almost eight hours of traveling in a day....And that's on bad roads, and you have to figure out, where are we right now? . . . Sometimes Google Maps doesn't know the roads . . . and it will tell you the trip is two hours, and the actual trip is five or six hours. And you just keep on going, and these guys keep on asking, "Oh, OK, how far are we?" And you say, "Four hours away." And they're like, "Oh really, Google Maps told me two hours," and I'm like, "I know, [but] it's wrong." (Pers. comm., May 2016)

Muasya describes a situation in which his clients were operating within a very particular temporality and spatiality being produced by a major global media corporation. The clients assumed that the ostensible ubiquity and credibility of the Google brand would serve as the best possible guide in the field. Yet, in this instance, Muasya knew from experience that Google's notion of time was starkly different from the realities of the road being traveled. Muasya's job was to grapple with the temporal and spatial realities that Google Maps could not recognize.

Both Muasya and the anonymous fixer working in Moscow imply that logistical planning is an art and a science that depends on the fixer's "knowledge of the material conditions" (Burne 1944, cited in *OED* 2017). While global news organizations and media companies may feel that they can swiftly obtain this knowledge through professional networks or digital technologies, these fixers suggest that the logistics of a foreign news story cannot be adequately navigated at a distance. This is because the very practice of foreign news reporting can spark a collision between drastically different conceptualizations of time and space, requiring a cultural mediator to interpret these differences and to navigate the journalist through them.

Making the Arrangements

Fixers begin their logistical labor as soon as they are certain that the journalist will be visiting the region. According to Swedish fixer and producer Niclas Peyron, the clients "say at some point, 'Let's talk about money.' I say, 'Okay, it's going to cost this, and if you want the hotel rooms, you can pay for them yourself, or I can pay it for you. They're going to be about this much—normal, standard, middle-class hotels. And then we'll need a car, and if we drive loads, we'll also fill it up with gas'" (pers. comm., September 2016). In Peyron's view, it is much more efficient for the locally based fixer or producer to make these arrangements, because the clients often do not have a clear understanding of what they will need once they arrive in Sweden or of what these needs might cost. They know that they will have to stay in a hotel, but which hotel? And at what price? These are issues with huge ramifications for the clients' efficient navigation of the unfamiliar space in a reasonable time frame. Answering these questions requires special knowledge of the material conditions on the ground.

Once the journalists arrive in the country where they will be working, they often depend on a locally based fixer to help them get situated. Kenyan fixer Michael Kaloki says:

> The first thing, physically meeting them ... will be to pick them up at the airport. Most crews, apart from a very few, usually need help going to their hotel. I'm just sort of giving a rough schedule for what it usually is like for me. Checking in at the hotel, because a lot of times they arrive with the evening flights. If they arrive on the morning flights, [I find out] if they want to sort of check in first. (Pers. comm., June 2016)

A Spanish fixer working in South Africa says that on top of guiding his clients to their hotels, he also helps them with "renting a car, because they need a car. 'Can you rent a car for us?' And that's part of the job that you must do, because you must provide them with whatever you need to cover the story they want to do" (Velazquez, pers. comm., September 2016).

In both Velazquez's and Kaloki's cases, the logistical tasks required of the fixer seem to be incredibly straightforward. The fixer picks the client up from the airport, takes the client to the hotel, and rents a car for the client. Yet, it is important to note the high level of cultural dependency that these tasks suggest. In many cases, the visiting journalists cannot even get to the hotel on their own, nor can they rent a car by themselves. This is remarkable, considering that the correspondents are visiting the "foreign" place specifically so that they can represent and explain that place to a distant audience.

Of course, not every client depends so heavily on the fixer for travel bookings. Valentin Savenkov, a cameraman and fixer in Moscow says that he prefers that his clients make their travel arrangements from a distance: "before the internet, they asked me to book hotels, to buy tickets for them, to book tickets for them. And now they can make this from their phone. So, it's less of a problem for me." Still, Savenkov takes care of numerous other arrangements: "I can rent proper transport for them. I can hire the translators if they need it. I can hire any facilities" (pers. comm., January 2017). As

Savenkov suggests, almost any news fixer will, at some point, be called upon to make logistical arrangements for the visiting journalist.

The labor of making all these arrangements can be exhausting. Muasya says, "Sometimes I make as much as one hundred calls a day. How could someone do [their work] when they're talking, you know?" (pers. comm., May 2016). Muasya implies that he must inhabit multiple times and places at once, making 100 calls a day while also dealing with the clients' constant requests. Not all of these requests are possible to fulfill:

> For me sometimes, you just have to be adamant and say, "No, I'm not going to drive you. We'll get a driver and car, you know? And we're going to get a car big enough to fit all of you, because some of you guys, especially from America, are really big. And you come, and you have to climb in a small car, by mid-day you're grumpy." So, I say, "Please, just pay for a van, pay for a truck, so that all of us can fit, so that you can comfortably fit in, and you guys can relax." (pers. comm., May 2016)

Muasya's story reveals that the fixer has to foresee the cultural differences that might affect the client even in a case as simple as choosing the proper car. Rather than following his clients' request to choose the cheapest car possible, Muasya feels he must push the client to pay the extra money for a car that will accommodate people who tend to be taller and bigger than Muasya. In the process of booking the proper vehicle, Muasya is actively ensuring that he is always "a step ahead," to use Almog's words (pers. comm., May 2016). To remain a "step ahead," Muasya must foresee the cultural differences that will impact the client's navigation through particular spaces in specific allotments of time.

Greek fixer Lamprini Thoma also observes that the process of making arrangements requires the fixer to act as a cultural mediator. She recounts one incident with a visiting client:

> The guy said, "I want a four- or five-star hotel." And there on the border, there are no three-star hotels, there are no two-star hotels, there are just rooms. You cannot have it, so it's not my fault, I cannot build it, you know. You cannot find it; it's like that. So, you have to explain to them the situation, and it again depends on the people, but you have to give them some guidelines. (Pers. comm., September 2016)

In Thoma's case, the mere act of booking a hotel can require the fixer to make a particular place more culturally legible to a visiting journalist or documentarian. Thoma's client did not comprehend that he was traveling to an area where his usual level of comfort simply could not be accommodated. On one level, this anecdote reveals the disjuncture between clients' expectations of time and space, and the sometimes very different articulations of time and space as they unfold in the field. On another level, this testament reveals something even more disturbing—the client, who was covering a story at the border, did not even know enough about that region to understand that there were no proper hotels in the area. Because of this, he needed a fixer to fill in the gaps in his knowledge and to interpret the space for him.

Even Thoma suggests that not all clients are so flagrantly out of touch with the material conditions on the ground. Most of my interviewees say that there are journalists and documentarians who do their homework, and there are those who do not. Fixers tend to feel that their job is to be prepared for both types of client so that they can ensure that the process of covering a "foreign" news story goes as smoothly as possible. The tricky labor of navigating the logistics of travel arrangement typically falls under the radar of news audiences, who are often led to believe that the authoritative eyewitness—the correspondent—has single-handedly traversed the vagaries of the "foreign" space in order to bring the story to readers and viewers located in other parts of the world. However, Thoma's and Muasya's narratives reveal the messiness of this process and the stickiness of cultural difference, even at the most basic levels.

This "stickiness" also becomes visible when journalists or documentarians go through the process of securing the proper visa to enter a particular nation. Gloria Samantha, a fixer who works in Indonesia, says that getting the proper documentation is crucial: "One of the things I often do is to get them [journalists] quick, immediate, information about the working visa" (pers. comm., June 2016). Samantha states it is critical that her clients get a working visa rather than a tourist visa to enter Indonesia. Distinctions like these are no small issue, since they can determine how long a journalist may legally inhabit a foreign country. For instance, the Iraqi fixer and producer Haidar Adbalhabi says that journalists who are not affiliated with a bureau in Baghdad are typically allowed only one or two weeks of stay in the country (pers. comm., May 2016). In these cases, the client's idea of time might collide with Iraqi authorities' notions of how long a foreign journalist should stay in Iraq. If these journalists overstay their welcome, they can lose access to the space. So, too, can journalists or documentarians who are caught moving through a particular region with the wrong visa.

This risk does not stop some clients from trying to enter a given nation with the incorrect paperwork. Russian news fixer Ksenia Yakovleva says that gaining

> accreditation to come here [to Russia] as a journalist for a two-week period is really, really difficult. It's not the easiest place to get a visa. But then, to get a journalistic accreditation—it can be a nightmare. You have to have official permission. So many journalists come here on

FIGURE 2.1 Camera crew filming in Moscow's Red Square. Fixers working in the area say it is difficult to get formal permission to shoot professional footage in this part of the city. Photo by the author.

the tourist visa, and then for them, shooting [video]—you always have
to think about kind of covering it up . . . .because we don't have three
months to wait for rotation for permission to shoot in Russia. (Pers.
comm., January 2017)

Here, Yakovleva highlights the interconnection between securing the
proper visa for a client and securing the proper permissions to shoot video
in places like Moscow's Red Square (figure 2.1). According to Yakovleva, it
is technically illegal for correspondents and documentarians to film in Red
Square without that very specific documentation.

Because Yakovleva knows that obtaining the journalist's visa will typically
take much more time than the client can afford—clashing with the temporality of the journalist's deadline—she sometimes helps her clients "cover up"
the fact that they are filming without the proper papers:

There is a big question if you can record on Red Square or not. They say
that you have to have a special permission to record. But from my experience, I shot [video] like four or five times. As long as you don't have
a tripod, no one cares about it. I [felt] that it was more difficult before,
but right now it's quite lax. (Pers. comm., January 2017)

For Yakovleva, then, the issue of permissions is a contingent issue; something to be interpreted and negotiated. If the journalist can avoid appearing
too "professional"—in other words, if he or she can avoid using a tripod—
then Yakovleva feels that the journalist can get away with filming in Red
Square without obtaining permission. By advising the journalist to appear
less professional, Yakovleva is in turn engaging in the performative work of
cultural mediation, suggesting that the journalist adhere to regionally specific
interpretations of what a television correspondent should look like and what
kind of equipment he or she might use.

According to Savenkov, in Russia, "You must ask for permission in advance, in a week or two weeks, and you must ask for an application, send in
the application and write what are you doing, what are you going to shoot
and what for" (Savenkov, pers. comm., January 2017). The problem is that following these rules can upset the temporalities according to which journalists
and their news editors are operating, in turn, upsetting their access to particular spaces. This is especially difficult within the current milieu, where news
outlets are competing with one another in an increasingly interconnected
set of global news markets. The temporality of these markets sometimes

demands that journalists push back against regionally specific temporalities, a conundrum that often surfaces in news fixers' professional narratives about navigating the logistics.

Yet, if journalists push back too much, they also risk losing access to the story, as Suzan Haidamous, a fixer and news assistant working in Lebanon, remarks. "I follow every day the news. I know when I can go there and when I can't. I know who's the right person and who's not. I know the permissions, who to take permission from. You don't want to end up in an area two hours away from Lebanon and they [the clients] can't do anything because you didn't talk to [the right people] for example" (pers. comm., June 2015). In this statement, Haidamous reveals the importance of remaining "a step ahead" of the client by relying upon her "material knowledge of the conditions" on the ground.

Thoma also notes how important this is, describing how she deals with her clients' inevitable desire to film in the Acropolis:

> If they need an archaeological site, [they think] that we can get there in a week or so. It takes more than two months to get the permit. So, you have to tell them that stuff, and they have to know that if this is the way they want to do it, we need that time. So, you cannot do it, you know. If you're coming next week and you're staying here for five days, you cannot do it. And nobody will do it, you know, it's like that. Or they think that they can get in the Acropolis and film there. What I do, is, I write back to them every time. I scouted Athens, I rented some balconies for my clients if they want to have a very near view of the Acropolis for their shot. I have found the best balconies in Athens; I rent them from the owners for the day they want to work. (Pers. comm., September 2016)

Thoma's method of staying "a step ahead" ensures that her clients still capture some of the region's most iconic buildings in their video shots, even if they did not foresee the competing temporalities that inform the process of obtaining journalistic access to those spaces. In this way, Thoma not only anticipates her clients' needs, but she also anticipates how those needs cannot be met and which alternatives to pursue. By the time her clients tell her they need to shoot from within the Acropolis itself, Thoma already has an alternative in place. Thus, Thoma's account suggests that even in the seemingly mundane process of dealing with video permissions, the news fixer is essential to the international reporting process.

Sometimes, the journalists will have obtained the correct permissions, but they might still encounter resistance from the authorities who are posted at the filming site on any given day. In these cases, the fixer must try to build a connection where a disconnection is in danger of occurring. Larisa Inic, a fixer working in eastern Europe, handles these situations this way:

> They [authorities] say, "You can't approach here." And I say, "but we wrote to the ministry and we have an approval, you know, they approved us." And they say, "Nope, no one can approve." And I say, "Sorry, but there is a press room in the ministry of interior, you know in the ministry, and we wrote to them." [They reply,] "I never got that email." "Okay, can you please check, sir? Because I'm quite sure that you received it, because I received it." "Okay." And then he searches: "Oh, it's here." So sometimes it's just people are lazy to do their work or they are cross because of something that happened earlier. (Pers. comm., August 2016)

Stories like Inic's reveal that the fixer's work is informed by moments of disconnection as well as connection, and with miscommunication as well as communication. For every case where the fixer is able to mend the divide between the journalist and the authority on the ground, there might be another case where the fixer cannot successfully persuade the authorities. My interviewees suggest that this potential for disconnection is simply the reality of international news reporting.

The news fixer acts as cultural mediator, pushing local authorities in ways that only the fixer knows they can be pushed, and guiding the client through the confusing red tape specific to particular geopolitical regions. Sometimes this mediation works, and other times it does not. On top of this tricky task, fixers say that they also engage in a more literal aspect of logistical navigation: accompanying and guiding their clients as they physically travel across unfamiliar geographical terrain. Acting as the clients' guide requires an intense level of familiarity with the material conditions, conditions that can sometimes threaten the journalist's safety.

Traveling the Terrain

News fixers routinely accompany their clients across unfamiliar terrain, although foreign journalists may initially congregate in certain hotels or

FIGURE 2.2 The Commodore Hotel in Beirut's Hamra district. During Lebanon's civil war of the late 20th century, foreign correspondents used this hotel as their base. Photo by the author.

FIGURE 2.3 Beirut's Mar Mikhael neighborhood, currently a favorite place for foreign journalists. Photo by the author.

neighborhoods within the news hubs to which they travel (see figures 2.2 and 2.3 in Beirut for example).

Foreign correspondents are eventually expected to leave their makeshift comfort zones and venture into spaces that can be physically and culturally challenging to them. News fixers are supposed to help their clients navigate these spaces. Sometimes fixers hire drivers to help them transport the journalist, and other times, the fixers drive. Either way, guiding a foreign correspondent through a particular urban or rural landscape is not a simple task. When foreign correspondents hire fixers to guide them through unfamiliar territory, they do so with two seemingly contradictory goals in mind: (1) to help them find the most compelling (and often dangerous) places to visit, and (2) to help them stay safe. This contradiction is a product of the increasing competition that defines the transnationally interconnected news markets in which journalists work.

For instance, Finnish journalist Iida Tikka says that some fixer-drivers eschew the unpredictability of the most dangerous spaces, becoming nervous in war zones; yet, other drivers embrace the danger (pers. comm., January 2017). Tikka tells of a driver she once hired in Ukraine, whose car had a bullet hole in it: "When I got to the car and I was trying to put my seatbelt on, he [the driver] started laughing, like, 'How are you going to run from the car when they start shooting at you and you have your seatbelt on?'" Later, Tikka says, "this driver was driving like 160 kilometers an hour. . . . And there were giant holes [in the road], and he's still driving, and I'm like, 'We are not in a hurry.'" Despite this harrowing experience, Tikka—like many correspondents— reflects that "for a journalist, that part of the driver is needed. Because you need somebody to take you to those places" (pers. comm., January 2017).

Journalists need "somebody to take [them] to those places" because their editors expect them to get the most compelling stories in a tight window of time. Of course, this pressure to meet deadlines has always informed the work of foreign correspondents (Hamilton 2011; Palmer 2018). But in the 21st century, when news bureaus are relying more and more on freelancers and parachute journalists (Sambrook 2010; Williams 2011), and when the convergence of media technologies and platforms have resulted in a competitive 24-hour-news flow, news reporters find themselves pushing the boundaries of local spatialities more than ever before. Because of these issues, journalists like Tikka suggest that they need drivers and fixers who are willing to accompany them to the dangerous spaces that will make their news reports more marketable.

Rather paradoxically, some journalists also feel that they need a fixer-driver to help them travel safely. A Turkish journalist who covers events at the Turkish-Syrian border for a major US newspaper emphasizes this need, asserting that at the border, people drive like mad, and so you have to have a local driver. You know, a good local driver who knows his way around, who knows the people, who's on your side, and who you can talk to about security. So that they can also be aware, like saying, "Hey I don't like that." So, you can realize if a car is following you. (Pers. comm., July 2015)

Significantly, this journalist highlights the fact that reporters working in dangerous areas do not simply need a driver for transport—they need a "good" driver, one who has been vetted and thus, can be trusted to strike the proper balance between embracing and eschewing danger, in order to get the story. Successfully striking this balance can make the difference between life and death. A good fixer-driver is one who will take the journalist to dangerous spaces, but who is also quite familiar with the material conditions on the ground. Journalists and news editors tend to view this familiarity with the material conditions as a key element of their safety as they travel through unfamiliar zones (Palmer 2017).

Echoing the discourse of foreign correspondents and their editors, news fixers also tend to cite the importance of physically accompanying journalists into particular spaces. While they are certainly aware of their role in keeping the journalist safe in certain areas, fixers suggest something more complex about the task of transporting their clients through different sites in the field. News fixers imply that in the act of guiding their clients through unfamiliar geographical territory, they are engaging in creative labor. Even in the most mundane aspects of their role as guide, news fixers suggest that they must "translate" particular spaces for their clients, making it far more likely that the journalists will get the material they need for their stories.

For instance, Velazquez tells of a time when he had to rent a car in his own name, pay for the car on his own credit card, and then drive a particular journalist around South Africa: "She didn't want to drive, because in South Africa, they drive on the left side [of the road]" (pers. comm., September 2016). In the simple act of transporting his journalist from one site to the next, Velazquez had to play an interpretive role, bridging the gap between the journalist's knowledge of what it meant to drive a vehicle in one cultural environment versus another. The roads themselves were barely "legible" to the visiting journalist, requiring Velazquez's guidance through that space.

Peyron also describes this phenomenon in his own production narrative, saying that

on a red light, if you turn right on a corner with your car, most states
in the United States you can go there, even if it says, "don't turn right,"
even if there's a red light. But you can't do it here [in Sweden]. You
can do that in United States, but you can't do it here. (Pers. comm.,
September 2016)

For Peyron, even something as uncomplicated as basic traffic laws are a matter
of cultural mediation. He has to explain to his clients that the laws are simply
different in Sweden, and that if the journalists or documentarians want to
avoid an infraction, then they need to listen to him.

In some places, the traffic laws are not the biggest challenge—instead, the
clients struggle with understanding the road signs: "In Tokyo, the maps and
signs are very bad," says translator and fixer Kosho Sato. "So almost all the
time, they [the clients] have lost where they're going. It's not very helpful,
people who don't speak, who don't read Japanese in Japan" (pers. comm.,
August 2016). Sato suggests that part of his job is to guide the client through
a culturally distinct sign system—both in terms of the tricky road signs themselves as well as at the broader level of language and semiotics. Since he knows
Tokyo's quirks, and since he can read the road signs, Sato is able to use his
knowledge of the material conditions on the ground to help his clients find
their way around the city.

These material conditions can include anything from different traffic
laws, poor signage, or extreme weather—brutal cold during some months
in Russia, for example (Pimanova, pers. comm., and Smith, pers. comm.,
January 2017), and wilting heat during some months in Kenya (Muasya, pers.
comm., May 2016). Peyron asserts that fixers can help visiting journalists
and documentarians prepare for these issues—but only if the foreign
correspondents bother to seek their help in the first place.

Sometimes there's crews calling me, "Oh we're here, we're shooting
this and that, and suddenly, we're doing this, and it doesn't work."
And I tell them, "Well, what local people do you have?" "Oh, no one."
"Yeah, OK, well, then you know, you're in trouble." Yeah, they get in
a car in the north and it's freezing cold, and they ran out of gas. "Oh
yeah, no gas." You should have someone local [with you], it's minus
thousands of degrees, you'll die, you know. You've got to trust the
locals. (Pers. comm., September 2016)

For Peyron, traveling safely through a Swedish winter is tantamount to trusting the fixer's knowledge of the material conditions. Though, as Peyron says, there are plenty of journalists who still try to travel through unfamiliar places (with unfamiliar climates) on their own, Peyron views this as a dangerous choice to make. In Peyron's view, it is safer for visiting journalists to trust the people more directly familiar with the area rather than braving the elements on their own.

Extreme weather conditions are not the only potential obstacles that news fixers can help their clients overcome. When fixers accompany their correspondents into specific spaces, they might in turn secure the trust of other people located at the site—people who may not otherwise welcome the foreign correspondent's presence. Samuel Okocha, a news fixer working in Nigeria, tells this story:

> This is what he [the client] wanted in Lagos, so he took pictures, and with my presence and [that of the] friends of a friend, he had a little more confidence to move around. We took him places where a white guy, a foreigner, would be afraid to go. (Pers. comm., May 2016)

In this account, Okocha describes how the work of fixing can sometimes be explicitly racialized: the news fixer accompanied the foreign journalist or documentarian to an area where the client's cultural difference—his foreignness, his whiteness—might have otherwise cast him as an outsider who was trespassing in a forbidden space. As Okocha asserts, his presence gave the client more confidence to "move around," to go into areas in Nigeria where "a white guy, a foreigner, would be afraid to go" (pers. comm., May 2016). Crucially, Okocha suggests that his presence was tightly linked to his blackness and to his national identity as an insider to Nigerian citizenship (unlike the client, Okocha was not a "foreigner"). Thus, Okocha's story suggests that the client was directly dependent upon Okocha's racialized "presence," accompanying him into the field, in order to get the photographs that the client needed.

At different moments, news fixers find it useful to accentuate particular aspects of their cultural identities over others as they physically travel with their clients into tricky areas. For example, Ukrainian fixer Anna Nekrasova finds it useful to play up her status as a woman: "You can ask something and say, 'Please, can you help us,' or 'I need these things,' and you smile, and it works better than if you're a guy telling the same problem, it works better than being a man" (pers. comm., August 2016). Nekrasova suggests that in the regions where she works, she can convince people in the field to let her clients do what they need to do. By playing up her ostensible vulnerability as a woman (asking, "please, can you help us?") or by establishing feminine cama- raderie (with a smile), Nekrasova can open doors that might otherwise have been closed to the foreign journalists traveling with her. Thus, like Okocha, Nekrasova performatively deploys certain aspects of her cultural identity in a mediating fashion, acting on behalf of her foreign clients to build trust with people in the field.

Still, there are limits to cultural performativity. Some aspects of cultural identity are imposed upon certain social subjects in ways that are difficult to disrupt. What this means for news fixers is that, sometimes, particular aspects of their cultural identities can actually impede them from helping their client navigate the logistics of the story. Maritza Carbajal, a fixer working in Mexico and Central America, shares this example from a time she was working in Honduras:

> I was in charge of logistics on this very, very important, big documen- tary project. The production company hired this company [based] in the UK which is called TAFFS. [The UK company] was providing assistance to gun crews in harsh environments. All of these guys, the guys that are working for TAFFS, are ex-military from the UK. So, they hired me to be the logistics on this project. And they sent me to a meeting in Honduras. And this one guy, when I said hi and I introduced myself, and I said, "I'm here for the meeting," he said, "Oh no, no, no, no, the guys from the UK, they told me they were sending somebody to review the logistics of this project." And I'm like, "Yes, that's what I'm here for." [And the guy said,] "Oh, no, I was expecting a man." (Pers. comm., March 2017).

Though Carbajal says that she eventually "got the job done," she also says that the TAFFS employees withheld information from her until some of her male clients vouched for her. Thus, in this particular case, a certain aspect of the news fixer's culturally-imposed identity—her legibility as being female— inhibited her from helping her clients navigate the logistics of the assign- ment. This is a phenomenon that surfaces in other news fixers' production narratives as well; in one case, the clients themselves imposed a static notion of femininity onto a female fixer by refusing to let her accompany them into a potentially dangerous area (anonymous news fixer working in Moscow, pers. comm., January 2017).

In other cases, it is not the news fixers' gender but notions of geopolitical citizenship that keep them from accessing certain places. For instance, an anonymous fixer and freelance journalist working in the Palestinian West Bank describes the challenges she faces:

> I'm not allowed to go to Gaza. I'm not allowed to go to Israel. The area that I cover is the West Bank. Do you want to call that a challenge? Yeah, I call that a challenge. I mean it's being hindered, being hindered from doing your job because of who you are, because of your nationality. You have journalists who come from the States who have access to everything else, whereas me, because I'm from this place, I'm not even allowed to cover it as I should. . . . You're always going to be at a disadvantage in that sense, because as a journalist, your number one asset is access. (Pers. comm., July 2013)

Nekrasova echoes this issue, explaining how her ability to help foreign journalists cover the crisis in Ukraine has been affected by her place of birth:

> In our passport we have a registration, a stamp. Where you can find where you were born and where you live. [During the 2014 conflict], if you [went] to Donetsk, you might have problems if you ha[d] a registration stamp from Kiev. If you understand what I mean. So that's why I never even tried to go there during the conflict. So, I always pass[ed] it to my colleagues who were born there or who ha[d] registration there. So, they work[ed] there, and I work[ed] in the outer part of Ukraine normally. (Pers. comm., August 2016)

In both of these accounts, the news fixer is decisively limited by the broader geopolitical contexts that shape the material conditions on the ground. The fixers' locally based knowledge and their status as "insiders" to certain cultural groups are simultaneously a benefit and a disadvantage in these cases. For the first fixer, being an "insider" to Palestinian culture also means that she is physically barred from traversing the border into Israel. For Nekrasova, being "Ukrainian" during wartime is not enough—she must also have been born in the "right" place if she wishes to work in particular parts of the country. The anonymous fixer from Palestine especially highlights the injustice of this situation from a fixer's viewpoint: foreign and Israeli journalists have all the access they need, but she personally does not. As she stated, "as a journalist, your number one asset is access" (pers. comm., July 2013).

This is especially true for news fixers, who must help the foreign correspondent successfully navigate the spaces and temporalities that sometimes
differ from those with which they are most familiar. Whether or not their
crucial labor is made transparent to news audiences, news fixers are hired to
complete a number of tasks that place them in the role of cultural mediator.
One of these tasks is that of accompanying journalists through geographical
regions in which they might be read as "foreigners." Yet, the larger geopolitical contexts that often draw journalists to certain areas in the first place
can, at the same time, inhibit their news fixers from successfully mediating on
their behalf. This points to the inevitable moments of disconnection that are
inherent to the process of cultural mediation. Not only does the fixer perform
multiple identities and negotiate competing agendas to help the journalist
get the story, but they also occasionally experience the imposition of certain
identities upon themselves, along with the lack of access that this imposition
can entail.

News fixing often involves such moments of disconnection. My
interviewees suggest that the labor of accompanying their clients through unfamiliar geographical territory becomes even more challenging when there
are breakdowns in communication. One of the most difficult communicative breakdowns occurs when the foreign correspondent or documentarian
simply does not listen to the news fixer's advice about a particular place. Oren
Rosenfeld—an Israeli fixer and producer—tells this story about an Australian
television crew:

> They wanted to go to Gaza to work. And I told them, "Listen, if you're
> going to Gaza, I have my colleague there that can look after you and
> help you. And he's the equivalent of me. We're best friends and on the
> phone, all the time, and he's in Gaza and can help you out. Because as
> you know, Gaza is not a safe place to be walking around." And they
> said, "No, we have a recommendation about this [other] guy, do you
> know him?" And they gave me this name, and I'm like, "No, I don't
> know him, never heard of him—let me check with my guy, maybe he
> can tell me who he is." So, I asked my guy and he said, "Yeah, he's a
> taxi driver." . . . And I tried to put them off that silly idea, and they
> wouldn't listen. . . . And that night, they called me, and they said,
> "Oren, you must help us, this guy didn't know what he was doing. He
> got us arrested by Hamas, and can you please give us your guy?" (Pers.
> comm., May 2016)

In this narrative, Rosenfeld shares an example of what can happen when foreign journalists and media workers fail to listen carefully to their fixers' perspectives on the places they want to visit. Crucially, Rosenfeld did not try to obstruct his clients from traveling to Gaza, though he viewed it as an unsafe "place to be walking around" without the right guide. Instead, he tried to furnish them with a Gazan guide he knew and trusted. Yet, the clients did not listen to Rosenfeld's advice, and this landed them in detainment. According to Rosenfeld, his colleague in Gaza felt it was too risky to help the television crew once they had been taken into custody, and so they lost the story, along with several thousand dollars (pers. comm., May 2016).

Rosenfeld's testimony reveals the intricacy of the fixer's cultural mediation, a kind of mediation that is vital to the labor of international reporting. When news fixers help their clients navigate terrain with which the clients are unfamiliar, they sometimes have to tell the foreign correspondents not to travel to those places at all. In these cases, the fixers' role in mediating a particular space is informed more by disconnection than connection. And if foreign correspondents fail to listen to their fixer's advice, this breakdown—indeed, refusal—of constructive communication can lead to serious trouble for the journalists. This points to the fact that the practice of international reporting depends heavily on the news fixer's effort at navigating the logistics.

Conclusion

Global media scholar Sarah Sharma says that the term "temporality" can productively signal an "awareness of power relations as they play out in time" (2014, 4). Sharma follows postcolonial scholars in critiquing the notion of one "homogenous" time for the whole world, (Chakrabarty 2004; Chatterjee 2005), instead asserting that there is a "multitude of time-based experiences specific to different populations that live, labor, and sleep under the auspices of global capital" (2014, 9). In a similar vein, earlier scholars argued that spatiality is socially produced and multifarious (Lefebvre 1992; Massey 1994). Far from homogenous, and rather than serving as a passive vacuum that the world's most powerful subjects can possess and traverse at whim (McClintock 1995), the construction and comprehension of space can change a great deal, depending on who has the most power in a given situation.

My interviewees suggest that there are some foreign correspondents who would do well to remember this more culturally and politically complex understanding of time and space. Through the act of navigating the logistics, news fixers bring the cultural complexity of competing temporalities and spatialities into sharp relief. On one level, fixers are expected to make all the necessary arrangements for foreign journalists and documentarians: this includes securing a visa (or educating the client on how to do so); obtaining the permissions required to film or shoot video in specific places such as Moscow's Red Square; and booking flights, hotels, and travel vehicles. Since clients are often unfamiliar with the local language, they need fixers to do these basic tasks for them. But they also need fixers to do these tasks because there is more to making arrangements than meets the eye. Be it the choice of hotel, car, or which kind of visa the journalist should obtain, every choice a fixer makes must be reflective of his or her own effort at listening carefully to the spoken and unspoken needs of the client. The fixer must then reconcile those needs with the material realities of the places the clients are visiting.

On another level, fixers are also typically expected to physically accompany their clients as they travel across certain areas of the country they have chosen to cover. Many times, the client will not want to drive, and so the fixer may find him- or herself driving an entire television crew across Kenya, for instance. Even if the fixer hires a driver, visiting journalists and documentarians may want the fixer to be present, just in case there is some kind of encounter on the road that the journalist cannot comprehend—either because of language barriers or because of other cultural differences. Thus, the fixer serves as a guide who must interpret space and place for the client, in real time.

In some cases, the fixer mediates through the act of opening doors for the journalist or accompanying the client into a space that he or she does not know very well. In other cases, the fixer must say "no" to the client, on behalf of the local rules and realities that do not necessarily match the journalist's notion of time or space. As Masterman puts it: "You can't find snow in lower Austria in August. We don't have snow; it's just not there. I cannot call someone from the weather to give me snow, unless we get the snow machine. But otherwise, you won't have truthful snow in August in lower Austria" (pers. comm., September 2016). Masterman highlights the fact that cultural mediation is a complicated process, one that is not always about saying, "yes."

Gaining a clearer understanding of the fixer's logistical labor can help scholars and journalists better understand the continued relevance of cultural difference for international reporting, despite the popular notion that globalization is leading to an increase in cultural homogeneity. International journalists might especially benefit from accepting the vastly different articulations of time and space that complicate each news assignment, rather than climbing over barriers to certain holy sites, as Renato Miller once saw his client do in Mexico City (pers. comm., March 2017), or filming in Red Square without permission, an act that got Savenkov (and not his clients) arrested in Moscow (pers. comm., January 2017).

Fixers often find themselves in risky situations when they are engaging in cultural mediation on behalf of their clients. This is especially the case when fixers help journalists to interface with potential news sources. As the next chapter will show, there is a decisively vulnerable element to this important task, since fixers sometimes must calm an angry source or convince a suspicious source to continue the interview. In less extreme cases, the fixer can risk alienating the contacts that he or she has spent years building, for example, when a journalist says or does something that makes the source upset. In the process of interfacing with the people on the ground, the fixer struggles to build a bridge between people who sometimes see the world in very different ways.

3

Networking with Sources

*I have my WhatsApp, and on my WhatsApp I have at least
twenty people that I have to say hello to them, every day. . . .
I have Skype. When the Syrian crisis started, it was like one
contact, now I have fifteen hundred contacts on Skype. So,
I have to say to like thirty people, "Hi, hello," that are in my
contact list. Plus, Facebook. . . .Yesterday, it was Ramadan,
and I sent about fifty messages, "Happy Ramadan." Because
they are my contacts.*

—HWAIDA SAAD, news assistant and fixer in Beirut

FOR HWAIDA SAAD, networking with sources is a central part of her work as a
news assistant and fixer in Beirut (Saad, pers. comm., June 2015). Based in a city
that has long served as a hub for foreign journalists, Saad has spent years building
an intricate system of contacts with people all over Lebanon and Syria. Saad's
network includes members of Lebanon's Hezbollah group, Syrian soldiers, and
numerous other people whose perspectives might be useful to journalists visiting
from faraway. As a news assistant for the *New York Times'* Beirut bureau, Saad's
extensive network also benefits the foreign journalists who stay in the field for
much longer stints. According to Saad, her bureau colleagues rely heavily on her
networking skills, in hopes of setting up interviews with the people most relevant
to the story. Thus, Saad's network of contacts is beneficial to journalists who live
at the site for months at a time as well as to those who visit Beirut more briefly.

Another former news assistant in Beirut, Nabih Bulos, asserts that "the
value of a fixer to a parachuting journalist is the contact list more than anything else." This is "because [parachuting journalists] just don't have time
to actually make those kinds of relationships" on their own (pers. comm.,
June 2015). Bulos points to an important aspect of the labor of networking
with sources: the emotional aspect. Building these vital networks is not
simply a matter of adding someone's contact information to the fixer's smartphone. Instead, building the network of contacts is also a process of building
relationships, a process that requires a great deal of emotional engagement.

As the epigraph to this chapter suggests, Saad is constantly checking in with thousands of potential sources, asking them how they are doing and wishing them a happy Ramadan. Sometimes, Saad must answer her messages late at night, even when the source might only wish to say "hi" (pers. comm., June 2015). No matter how tired she might be, Saad cannot risk ignoring a message from a potential source, because what starts out as a simple "hi" might turn into an important news story.

This points to another element of networking with sources that news fixers describe in their production narratives. Not only do fixers work overtime to build their networks of potential interviewees, but they also assist their clients in navigating the different cultural mores that might be significant in convincing a source to open up and share the information that the journalist needs. According to Saad, sources in Lebanon might expect the visiting journalist to engage in conversation with them for some time, before delving into the correspondent's official questions (pers. comm., June 2015). A number of the other fixers I interviewed have made this observation as well. In fact, my interviewees suggest that the tendency for some journalists to be in a hurry, or to be too direct with their questions, can hinder these journalists from getting good interview material at all.

In those cases where the client does not follow the proper cultural protocols during an interview, the fixer runs the risk of losing an important contact. The trust that the fixer has sometimes spent years building can crumble in seconds, leaving the fixer with one less source to offer the next journalist who comes along. For this reason, news fixers often find themselves carefully playing to both sides, striking a balance between satisfying the client and alienating the contact. The source can be alienated simply because a journalist refuses to sit down for tea, or because the journalist shows no compassion for the source's suffering in a moment of trauma. In more extreme cases, the client's behavior can put the entire news team in danger, especially when the potential source is a militant or someone in a position of political power.

Chapter 3 shows that fixers' lucrative networks are human networks, constructed through emotional engagement and riven with material risk. These networks are far more than a contact list on Skype, and they are indispensable to the foreign reporters and documentarians who often do not know many people in the area they are trying to cover. In the context of international reporting, the labor of networking with sources is also highly performative. By engaging in this important work, news fixers draw upon multiple aspects of their own cultural identifications to build trust with potential interviewees, and they constantly negotiate with sources who may not feel comfortable speaking on the record.

Though most professional journalists network with sources, this chapter also shows that international reporters tend to outsource this particular type of labor to their "local" guides—a fact that they rarely make transparent to their audiences. Because of the intensifying competitiveness of international reporting in the era of media convergence and slashed foreign news budgets (Paterson and Sreberny 2004; Williams 2011; Palmer 2018), foreign correspondents depend heavily on their news fixers to connect them with sources, especially in regions where the journalists may not know how to properly communicate with people on the ground.

According to my interviewees, some journalists hire certain news fixers in hopes that these locally based media employees will be able to connect them with specific *types* of contacts, with sources who are expected to appear in international stories on drugs, war, or protest, for example. Because of the sometimes stereotypical narratives that circulate across the world's increasingly interconnected news markets, certain fixers might actively build a specialized contact list, one that will make them more marketable to journalists who want to interview particular "stock characters" for their stories. In other cases, news fixers focus on building a "generalized" list of contacts, in an effort at being marketable to as many potential clients as possible.

In the process of networking with sources, fixers must constantly operate across multiple identificatory boundaries, building cross-cultural connections that the journalists cannot build on their own. The labor of networking suggests a nuanced definition of the word "connection." On one level, the fixer links him- or herself with certain contacts, and then links these people with foreign journalists. Working within this liminal space, news fixers imply that they, themselves, are the connection between foreign journalists and potential news sources. But in another sense, news fixers suggest that networking is also about the constant effort at grappling with disconnection. Engaging in this particular type of work can regularly result in failures of communication between the journalist and the source. Sometimes, a source will simply refuse to talk, no matter what the fixer says. And sometimes the source will be so different from the journalist that the news fixer will have to explain the journalist's behavior to the source—and vice versa.

In the most extreme cases, news fixers say that they must actively remind the foreign journalist to remember the dignity of the source. Sometimes, reporters and other media workers who travel to different geopolitical regions simply do not understand the cultural mores that they should observe in order to show their interviewees the proper measure of respect. This is an issue of great relevance to scholars, students, and journalists. News fixers' professional narratives reveal the need to gain a clearer sense of the best practices for dealing with people who might be traumatized, injured, or afraid of talking to media workers from different parts of the world. Whether or not the client trusts or even likes the source, my interviewees suggest that considering the basic dignity of the people on the ground is vital.

In order to emphasize these points in more detail, chapter 3 first examines the methods through which news fixers say they build their valuable network of contacts. The chapter will then look at examples of news fixers' strategies for culturally interfacing with potential interviewees. Finally, I will close with a discussion of the dignity of the source. News fixers' production narratives have much to tell us about the people whose testimonies surface in international news reports. Ethically considering the dignity of news sources in the international context could eventually pave the way to better cross-cultural understanding, for both journalists and the scholars who study their work.

Building a Network of Contacts

Foreign reporters appear well aware of their dependence on locally based fixers in connecting with potential sources in the field. Alasdair Baverstock, a freelancer based in Mexico City, puts it this way:

> As a journalist, it's all about building your contact book. If something happens tomorrow at the Ministry of Education, I have three people in my list of contacts who I call immediately to then cover that story. But if I'm in Reynosa, I know nothing about the city, I don't know which neighborhoods are good, which neighborhoods are bad, so I need someone who knows that information and knows who to talk to in order to cover that story. So that's why I'll use a fixer. (Pers. comm., March 2017)

Baverstock says that he can generally rely on his own personal networks when he is working in Mexico City, where he also lives. Yet, the moment he ventures outside the city and into Mexico's more distant states, he needs a fixer to connect him with the right people to help him tell the story. Baverstock also notes that relying on the fixer's network of sources is, in of itself, a safety precaution. A fixer in Reynosa would know "which neighborhoods are good, which neighborhoods are bad," and could thus connect Baverstock with sources located in safer areas. According to Baverstock, journalists rely on fixers' networks not only to help them tell their stories but also to help them stay safe in the field.

Rather paradoxically, journalists also sometimes look for fixers who they feel are connected with the more "dangerous" people in the field. Anna Lekas Miller, a freelance journalist based in Beirut, says, "the best fixers here are the ones that are typically really shady men who were in the military at some point, and [who] have a bunch of military contacts" (pers. comm., May 2015). Another freelancer in Beirut agrees, remarking that he uses certain fixers specifically to get interviews with members of Hezbollah (Wood, pers. comm., June 2015). This is because, as Saad also suggests, foreign journalists cannot simply call someone from Hezbollah on the phone and quickly set up an interview. Members of Hezbollah will want fixers like Saad to smooth the way, to speak on the journalist's behalf, and to assure them that the journalist is not their enemy (pers. comm., June 2015).

Jaime Velazquez, a Spanish correspondent who also works as a fixer in South Africa, indicates that journalists contact different fixers to get in touch with different types of sources. This is because journalists sometimes view certain fixers as being "insiders" to the political or social groups of the people they are trying to represent in their stories:

> If you want to go to a township, for example, [to a] township that is the most dangerous place in South Africa, for example, if you want to interview drug dealers. And you want to see their guns and you want to see the stuff that they are dealing with, and all this. And, of course, you as a local journalist, you may have that information and those contacts, because you have found a similar story before. But normally, it's very difficult to get into those environments. So normally, you have people that belong to that township. . . [like] this guy [who] has started to work with the media, and he's starting to build himself as a fixer for that particular area. (Velazquez, pers. comm., September 2016)

Velazquez emphasizes that possessing the contact information of certain "dangerous" people is not enough; the journalist also needs to have built a deeper connection with these people or to find someone else who has "started to build himself as a fixer for that particular area" (pers. comm., September 2016). Once a fixer builds enough trust with people in a given neighborhood or city, Velazquez suggests that "contact information" becomes a real *contact*—a deeper connection that can be shared with a visiting journalist.

Each of these foreign journalists suggests that they depend on news fixers to help them get sources for their stories. Yet, their statements also reveal that correspondents might seek out certain news fixers to help them find specific *types* of contacts. Just as journalists might visit a particular region with a preconceived story already in mind, so might they also search for news sources that fit into a preordained category: the Mexican drug trafficker, the Syrian army defector, the person living in a Johannesburg township, to name a few examples. When foreign correspondents operate in this way, they are responding to their respective industrial imperatives—what types of perspectives their editors (and their audiences) expect to see in their reports. In the 21st century, foreign correspondents are also responding to the intensifying interconnection of disparate news markets around the world, to the technological and economic convergence that is leading to more and more competition between journalists on a transnational level (Tumber and Webster 2006; Cottle, Sambrook, and Mosdell 2016; Palmer 2018).

This interconnection does not mean that there is only one streamlined global news industry however, nor does it erase the existence of stubborn and confusing cultural differences. Even when journalists from diverse news markets are seeking "stock characters" for their stories, news fixers must draw upon their regionally specific expertise to secure these interviews. For instance, Mostafa Sheshtawy, a fixer who worked in Cairo during the post-Mubarak uprisings, says that he was able to get a great deal of work during that time because he was personally connected to a number of the Egyptian activists whose particular perspectives were in high demand (pers. comm., July 2015). The correspondents who hired Sheshtawy could not uniformly get these contacts on their own.

In turn, Chris Knittel, a fixer working in the United States, says that his "specialty is in gaining access to subjects within the criminal underworld. A few examples of stories that I've worked on include underground dog fighting, gun trafficking, gang warfare, MDMA distribution, and many others" (pers. comm., September 2016). Thus, Knittel has built a very particular contact list that might be useful to clients from a variety of news outlets. Without Knittel to smooth the way, however, journalists and documentarians from vastly different regions of the world might not be legible (or trustworthy) to the contacts they seek.

Each of these news fixers identifies a distinct group of people with whom they are specifically connected, suggesting that this unique contact list is something of value to the diverse journalists and documentarians who seek them out. Yet, not all fixers focus on cultivating specific types of contacts. Some of these media workers are more "generalists" than "specialists," a strategy that also leads to broad marketability. Paulina Villegas, a news assistant with the *New York Times* bureau in Mexico City, says that she is held responsible for building and maintaining a wide network of sources in the area, both in and outside the city (pers. comm., March 2017). Suzan Haidamous, a news assistant and fixer working for the *Washington Post* bureau in Beirut, says that she arranges all the bureau's interviews in both Lebanon and Syria (pers. comm., June 2015). And Immanuel Muasya, a fixer working in Kenya, says that he developed a broad range of contacts in his former life as an actor and a salesman, contacts that complement the newer networks he has built while working as a fixer (pers. comm., May 2016).

Thus, some fixers build networks that are "broad," while others build networks that are "deep." Some build networks that are made up of a certain professional class (such as politicians), while others build networks that target a certain ethnic group. Some fixers are cultural "insiders" to the networks they build, and others are not. My interviewees suggest that there are different strategies they can deploy in the process of networking with potential sources, and each strategy is geared toward making the news fixer more valuable to the world's varied journalists—each of whom increasingly works within a competitive and interconnected set of news markets.

A central part of this marketability is the fixer's cultural savvy, something that is indispensable to the process of building these human networks. Whether fixers connect with a source over a long duration of time or in the five minutes before the interview happens, these media employees engage in an intricate dance of cultural mediation, just in the process of reaching out to the diverse individuals who might eventually appear in a foreign news story. This is why fixers describe the process of networking in very active terms:

> Networking, making connections, and assisting others in different capacities, has been something I've always been adept at. Not just any access, a good fixer must provide safe and secure entry to the subjects you are trying to film. From using your reputation and knowledge, your connections and/or working the chain to find new types of access by thinking outside the box. (Knittel, pers. comm. September 2016)

In this statement, Knittel emphasizes the "adeptness" required to connect with sources who might be dangerous—both to the fixer and to the journalist or documentarian. He also notes that the fixer must actively draw upon his or her own reputation and knowledge, as well as "working the chain to find new types of access" when the work demands it (pers. comm. September 2016). This suggests the need for the fixer to perform multiple identities and to constantly negotiate with potential sources who may not feel comfortable talking to journalists or documentarians.

Sometimes this work is directly emotional in nature. Ingrid Le Van, a European fixer working in Brazil, finds that a lot depends on the fixer's effort at making "informal" connections with people (pers. comm., August 2016). In a similar vein, Lamprini Thoma, a fixer working in Greece, notes that

> if you establish a good relationship with them [potential sources], things are getting easier for you. I never forget to send flowers on their name day. We don't have birthdays so much here; we have name days. And I call them and say, "Have a nice summer." I'm trying to have those people near me and use those people when I need them for my clients. (Pers. comm., September 2016).

Similarly, Luna Safwan, a former fixer working in Beirut, remarks:

> These contacts, I built them from personal friendships. I went to Tripoli many times and had tea with this person who is an extremist. And my family and my friends would tell me, "You have a lot of weird people on your contact list. You know, very weird people. You go to very weird places. You have coffee with strangers." I know these people. And I can't only reach out to them when I need information. (Pers. comm., June 2015)

In each of these accounts, the fixer underscores the many extra hours of connecting with potential sources on a different level, outside the purview of the "professional." For Le Van, it is essential that she have some kind of informal engagement with potential news sources in Brazil, because she feels that this informality is where the connections really happen (pers. comm., August 2016). Thoma highlights that she always remembers people's name days and checks in with them to see how they are doing; this extra work of connecting emotionally in turn helps her to connect these sources with her clients. And Safwan observes that sitting down and having tea with an "extremist" can result in a "personal relationship" that will then be helpful to foreign journalists who could not easily make those contacts on their own.

Building this type of emotional connection can be psychologically taxing, especially when the source becomes important to the fixer in one way or another. Safwan tells of the deep connection she eventually began to feel with her Syrian activist contacts, though she is not Syrian. And Saad tells of a Syrian soldier—with whom she had been in contact for over a year—who suddenly died in the civil war, just after contacting her a final time: "He texted me, he said, "'Goodbye.' He told me poetry, two lines of poetry, it was from a famous Syrian poet. He told me the poetry, and then he's gone" (pers. comm., June 2015). In some circumstances, the contacts that fixers build can impact their emotional lives, pointing to the important fact that these networks of sources are human networks, in which the fixers are deeply entangled.

This is why the concept of trust is so prevalent in the stories that news fixers tell about building their networks. Even for those fixers who do not overtly emphasize the need to build personal relationships with sources, the issue of "building trust" looms large as a sociocultural and psychological necessity of the work. For instance, Knittel highlights "the difficulties [that] arise from the inherent danger in filming hitmen, gangsters, paranoid drug dealers, smugglers, and the like," pointing to the fixer's precarious positioning between "paranoid" sources and journalists or documentarians who want to publicize their stories. For Knittel, it is crucial to cultivate trust with his network of sources in order to successfully gain "access [to] that world" (pers. comm., September 2016).

Abd Nova, a former fixer who worked in Lebanon, similarly asserts that "building trust with the journalist is not as important as building trust with the contact." This is because the journalist "comes working for a few days and then leaves. Not important" (pers. comm., June 2015). For Nova, the network of contacts is more important because those relationships need to be maintained long after the journalist has gone. Indeed, these contacts are what the fixer will be able to offer other journalists who come along later. Nova observes that when he was working in Beirut journalists most often sought him out as a fixer for two reasons: (1) to act as a translator and (2) to share his contacts with them (pers. comm., June 2015). But even the act of sharing a contact with a journalist can be risky for the fixer, as Safwan remarks:

> It takes a great deal of courage in Lebanon to actually share contacts and to get your contacts to talk to the media. It's challenging, people are always afraid. The contacts are always afraid of the media misusing their quote. Dragging them into complications with their families. Especially when a contact's situation is a little critical in terms of political opinion. When they have a different opinion from their sect,

when they have a different opinion from their entourage or the area in which they live, or their work environment is a bit different. (Pers. comm., June 2015)

This risk becomes all the more pressing in an era when people from one part of the world can see news coverage aimed at audiences in another part of the world. Foreign correspondents like the former ABC bureau chief Ray Homer have increasingly commented on this dilemma, noting that, at one time, their reports would never have been seen by the people they were interviewing (pers. comm., June 2015). Yet, now, a news source based in Beirut can more easily access a US correspondents' news report online or on satellite television.

Safwan's statement gestures at this same phenomenon, suggesting that this increased visibility in the digital age further contributes to the need for the news fixer to build trust with the source—both before and during the interview with the visiting correspondent. Yet, a variety of cross-cultural *dis*connections can make this task very difficult. Sometimes the fixer has to convince the potential source that there is a direct benefit to speaking with foreign media. At other times, the fixer has to convince the person that there is no direct danger. And the entire complex process can be complicated further by the ignorant behavior of the visiting journalist or documentarian.

Interfacing with Interviewees

Helping foreign journalists to secure compelling interviews is something that can make a news fixer very proud. For instance, Yizhou Xu, a Chinese-American who used to work as a news assistant and fixer in Beijing, tells of a time when a client was doing a story on a Chinese dissident who had been in prison for 20 years: "I got the first interview with his wife, who was under house arrest at the time" (pers. comm., January 2016). Being the person to "g[et] the first interview" was something of note for this former news assistant. This is because the act of successfully scoring these interviews can be as simple as calling one of the fixer's contacts on the phone. But it can also be very challenging. Even when news fixers have spent years building their intricate system of contacts, they might still find themselves finagling strange interview requests with very little notice. In other cases, news fixers struggle to get their contacts to keep their word and show up for an appointment.

This is especially the case in societies where appointments with foreign journalists do not necessarily carry the same weight as they might in other places. For instance, Haidamous tells this anecdote:

> There was a story in Tripoli. I talked to him [the source] three days before the interview, and he said, "Yes, at eleven" and gave me a date. I went with a journalist. I called ahead, his line was off. Kept calling. We waited. I tried to find him, I went to the mosque, he was not in the mosque. Then I decided, "I will look for his house." So, we were looking for his house, and fortunately we found his house. . . . I was ringing the bell from downstairs, and no one was answering. Then after about half an hour his wife answers. She says, "Yes, please hold on." And I said, "Hi. I'm Suzan, I talked to you three days ago." [He said], "Oh, I forgot." (Pers. comm., June 2015)

The phenomenon that Haidamous describes does not only occur in Lebanon, where Haidamous works. News fixer Anna Nekrasova observes, "Ukrainians can be difficult to plan the interview one week before. Even a very serious politician will say to you, 'OK, call me one day before.' Because no one is used to planning something beforehand more than a day before" (pers. comm., August 2016). And a fixer working in Nepal, Sharad Chirag Adhikaree, says:

> Most of the clients I've worked with, they want to do an interview with someone, for instance a common official or some other person. They ask me to arrange the meeting. But sometimes people are so laid back that even if you have fixed an appointment, sometimes they don't inform you, but they just simply go somewhere. And they say, "OK, I really forgot that." So, you have to remind them. That is what we [fixers] do. I mean, it seems very simple, but you have to remind them, "OK, we are meeting tomorrow," one day before, and then the same day before you leave to go to the interview. You just say, "OK, I am on the way to the interview," to make sure. (Pers. comm., August 2016)

Because potential sources do not always think about keeping appointments in the same way that foreign journalists might, the task of securing the interview falls to the fixer. In such cases, the news fixer must actively interact with the source in order to ensure that the connection is maintained and that the journalist gets the information needed for the story. In other cases, the fixer must engage in a much more intense level of interfacing because the source does not feel comfortable speaking with foreign media.

For instance, one anonymous fixer and documentarian working in Russia says that there are particular difficulties involved in getting certain Russian officials to speak to foreign media, especially if they are suspicious of that media organization's political stance. Because of this, the fixer must serve as an interface between foreign journalists and Russian officials, making each more legible to the other:

> I [told the officials]: "If they [the foreign documentarians] do not listen to you, then the only people who will be in the film will be the guys from one position. So, don't you want to say what you think? Just articulate it in the film, you know." And then they thought, "Yeah. Well, why not? We should do it." Sometimes maybe you can mention that some guy recommended them who is kind of well-known in Russia. Many different approaches. (Pers. comm., January 2017)

This statement points to the fact that, on the one hand, the fixer must maintain trust with the contact, perhaps invoking a familiar name—of "someone well-known in Russia," for example—who sanctions the source's interaction with foreign media. On the other hand, the fixer might encourage the contact to think "globally"—to consider the possibility that this particular documentary or report will be circulated outside of Russia, and that this broader distribution poses an opportunity for the source to get his or her opinions heard. Crucially, this effort at assuaging the Russian official's concerns is also an effort at securing a compelling interview for the client. In this sense, the fixer serves as an interface, where the foreign journalist and the Russian official can successfully connect with each other.

In other circumstances, the fixer might focus more intensely on emphasizing "local" connections. For instance, Swedish fixer and local producer Niclas Peyron says, "in Scandinavia, business is 'local, local.'" This means that a Swedish fixer like Peyron

> can open a door or get in contact with someone much easier than a foreigner. . . . If someone says, "Oh, I'm calling from Fox News, you know, we have billions of viewers," I say, "Oh yes, that's fine, stand in line." But if [the fixer] calls them and says, "Hi, I've got this Fox News crew coming in, and I'm Swedish," then that opens the doors much more easily. (Pers. comm., September 2016)

For Peyron, being a cultural insider is more useful than dropping the name of a global news organization. Yet, for the anonymous fixer and documentarian in Russia, appealing to the possibility of global distribution can be a powerful approach. As this fixer suggests, convincing cagey sources to talk requires "many different approaches" (pers. comm., September 2016). Some of these approaches involve a direct appeal to the source's notion of the "local," while others involve a direct appeal to the concept of the "global."

A fixer working in Lebanon, Moe Ali Nayel, says that it can be especially difficult to convince certain sources to speak on camera, where their faces will be seen. This is why he particularly dislikes working with television crews:

> I probably had a problem in the past, because I wouldn't want to impose on anyone to be on camera or to do it in a way where I pressured them so much that they can't run away from it. They are being so nice, and so they end up being on camera or they end up speaking to me about issues they don't want to speak about. I'm not for pressuring people. (Pers. comm., June 2015)

Nayel's statement addresses the vulnerability of some sources, the dangers they feel they might face if they can be identified in a foreign news story. Part of the fixer's job is helping to assuage this sense of vulnerability; yet, as Nayel suggests, not all fixers relish the task, especially when they feel that the foreign news team is being exploitative.

Even when the fixer does not feel that the clients are exploiting their sources, it is challenging to convince some people to appear in a foreign news story. Irene Lioumi, a fixer working in Greece, says:

> I am an expert in the refugee crisis. So, everybody here now calls me in northern Greece to arrange interviews, or documentaries, with the refugees. It's very important and very difficult to persuade them to talk to you. First of all, they don't speak English, they don't speak Greek, they speak other languages. So, you have to find, first of all, a translator. Then you have to find the refugees who are willing to speak to you. (Pers. comm., September 2016)

Here, Lioumi implies that the news fixer does not necessarily have to be a cultural "insider" to secure interviews with people who may not initially wish to speak with the foreign press. She does not speak the same language as the population that she has become an "expert" on—in fact, she has to hire her own cultural mediator to communicate with these contacts. Yet, Lioumi has been successful enough at interacting with this population that she is now one of the "go-to" fixers for clients who want to interview refugees in Greece. Part of this success may stem from her passion for helping the refugees: "This is very important for me, the ethical [aspects], you know, because many refugees are already in Europe. Because we helped them one year and a half before. That's why I love this job. Because it's not only a job, not only a profession, but you can help people" (pers. comm., September 2016). Lioumi has created a personal, emotional connection with the network of contacts she has built, despite the fact that she is not a cultural insider to this group of refugees.

Still, other fixers do tout the usefulness of cultural proximity in the process of interfacing with sources and convincing them to give an interview. For instance, an anonymous fixer working in Palestine tells this story:

> PBS contacted me to work on a piece about Jenin, which used to be known as like, I'm making quotation marks in the air here, you know, the "hotbed" of suicide bombers and a "breeding ground" for suicide bombers and terrorists. It had been turned around by US government participation and a security program to clean up the street and get the resistance fighters to turn in their arms and not fight against Israel anymore. They wanted me to find certain government officials involved in this program, but they also wanted me to track down and get interviews with former resistance fighters, who were kind of in a martyr's brigade, kind of militant wings of political groups. It was a good challenge. I found them, we went into the Jenin refugee camp and they [PBS] wouldn't have been able to do this work without me because I was considered—you know, people ask, "Who are you? What's your last name? What's your family name? Oh, ok, do you know, are you related to this person, that person?" So, I was in some cases a local or an insider, who was able to get these interviews. And when the crew was getting suspicious looks, somebody would say, "No, no, no, they are with her. She's OK, we can trust them." (Pers. comm., July 2013)

In this narrative, the fixer emphasizes the fact that PBS wanted to interview a group of people who had been involved in potentially controversial and dangerous activities. Crucially, it was this fixer's cultural proximity to the militants—her family name, which gave her special status as a local or an insider—that directly helped her to get interviews with these people. Because she seemed culturally familiar to the sources, this fixer was able to build enough trust to get them to speak to PBS. In this way, the fixer served as an interface at which the sources and the PBS correspondents could connect with each other.

Abd Nova also emphasizes the usefulness of cultural proximity, even when that proximity is not necessarily very precise: "Especially if it's a refugee story or a contact in Lebanon. I did work on the Lebanese conflicts in Tripoli, between two areas in Tripoli, and it's a trust factor of having an Arab or someone—the contact would see that he [the fixer] comes from his background and he's saying, 'OK these guys [the journalists] are good. You can talk to them'" (pers. comm., June 2015). Nova suggests that his status as someone who was recognizably "Arab" helped him connect his clients with sources in Tripoli. He did not necessarily need to identify as Lebanese—Nova was a Syrian refugee, after all—but a broader cultural proximity still assuaged the concerns of his clients' potential sources. Because he appeared to these sources as an "Arab" like them, Nova says that he was able to convince them to give an interview to the foreign media. Significantly, it was not some vulgar sense of the "local" that allowed Nova to connect his source with his client. Instead, it was a shifting element of cultural identification that Nova was able to accentuate for the comfort of the source, while still keeping his clients' needs firmly in mind.

This performative effort at building trust with the source does not necessarily have to unfold along strictly ethnic lines. Fixers can also play to certain religious affiliations, for example, or they can perform particular gender roles in the process of "playing to both sides." A number of my female interviewees say that, as women, they can inspire confidence in female sources who may not feel comfortable speaking with male journalists from another region. Yet, female fixers also say that accentuating their femininity helps them inspire more confidence in men. For instance, Le Van notes, "sometimes you just have to play around with the fact that you're a woman, to flirt with people, to get the interview. . . . Often people just speak more freely when it's a woman interviewing them, and they just relax, and they smile" (pers. comm., August 2016). Significantly, Le Van describes this phenomenon as "playing around with the fact that you're a woman," highlighting the performative element of drawing upon gender to "play to both sides."

Some fixers do not necessarily like drawing upon gender performances to get an interview with a male source, but they note that "at the same time, it's like, 'oh well, OK fine.' If I talk nicely to him, he's going to let me interview him. Then I'll talk nicely" (Saidi, pers. comm., May 2013). This statement emphasizes the pragmatic quality of accentuating expected gender roles in order to help journalists get an interview with the client. Part of the job is smoothing everyone's suspicions and helping the source relax so they will speak freely. Female fixers especially say that they can do this by acting more "feminine." As Lekas Miller observes, "A lot of it with fixing is making everyone feel relaxed and at ease. Making the sources feel relaxed and at ease in order to tell the journalist their story. I think that's a little bit gendered as well. I feel like I'll be in the room, [and they think] 'Oh, Anna's here. She's cute, my friend, whatever'" (pers. comm. June 2015).

Part of acting more "feminine" is making sure not to intimidate the source, especially if the source is male. Catalina Hernández, a fixer working in Colombia, says that when she is interacting with sources, "I try not to be aggressive, I try to joke about it and stuff. And I also, when they start giving their opinions, whether I agree with it or not, I'm always like, 'Oh, yeah, you're absolutely right, yeah, that guy's an idiot.' So that sort of calms them down" (pers. comm., August 2016). Haidamous echoes this, saying: "I try to make him [the source] feel that he's comfortable telling me, and I play [as though] I'm stupid to an extent. I don't show them that I know, because this will scare them. I just show them that I am willing to learn from them what is happening" (pers. comm., June 2015). In both of these cases, the female fixer feels the need to hide her intelligence and professional expertise—qualities that make her marketable to her clients—to gain the trust of the men the client needs to interview. Hiding these aspects can serve as one useful strategy in the complex process of interacting with sources.

In other cases, female journalists like Hernández engage in an entirely different performance, pointing to the shifting performativity of "playing to both sides," and serving as the interface between the client and the source:

> Sometimes with guys who are very overpowering, it helps to interrupt. It sort of surprises them and they stop. Here in Colombia. So that, I think that you have to be strategic about it, because if you're a man that's doing the translating, then they'll want to talk to you a lot more. And maybe they can be a bit more confrontational, because there's always the "competition" sort of thing, especially in Latin America and in the social classes that are more impoverished. There's always sort of like a gender jealousy kind of thing. (Pers. comm., August 2016)

"Being strategic" about interfacing between the client and potential interviewees is part of the fixer's labor for the visiting journalist. The very process of relating to locally based people by accentuating some aspect of cultural identity is also the process of relating to the foreign journalist—because, ultimately, the goal is to produce a news report or documentary for an audience that is typically based far from the people being interviewed. In this sense, the work of interfacing with sources is always about "playing to both sides," especially because foreign journalists might intentionally choose a fixer who can more directly identify with the potential source. An anonymous female fixer working in El Salvador says that

> foreign journalists prefer to work with women. Because it's easier to talk with people. . . . If you're working on abortion, for example, on this topic, and you go to talk to girls that have been raped and they had an abortion and things like that—they're not going to be very open with a man. They'd rather have a girl. And that's why, I think girls are more—[journalists] prefer to work with girls. (Pers. comm., August 2016)

Similarly, an anonymous news assistant and fixer who formerly worked for a major US newspaper in Moscow says that in some cases her bureau colleagues took her on an assignment "because I was a woman. [I] was expected to pose less danger to some potential sources." In turn, the journalists asked this news assistant to "call someone and just kind of be more like nice, sweet" (pers. comm., January 2017).

Foreign journalists sometimes choose fixers specifically because they might be able to convince sources to talk, based on the cultural identifications that the fixers can accentuate. This is the same with the journalists who choose ex-military male fixers in Beirut when they want to talk to a different type of source who would only trust a man with whom they had made previous contact (Lekas Miller, pers. comm., May 2015). Because of this, fixers find themselves drawing upon certain aspects of their sociocultural identities in order to convince a local source to speak while, at the same time, working to maintain their connections with the foreign journalist who has an entirely different audience in mind.

This effort at interfacing, at "playing to both sides," requires skill—so much, in fact, that some fixers invoke the notion of diplomacy when describing this work. For instance, Haidamous attributes her skills in dealing with sources to a course she once took in diplomacy (pers. comm., June 2015). And a British fixer working in Italy says that the fixer must "be a consummate diplomat. You must also protect both parties in any negotiation while satisfying both. While clearly your prime loyalty is to [the person] who hired you, this needs to be set against one's long-term interests to avoiding being cut off entirely by any given body" (pers. comm., September 2016).

The fixer risks "cutting off" a long-term source, most especially when the visiting journalist or documentarian makes the source feel offended or threatened. This typically happens as a result of cross-cultural disconnection— as a result of miscommunication, misunderstanding, or—in the most extreme cases—the client's lack of interest in the dignity of the people being interviewed. Since maintaining a network of contacts over the long term is vital to a fixer's livelihood, fixers sometimes find themselves working to educate their clients on how to interact with interviewees in the most respectful and productive ways. Often the visiting journalists listen to their fixer's advice—but sometimes they do not.

The Dignity of the Source

According to Renato Miller, a fixer working in Mexico City, "the most important thing you can do is to really make [your interviewees] feel like you respect their dignity." Miller adds that if "you think, oh this guy is full of shit—they'll read it, they'll read it off of you, and they'll close their doors" (pers. comm., March 2017). In other words, sources can tell when foreign journalists hold them in contempt; this is the kind of thing that translates across linguistic divides. For Miller, respecting the sources' dignity means listening carefully to what they have to say—and even trickier—trying to gain a clear sense of what it is that they are trying to communicate (pers. comm., March 2017). In Miller's experience, showing sources this kind of respect will often result in new alliances. For example, the sources might share useful tips with the journalist or try to help the news team find a place to eat or rest.

For other fixers, respecting the dignity of the source also means observing the proper cultural protocols on how to interact with each other. Swedish fixer Niclas Peyron says:

> You've got to shake everyone's hand, you don't just shake the boss's hand. It's a democracy, it's very flat-based, you know? [Also,] a typical Swedish thing is, be on time. If it's a meeting that's at six o'clock, it [the meeting] is six o'clock, you know. If you're five minutes past, or two minutes past, they'll have probably left, or started another meeting. And some people don't understand that....Those kinds of little things, I know have destroyed loads of stories that people want to do. (Pers. comm., September 2016)

Peyron describes a cultural expectation specific to Sweden, pointing out that the client's failure to observe these traditions can result in the loss of a good story. According to Peyron, it matters that the journalist makes sure to shake everyone's hand. This differs drastically from other parts of the world, where it might be considered very rude for a foreign journalist to try to shake hands with religious leaders or women. Variations like these point again to the continued "stickiness" of cultural difference, even in the era of globalization.

Michael Kaloki, a fixer working in Kenya, says that he tries to actively provide his clients with some guidelines on how to comport themselves in a way that is respectful of regional traditions. "For example, if you're filming in Mombasa with a Muslim family," says Kaloki, "I give advice for how she [the reporter] can dress, how we should we behave generally, if there's anything that we should or shouldn't do" (pers. comm., June 2016). Kaloki says that most of his clients listen to his advice and do their best to try to heed the important cultural differences. Yet, without someone like Kaloki, the journalists who travel quickly from one region to another would have a difficult time even knowing what traditions they need to observe. Especially in the current international news environment, where journalists often parachute into one zone and then leave just as swiftly for an entirely different place, fixers play a vital role in helping their clients respect the dignity of the source, simply by educating the client on how they should act during the interview.

Haidamous tries to have a conversation with each client before they meet with the source:

> "I want you to be patient," I will tell the journalist. "It's not that you just arrive and start asking questions. You have to be friendly at first and nice. And sometimes we cannot approach directly the subject." . . . Because if you ask it directly they [the sources] are going to say, "Oh no. That's not true." So, it's not that I trap the person, I approach them in a way to be comfortable to say what they really think. (Pers. comm., June 2015)

Haidamous argues that—at least in Lebanon—treating the source with dignity requires a certain tone on the part of the person asking questions. The directness so often associated with the hardboiled reporters in Hollywood movies is not at all appreciated in Lebanon, and it will very likely shut down the entire conversation. For people to "say what they really think," they have to feel that they are generally respected and not under personal attack.

Listening is key to creating this environment of mutual respect. An anonymous fixer working in the West Bank says:

> I like to go to people's homes when they invite me and listen to everything they say even if it is not pertinent to what I'm doing. I don't do what some journalists do which is: "No, no, no, that's not the question I'm asking. I want to know about this other question." I let people do whatever they want and rattle off because (a) you will get something out of it maybe that you haven't thought about, and (b) it's about respect. These people are bringing you into their home, and they are not your subject. They are not something you can use and forget about the next day (Pers. comm., July 2013).

Kaloki also observes this tendency for some journalists to interject too much during the interviews: I'll give you an example: Waiting for an elderly person to finish speaking before you speak to them." Kaloki says that sometimes, the journalist "wants to get the story quick and can't take up too much time, and he cuts in between the sentences of the [elderly] interviewee. In some Western countries, maybe that might be taken OK, but in rural communities [in Kenya], they might take offense to that" (pers. comm., June 2016).

Both Kaloki and the anonymous fixer working in the West Bank—two very different people from disparate geopolitical regions—emphasize how important it is for the foreign journalist to *listen* rather than merely speak. In Kaloki's view, the problem arises in the correspondents' occasional tendency to cut the interviewee off and interrupt that person—something that is especially frowned upon if the interviewee is older than the journalist. In the case of the anonymous fixer from the West Bank, the foreign journalist might try to control the conversation rather than letting it flow naturally. Indeed, this fixer reads this effort at controlling the conversation as an ethical problem, suggesting that doing so is tantamount to treating the sources as though they are "data"— "your subject . . . something you can use and forget about the next day" (pers. comm., July 2013). Instead, this fixer asserts that sources are human beings who deserve respect. She implies that journalists can show such respect by dropping the authoritative performance and by listening much more carefully.

Kaloki's statement especially highlights the reason why some journalists struggle to engage in this active listening in the field: he mentions that the client might frequently interrupt the interviewee because the client is in a hurry. Foreign journalists are harried by the tight deadlines inherent to news production in the 21st century, and this systemic stressor can in turn cause them to treat people in the field without the proper dignity. Ksenia Yakovleva, a fixer working in Moscow, echoes this concern, saying that her clients "just keep asking questions even though you can see the person is already really tired, they [the clients] just keep—well, they need material. They need to talk, which they would use in their movie. So, of course, they would risk everything to talk to a person for as long as possible" (pers. comm., January 2017). Like Kaloki, Yakovleva recognizes that much of the client's "rude" behavior is due to the intense pressures of trying to produce news and documentary films in a competitive international milieu. But like Kaloki, Yakovleva also recognizes the danger in letting these deadlines dictate journalists' treatment of the interviewee: in pushing the person to talk "for as long as possible," Yakovleva says her clients "risk everything."

In more extreme cases, fixers note that their clients not only give the impression that they are not listening to their sources, but they also give the impression that they do not care about them on a basic human level. Irina Minaeva, a Russian fixer working in Mexico, gives the example of some Russian journalists who wanted her to travel to Guadalajara to interview the families of a group of people who had just died of food poisoning: "This is their family. Can you imagine?" (pers. comm., March 2017). In a similar vein, French fixer Benjamin Zagzag notes: "Working with some Americans, a lot of times, they want to interview survivors [of terrorist attacks]. And it's hard to make them understand that you know, a survivor, like it's something in France, you're not doing it" (pers. comm., September 2016).

Another fixer also says that he has noticed this problem: "I once had an argument with a journalist who I thought had no understanding of the situation and no empathy for the victims. Being an American and having lived through September 11th made her think she could lecture me. And I thought it was not accurate" (pers. comm., September 2016). In this particular case, the fixer suggests that his client believed that her personal experiences somehow negated the need for her to treat her sources with the proper level of dignity. Yet, as this fixer implies, one experience of trauma—in one particular geopolitical region, at one distinct moment in time—cannot be conflated with an entirely different experience of trauma. Thus, news fixers like this one hint that journalists should not assume that they are familiar with a source's suffering. They also should not assume that because they personally have overcome their own suffering, so, too, should the source.

Failure to consider the dignity of the source can seriously damage the fixer's relationship with the contact, a relationship that sometimes takes years to cultivate. One fixer who wishes to remain anonymous recounts how she once helped a team of journalists interview sources for a story that they ultimately interpreted (and wrote) in a highly negative fashion. For the fixer, this ideological twist was a betrayal—most especially, a betrayal of the people the journalists interviewed:

> You know, those people accepted them [the journalists] into their homes and they honestly talked, they gave them statements that were honest and sincere. . . . They [the sources] are not scammers or anything, they're normal, regular people. Some of them are artists and lawyers. . . . And the final story was so bad. (Pers. comm., August 2016)

For this fixer, the journalists' xenophobic treatment of the people they interviewed was not only a problem of misrepresentation, it was also a problem of communicative disconnection and sociocultural misunderstanding. As far as the fixer was concerned, her clients did not properly hear and consider what the sources were trying to say, nor did they value the fact that the sources invited them into their homes and gave them their time.

What the fixer viewed as her clients' betrayal of her sources in turn led these contacts to hold the fixer accountable for the negative story: "All those people were cross at me, because they had trusted me. Because I am very respected in my town, and they know me as a professional, a journalist. And I called them [the clients], and I said that if they don't remove the story from the internet that we will sue them, because they lied" (Pers. comm., August 2016). Since the fixer's sources trusted that she was a professional journalist, they believed she would act as cultural mediator, helping them to communicate their perspectives with the foreign journalists they invited into their homes. Yet, when the fixer's clients published this damaging story, her sources began to question their trust in her, putting her in danger of losing a number of important local contacts. This is the danger that most fixers face when their clients fail to treat their sources with dignity.

Stories such as this one point to the most extreme cases of disconnection between sources, fixers, and journalists in the field. As Muasya asserts, "It's not every journalist" who shows such disregard for the people they wish to interview. In fact, Muasya says:

> I think as I've doubled up in my fixing career, I think the journalists who come down these days, because there's been a lot of media about Africa, you get people who are more well behaved, and they know the

ethics of the work. And it's not like when I started out two years ago, when people would just come and shove—there were some really rude cameramen, it was nasty back then, but these days I say that's changing. And these days, if you're shooting with a cameraman, he'll come and ask you, "Oh, can I take pictures, or do you think it's right for me to do this?" or "Do you think it's OK for me to do this and that?" (pers. comm., May 2016).

Other fixers agree that most of their clients are quite conscientious about observing the proper cultural protocols, relying heavily on their fixers' knowledge when they do not know how to act. And even those clients who have crossed a line can still make amends—the anonymous fixer's clients finally consented to taking down the news story that offended her sources, for example (pers. comm., August 2016), while the anonymous fixer chose to work again with the journalist who felt that her experience with the trauma of 9/11 made her an "insider" to the trauma of her news sources (pers. comm., September 2016).

Still, it is important for journalists and scholars to be aware of the problems that do arise for fixers as they engage in the work of networking with sources. Significantly, Muasya overtly says that these are "ethical" problems—his clients either do or do not understand what he calls "the ethics of the work" (pers. comm., May 2016). Muasya's testimony intimates that news fixers have their own diverse perspectives on what ethical news production should look like, especially when the client is visiting from another geopolitical region. According to my interviewees, respecting the dignity of the source—as well as considering the fixer's precarious role as the connecting force between journalists and potential interviewees—is a vital part of this ethical news production.

Conclusion

Global media ethicist Herman Wasserman believes that if journalists would make a more active effort at ethical listening—at *difficult* listening (Dreher, cited in Wasserman 2013), the kind that demands the journalist try to understand the sources' experiences and affirm their right to be heard—then these journalists would also "afford [news sources] their human dignity" (80). This ethical practice "mean[s] listening attentively to the stories people have to tell—especially those people who might otherwise not be heard because they find themselves too often in the shadows of the public sphere" (80).

In many ways, news fixers appear to be recommending this concept of ethical listening when they describe journalists' occasional tendency to forget the dignity of the source. Compellingly, fixers' production narratives also suggest that all too often it is not the people living "in the shadows of the public sphere" who comprise their lucrative networks of sources. This is because there is a market for certain types of news sources, and fixers have to make a living. Still, although some news fixers' networks are predetermined by the journalists' preconceived notions about a story, other fixers do try to connect their clients with sources who have vastly different perspectives than those the correspondents are used to hearing.

Either way, the labor of networking with sources is foundational to international journalists' ability to do their reporting. Without their fixers' living, breathing networks, there would be no life in international news stories. Foreign correspondents certainly seem aware that they need fixers' networks, because one of the first things they reportedly ask a fixer is: "Could you please come, or give me contacts, because I'm here just for a week and I don't know what to do" (anonymous fixer in El Salvador, pers. comm., August 2016). Some journalists value the contacts so much that they might pay the fixer for simply providing names and phone numbers, as was once the case for Samuel Okocha, a fixer working in Nigeria (pers. comm., May 2016). Yet, other journalists might contact a fixer, secure the fixer's contact list, and then disappear (Velazquez, pers. comm., September 2016; Riquelme, pers. comm., March 2017). Velazquez tells a story about a time when this happened to him:

> I gave [the journalists] some contacts, and then I didn't hear from them for a very long time. So, I was thinking, "OK, these guys, they are not going to show up." . . .Well, I stopped working, of course, once I stopped hearing from them, I stopped working for them. . . .They called me, three months later: "We are in Madrid, do you want to meet for a coffee?" And I was like, "No, I don't want to meet for a coffee. I haven't heard from you in three months, I gave you all these contacts, you never told me if you're going to pay me or not, I d[idn't] know if I [was] going to [be working] for you, and now you want to get coffee." (Pers. comm., September 2016)

Velazquez's story illuminates a problem related to Wasserman's analysis of ethical listening: the failure of some journalists to remember that a fixers' network of sources is far more than a commodity to be bought or sold. "Contacts," or "sources," are people with stories that they sometimes share at great risk. Even when they seem entirely "other" to the journalist visiting the region, the contacts that fixers like Velazquez build are human subjects, who must be courted, engaged, convinced, and put at ease. The emotional labor of building this living network can be costly for the fixer, especially if the client does not bother to pay for this labor in the first place.

The equally important task of securing the interviews that journalists want can also be costly for news fixers. One anonymous fixer tells of a time when she was working in Bahrain and a news team wanted interviews with people whom Bahraini officials would have viewed as a threat:

> I'm there on the ground. I had a residency permit, you know, I had a work visa in this country and was doing work that the government wasn't allowing to be done. The interviews we were doing were anti-government, and this is the only case that I've ever had to do something like this as a freelancer, something that was even remotely dicey or would put me in any danger. We got it done. It was extremely difficult, and I made sure that I charged them more than I normally would as a fixer or producer because it was dangerous. (Pers. comm., July 2013)

As the above statement suggests, sometimes fixers risk much more than alienating their contacts. Their interaction with particular sources can also put them on bad terms with governments or militant groups. For instance, this particular fixer was eventually called into a Bahraini government official's office to explain herself, a process that required her to accentuate her purported status as a "fixer" rather than a "journalist." She told the government official that she had simply been helping the foreigners with logistical work for a fee (pers. comm., July 2013).

In this way, the fixer engaged in a specific cultural performance that helped smooth the friction between foreign journalists and other people on the ground, "playing to both sides" in order to please her clients as well as the people who disapproved of her work after her clients had left. Fixers often have to accentuate one aspect of their sociocultural identities over others in order to interface between clients and sources in the field. Some fixers emphasize certain cultural interpretations of their gender, for instance, while others draw attention to a shared ethnic or religious identity. The anonymous fixer working in Bahrain accentuated an identity imposed upon her by some news outlets themselves—as a "fixer," she could be viewed as mere "support staff," not responsible for the conceptual part of the story. Luckily, this tactic worked, and this particular news fixer was not questioned further.

Even for those news fixers who do not face personal risk in the process of networking with sources, the effort at building and maintaining trust is quite difficult, pointing to the need for international journalists to also engage in ethical listening with their fixers in the field: "You gain this access gradually, it doesn't happen at once," says Nova. "First you meet the leader of this certain militia, for example. And then you meet the higher person and then they trust you. And then you tell them, 'Look I have a TV channel who wants to cover this, and I can guarantee that they won't shoot what you don't want to shoot. You tell me, and I will make sure they don't" (pers. comm., June 2015). If the journalists fail to listen to the fixer in cases like these, everyone's life could be on the line. At the very least, the news fixer risks losing a vital contact.

Because of this risk, fixers' narratives about networking with sources imply that it is not enough for correspondents to seek out sources and conduct interviews with them. Journalists also need to truly hear and consider what the sources are saying, even if they ultimately disagree with them. As Wasserman suggests, ethical listening does not require some false sense of consensus (2013). Instead, it requires real effort, "straining" to hear one another across cultural differences (Wasserman, 2013). One of the fixers' primary tasks is to tell foreign clients how they can do this, how they can respect the dignity of the people they call "sources." Since the concept of dignity itself differs across cultures, the fixer is indispensable, translating the journalists' actions and expectations for the source, and vice versa. The next chapter of this book further examines the issue of translation in international news reporting, focusing on the fixer's role in interpreting unfamiliar languages.

4

Interpreting Unfamiliar Languages

A fixer needs to be able to keep up the communication be-
tween two different languages, so that they [the journalist
and the source] can actually speak to each other.

—GENNY MASTERMAN, fixer working in Austria and Germany

Every place has its own idiosyncrasy, and there are cer-
tain terms, certain things, that just can't be translated.
Like [British] humor. I mean, you can't translate
[British] humor.

—Anonymous fixer and producer working in Mexico

AS GENNY MASTERMAN implies in the epigraph to this chapter, the ability of
the journalist and the source to "actually speak to each other" depends heavily
on the fixer's role as interpreter and translator (pers. comm., September 2016).
Abd Nova, a former news fixer in Lebanon, says that "half the time, you can
say, I'm contacted because of the language. And fixing happens along the way"
(pers. comm., June 2015). Another fixer working in Beirut agrees, noting that
while some journalists want her to do more heavy lifting in conceptualizing
the story itself, "others, they know everything, and they just want me to go
with them for two reasons: to translate and to make the introduction with the
locals" (Haidamous, pers. comm., June 2015). Russian videographer and news
fixer Valentin Savenkov also highlights the importance of interpreting for
clients, saying, "sometimes it depends on [the journalists'] budget. Sometimes
[their budgets] are very tiny, small, but they ask me to be translator if I can"
(pers. comm., January 2017).

In each of these cases, the news fixers illuminate the fact that, at the bare
minimum, their clients will likely need them to do some interpreting in
the field.

Even when the clients already know the stories that they wish to cover,
they will typically hire a fixer to help them understand the languages that are

FIGURE 4.1 On the HackPack website, journalists can search for fixers by the languages they speak. Screenshot by the author.

foreign to them. As Savenkov notes, this particular skill is so important that it tends to be a priority, even for the journalists and documentarians who are operating on a tiny budget. When the visiting journalists are not already conversant in the languages of the regions they are visiting, they will inevitably find themselves paying for someone else to build a linguistic bridge—to "keep up communication between two [or more] different languages" (Masterman, pers. comm., September 2016).

Yet, news fixers' production narratives also suggest that the labor of interpreting unfamiliar languages is not a simple process. An anonymous news fixer and producer working in Mexico City remarks on the untranslatability of some types of communication, pointing specifically to humor in a cross-cultural context: "British humor... doesn't translate to English speakers in the US. So, imagine translating that to Spanish. You've got to find ways. You've got to be extremely creative" (pers. comm., March 2017). With this assertion, this fixer points to the active nature of linguistic interpretation, to the "creative" and productive elements of mediating between multiple languages. Indeed, this fixer suggests that this particular form of cultural mediation requires the fixer to "find ways" of translating even the untranslatable, the cultural differences that do not have a counterpart in another linguistic system.

Though translation scholars have argued for the past few decades that translation—typically understood as focusing on the written word—and interpretation—typically understood as focusing on the spoken word—are active and creative processes (Venuti 1998; Bielsa and Bassnett 2009; Tymoczko, 2010; Bassnett 2014), professional journalists sometimes still think of translation as an act that should be very "literal" (Bielsa and Bassnett

2009, 1). In the world of international news reporting, there is not always a very clear distinction between translating the written word and interpreting the spoken word. These two terms are often used interchangeably. However, the acts of translating and interpreting are both viewed with a certain degree of suspicion in international news reporting. Some journalists and news editors conceptualize interpretation as a process that should indeed be "literal" (Bielsa and Bassnett 2009, 1), so that the journalist can remain impartial to the vagaries of cultural subjectivity (Holland 2017).

Perhaps it is this belief that contributes to foreign correspondents' occasional ambivalence toward their fixers and interpreters, an ambivalence that surfaces in the Anglophone news industry's discourse (Palmer 2017) as well as in journalists' accounts of their interactions with translators (Palmer 2007; Palmer and Fontan 2007; Murrell 2015). This distrust of the interpreter sits uneasily alongside the dire need for translators in the practice of international reporting—especially as various international news markets are becoming more interconnected in a global era. If translation is itself a "globalizing process," and if "globalization is quite literally unthinkable without the operation of translation and translators" (Cronin 2017, 491) then the intensifying interconnection of the world's various news markets points to the inevitability of foreign correspondents' reliance on the very skills that they also sometimes distrust. This is even more the case in the context of parachute journalism, where many foreign correspondents cannot practically learn all the languages that are used in every single place they visit.

This chapter first examines the market-driven need for news fixers' interpreting skills, investigating the tension between distrust and dependency that defines the process of interpreting unfamiliar languages. Though foreign journalists have been relying on interpreters for at least a couple of centuries, and though interpreters have more generally been operating for thousands of years, the age of globalization brings with it a new set of questions and a new sense of urgency surrounding the interpreter's labor (Bassnett 2014; Cronin 2017). What is more, there has been very little scholarly discussion of news fixers' perspectives on their role as interpreters. My interviewees tend to represent their language skills as crucial services that they can offer journalists operating within an increasingly interconnected set of news markets around the world. In other words, news fixers are aware of the international need for their language skills, and they know that their skills as translators can help them pay their bills.

But news fixers also understand the task of interpreting unfamiliar languages as active and creative work. Though a few of my interviewees suggest that they are mere "mediums," mechanisms that must transmit a coherent message from sender to receiver, even these news fixers simultaneously describe their work in highly active terms. At the same time, fixers' production narratives underscore the fact that the figure of the translator is often gendered, racialized, and looked down upon by both clients and sources in the field. Grappling with such challenges, my interviewees discuss the need to translate emotion as well as words, meaning as well as diction, and cultural context as well as basic statements. Some news fixers mention the need to re-work the very direct questions that journalists might ask an interviewee, pointing back to the fixers' task of interfacing with news sources, as well as highlighting the fact that many news fixers' translations are not direct, "literal" translations at all. Others talk about their active effort at building their vocabularies so that they can more accurately translate the "whole" of the sources' meaning for their clients (Nayel, pers. comm., June 2015). In each of these instances, the news fixer describes an active rather than a passive process.

Still, even the most active and creative effort at translation can sometimes result in disconnection rather than connection, in miscommunication rather than communication. Where translation is concerned, miscommunication can indeed be a very literal problem: struggling to find an equivalent word in two different languages, for example. Miscommunication can also occur because of broader cultural disconnections, such as cultural differences that have not been adequately considered, or a lack of cultural sensitivity that impacts the message itself. In the most extreme cases, cultural difference can lead to risky situations in which the news fixer might have to use his or her knowledge of multiple languages to keep the foreign correspondent out of danger. In these situations, the news fixer makes a quick linguistic connection with the client, but only to communicate the fact that there has been a major—and perilous—breakdown in communication and connection at a broader cultural level. This chapter will also examine these messier aspects of interpreting unfamiliar languages.

News fixers' production narratives echo the more recent scholarship on translation as a creative cultural practice. However, some journalists view this creativity with suspicion, worrying that it is tantamount to news fixers skewing the "objectivity" of the journalist's story (Palmer and Fontan 2007; Murrell 2015). Addressing this concern, this chapter will also discuss the radical potential of translation and interpretation for an increasingly interconnected set of news markets around the world. Because there is *not only one* global news industry, and because even professional correspondents differ drastically from each other, there is less and less to gain from the claim for one objective version of a news event—a version that should ostensibly look and sound the same in every language. Thus, this chapter will close with a call for scholars and journalists to consider linguistic differences more carefully, since these differences cannot be separated from the various cultural subjectivities that often collide in the process of international news reporting.

Distrust vs. Dependence: The Interpreter's Marketable Skills

Translation scholars increasingly argue that the act of translation is an act of negotiation: "There is no act of translation that is not also an act of negotiation. . . .Negotiation is inscribed in the very fabric of translation from both a linguistic/semiological and a historical viewpoint" (Tessicini 2014, 1). Because the translator facilitates this negotiation and thus occupies a position of cultural power (Cronin 2003), the question of "faithfulness" has historically been a part of the discussion and definition of the interpreter and translator (Tessicini 2014, 4; Cronin 2003). This question of "faithfulness"—of whether the interpreter will intentionally or accidentally misinterpret something—can inspire anxiety on the part of foreign correspondents working in a context where they do not know the regional languages.

For instance, when Western journalists covering Iraq began relying heavily on Iraqi translators and fixers, there was concern that these interpreters were unreliable because of their potential bias (Palmer 2007; Palmer and Fontan 2007). Rosie Garthwaite, a freelance journalist who went to Iraq in 2003 to work with a startup news outlet, directly addresses what she and her colleagues felt was the inevitable bias of their locally based interpreters: "We had seven or eight translators, all from different sects. We thought that was a good idea. So, we'd never be tied to one opinion. We wanted to be unbiased, that was our great dream" (pers. comm., February 2013). In order to achieve this goal of impartiality, Garthwaite and her colleagues believed that they could not rely on only one Iraqi translator. The implication was that any Iraqi translator would be biased in favor of the beliefs associated with their religious sect; therefore, Garthwaite and her colleagues reasoned that their safest bet was to use translators from multiple sects.

Garthwaite's statement reveals the distinct discomfort that Western journalists felt with their Iraqi translators during this time period, a distrust that continued after the US invasion of Iraq in 2003. In post-invasion Iraq, reporting from the region became more and more dangerous for white Anglo and

European correspondents. Though these journalists heavily depended upon locally based media workers to act as their surrogates and to navigate them through
the dangerous landscape (McLeary 2006; Ricchiardi 2006), they still struggled
to trust the credibility of their Iraqi partners—particularly where translation
and interpretation were concerned (Palmer and Fontan 2007; Palmer 2007).
Without their Iraqi partners, foreign correspondents could not have covered
the story of Iraq in the post-invasion years. Yet, the correspondents' dependency
sat uncomfortably alongside a marked level of distrust.

This tendency toward distrust did not disappear as the occupation of Iraq
began to fizzle, nor did it apply only to reporting from that particular nation.
Such suspicion informs the attitudes of foreign correspondents working in
other parts of the world as well. For example, an anonymous field producer
working for Al Jazeera says that unreliable translators are a big problem in
Iran: "Everybody has to get registered when they get there, and [you] get . . . a
translator assigned to you, who often doesn't translate things particularly fac-
tually" (pers. comm., April 2013). This field producer implies that, because
the translator is assigned by the Iranian government, he or she will skew the
translation, disregarding the facts and tampering with the truth of the story.

While the anonymous field producer is discussing an instance in which
the translator is government-assigned, other foreign reporters, editors, and
news commentators invoke the same fear of unreliability when discussing
translators who are *not* necessarily government pawns. Some of my previous
research reveals that the broader issue of unreliability specifically surfaces in
the industrial discourse on fixers who work for Anglophone news organizations (Palmer 2017). At times, this discourse reflects the fear that fixers might
not understand journalistic norms on how to properly use the linguistic testimony of a source—that the fixers might paraphrase an interviewee's statement, instead of translating it literally, or that they might omit part of what
the interviewee says (Palmer 2017).

News fixers are themselves aware of the tension surrounding the question
of linguistic "faithfulness." Moe Ali Nayel, a fixer working in Beirut, remarks
that by "not understanding Arabic, you [the correspondent] are like a dumb
person sitting there. So, you have to literally trust what is being told to you"
(pers. comm., June 2015). This statement points to two interrelated issues: (1)
the foreign correspondents' lack of linguistic knowledge, which places them
at a disadvantage ("you are like a dumb person"), and (2) the requirement
that the correspondent "trust what is being told to you." Nayel's assertion
underscores the coexistence of dependency and distrust, a tension that the
fixer also has to navigate.

Sometimes this tension can cause the fixer a great deal of stress. For example, Renato Miller, a Chilean fixer working in Mexico City, says:

> It's hard because, for example, sometimes I had interviews where the interviewee . . . for four or five minutes, he's looking for a word to say, and those four or five minutes he's mumbling. And then you're like, "How the hell do I tell the editor that there's four minutes of mumbling?" I mean he gets the tape later on and then he'll see, but it's funny like that. (Pers. comm., March 2017)

Here, Miller describes a situation where he might conduct an interview in Spanish, and then translate the interview into his client's language. Significantly, Miller mentions the discomfort he feels with giving his client a transcript suggesting that the source said nothing at all for four or five straight minutes. This discomfort surfaces in Miller's testimony because he is aware of the distrust that journalists sometimes feel for their interpreters, and he does not want to exacerbate this distrust by causing his client to think that he is intentionally leaving something out of the translation. Miller's statement points to the tension that informs the work of translation, tension that impacts both the journalist and the fixer.

Despite this tension, both news fixers and foreign correspondents seem to agree that the process of international reporting depends on overcoming the "language barrier." Nikolay Korzhov, a Russian journalist who works in China, notes that the language barrier can be prohibitive, and thus, foreign correspondents in China often have to hire translators at the very least (pers. comm., January 2017). This is because, as freelance journalist Alasdair Baverstock says, "if there's a language barrier you can't report a story" (pers. comm., March 2017). Baverstock's assertion points directly to the foreign correspondents' dependence upon locally based translators who are familiar with regional languages. For parachute journalists, and even for correspondents more permanently based at foreign bureaus, the work of translating between two or more languages is very often outsourced to a fixer or news assistant.

Some foreign correspondents, like former freelancer Ben Gittleson, work hard to specialize in another language, in hopes of getting around this dependency: "Speaking Arabic is a big advantage, because I don't have to pay fixers or translators for the most part. I know other freelancers who do, and it takes a big cut out of what they make" (pers. comm., February 2013). Gittleson's assertion clarifies why news fixers and assistants consider their linguistic abilities to be one of their most valuable services—services that

Gittleson tried to avoid when he worked as a correspondent in Cairo. But even when correspondents like Gittleson are familiar with more than one language, their linguistic skill level may still be too low to completely obviate the need for an interpreter. Artem Galustyan, a correspondent (and sometimes, fixer) working in Moscow, says of his assignment as a journalist in Ukraine:

> Ukrainian and Russian languages are quite similar. But anyway, when you are covering some statements or some speeches it is so important to cover it very correctly. . . . It's not simple . . . I realized, first I had to have an interpreter—a fixer-interpreter, because I need[ed] to have a very correct translation. (Pers. comm., January 2017)

Galustyan's statement reveals the uncomfortable fact that even those journalists who possess some familiarity with the regional language may not be properly equipped to act as their own translators. As Galustyan suggests, translating "is not simple."

Many journalists do not have the language skills needed to report a story in a part of the world that is foreign to them. Because of this, news fixers' language skills are an essential part of the broader work of international reporting. News fixers' production narratives bring this vital labor into the light, representing it as a special service that is highly lucrative in the era of interconnected world news markets. For instance, an anonymous fixer working in Moscow recounts how his language skills scored him a job with the BBC:

> About ten years ago. . . a [fixer] friend of mine asked me to cover for him. He got this gig with the BBC. . . . I have a [university] degree in translation and interpretation. So that's why. They were actually looking for someone to help them to interpret an interview. So, they reached out to a friend of mine, and then he was kind of busy at the time. So, he recommended me, so that was the time when I stared working with the BBC. (Pers. comm., January 2017)

This person's story points to the lucrativeness of a news fixer's foreign language skills, a lucrativeness engendered by the foreign correspondents' lack of linguistic knowledge. Sharad Chirag Adhikaree, a fixer working in Nepal, also stresses journalists' dependence on news fixers' interpreting skills:

> Though the younger generation [in Nepal], they somehow speak English and they can communicate . . . when you come to do a story

and you go to a news source—it's still more than seventy percent of
our civil servants, they don't speak proper English. And most people
that live in the villages, they don't speak English at all. (Pers. comm.,
August 2016)

Because of this phenomenon, Adhikaree says that the language barrier is one
of the major challenges that his clients face in the field. This is why Adhikaree's
language skills are so marketable, something that Luna Safwan, a former fixer
working in Beirut, also notes: "It's funny, because in Lebanon, it's not hard
to be a fixer. Because, if you're from Tripoli or the Beqaa and you actually
speak English and Arabic, you understand both languages" (pers. comm.,
June 2015). For both Adhikaree and Safwan, their ability to speak English
comes as a result of their particular cultural identity, one that is haunted by
the legacy of colonialism. This linguistic ability is also a special service that
Adhikaree and Safwan can offer the journalists and documentarians who visit
their regions.

Each of the aforementioned news fixers invokes the necessity of speaking
at least one particular language in order to be marketable: English. Not only
do journalists whose news outlets are based in Anglophone countries need
fixers who speak English, but, sometimes, so do journalists whose organizations are based in countries where English is not the primary language. For
example, Catalina Hernández, a fixer working in Colombia, says that when
she worked on a project with Al Jazeera Arabic, she and the correspondent
spoke English together in the field, because the correspondent was actually
Canadian: "if not, then it would have been a disaster" (pers. comm., August
2016). In Hernández's case, English served as a mediating language that helped
the fixer and the correspondent work together. Some of the Russian fixers
I interviewed also point to this phenomenon. For example, Alyona Pimanova
and Daniel Smith say that they have sometimes spoken English with news
and documentary teams for whom English is a second language.

The importance of the English language for news fixers points, in some
ways, to the hegemonic rise of English as a "global" language (Crystal 2012;
Pennycook 2017). Yet, Pimanova and Smith suggest that the stubbornness of
cultural difference impacts the fixer-client relationship even when everyone is
relying on English as a linguistic middle ground:

We had this Canadian [team who] was French speaking. The problem
was that they were speaking in French a lot between themselves, and
not letting—well, normally I could hear, if they speak English, I can

hear what they're talking about, and I can recommend advice and things. Like, "that's not going to work, this, don't even try it." But they had their own plan. . . .And then it doesn't work and then they're surprised why it doesn't work. (Pers. comm., January 2017)

In this statement, Pimanova foregrounds the problem of working with clients who use their own linguistic differences as a way to shut down communication with their fixer. Thus, the concept of English as a hegemonic, mediating language can only go so far. Just as clients and fixers can use a common second language as a site of connection, so too, can this common language be abandoned. This points to the slipperiness of mediation in general, to the inherent problem of disconnection as well as connection.

Alongside the logistical confusion of working on a multilingual news team, Pimanova and Smith also emphasize the complicated nature of their role as translators in these situations:

Sometimes that's very interesting, because if [you are] just [translating] from English to Russian, Russian to English, it's very easy. So, the director asks the question, then I translate, then the interviewer [speaks], and I can say [the words] back to the director. In [this other case] we had this really funny experience, because the presenter speaks in French. I don't speak French. So, she had to ask the question in French. Then the director translated it into English, then I translated it into Russian. (Pers. comm., January 2017)

Here, Pimanova describes a process requiring at least one extra translator, due to the linguistic differences that informed the entire assignment. Pimanova's narrative underscores the fact that translation and interpretation is a messy process, riddled with challenges that continue to resonate, even in the purportedly more "homogenized" and streamlined era of globalization.

Because of the complexity of working on a multilingual news team, some journalists and documentarians instead seek fixers who speak the correspondents' native languages, rather than relying on English as a middle ground. For instance, Diana Kultchitskaya says that there is an entire community of French-speaking fixers who work in Moscow (pers. comm., January 2017), while Irina Minaeva, a Russian fixer working in Mexico City notes that "it's very difficult to find anybody in Mexico and Mexico City and Mexico the country, who speaks Russian" (March 2017). Due to this phenomenon,

Minaeva possesses a unique skill that is quite valuable to a certain niche of Russian journalists.

In a similar line, Greek fixer Irene Lioumi says that on top of speaking Greek and English, she also speaks Spanish and French, revealing a formidable skill with language that helps her work with various types of clients (pers. comm., September 2016). And Ingrid Le Van, a multilingual European fixer working in Brazil says: "I mean, of course, you always find people who speak English, but, first of all, the level of English is pretty low in Brazil, and any other language, especially German and French, is even rarer. So, I kind of got these jobs out of the blue, thanks to that" (pers. comm., August 2016).

Linguistic diversity is a valuable service that fixers can offer the foreign correspondents and documentarians who do not possess those skills. Though the practice of international reporting appears to become more and more global in the 21st century (Löffelholz and Weaver 2008; Berglez 2013; Ward 2013), fixers' production narratives reveal that the cultural specificity of language continues to confound any simplistic concept of globalization as a homogenizing and unifying process, at least where news reporting is concerned. This phenomenon not only surfaces in the stories of news fixers who can easily fall into the role of translator, but it also surfaces in the stories of fixers who, at one point or another, run up again their own linguistic limits. For example, although Lioumi speaks several languages, she does not speak the languages of the refugees based in northern Greece (pers. comm., September 2016). This is despite the fact that she has become the "go-to" fixer for covering this particular refugee crisis. To combat her own language barrier, Lioumi hires translators of her own, outsourcing the labor of interpretation that has already been outsourced to Lioumi (pers. comm., September 2016).

As a former Chinese-American news assistant and fixer says, the fixer's translating capabilities become even more marketable when a story emerges suddenly. Yet, the contingent nature of the story can also limit the linguistic services that some news assistants and fixers can offer. Yizhou Xu says he was working as a news assistant for CBS in Beijing, when a series of protests erupted in Hong Kong:

> When we went to Hong Kong for the protest, I went there, and we hired fixers basically. Because we just basically grabbed students, just from the public who speak English to guide us through. Because, when I was in Hong Kong, I don't speak Cantonese, I'm useless. I can't fix whatever's going on. I can't even communicate in the local dialect, so we have to get local translators. So, in that sense, I think fixers come

with that sense of emergency and urgency. This applies to other parts of China too, because regional dialects, there are parts I just don't understand. I only understand Mandarin, so I don't understand all the regional dialects. So that's to me, fixers [fulfill] kind of a temporary, urgent need for either a translator or someone who can fix a story really quick. (Pers. comm., January 2016)

Here, Xu describes his linguistic limitations. Though he could offer his CBS colleagues his skill with the Mandarin dialect, he says he was "useless" when it came to Cantonese. Thus, he and his colleagues had to quickly locate some people who could speak both Cantonese and English, in order to address the contingent nature of the news story. Though Xu was CBS's full-time news assistant in Beijing, the urgent nature of the story suddenly created a market for a different linguistic skill, necessitating that CBS hire anyone they could find—even local students—to translate the events unfolding in Hong Kong.

News fixers' production narratives serve as a reminder that globalization is "unthinkable without translation and translators" (Cronin 2017, 491), highlighting the heavy dependence of the world's diverse foreign news industries on fixers' translating skills. Consequently, news fixers' narratives also suggest that the labor of translating and interpreting is not a passive process, but a process of active cultural mediation. Even so, this perception of translating and interpreting does not always match the attitudes of the journalists and news editors who might hire fixers. As some scholars have argued, "When journalists talk about translation, they tend to be thinking of what others might term, 'literal translation'" (Bielsa and Bassnett 2009, 1). Despite the fact that journalists "may genuinely aspire to impartiality," fixers who act as translators "are constantly forced to make decisions about what to 'lose' and what to 'gain' in the attempt to convey a message across languages and cultures—decisions that can only be made on the basis of their own (ultimately subjective) experience" (Holland 2017, 342). In other words, "translators must make choices" (Tymoczko 2010, 8), and news fixers' stories suggest that they are no exception.

Translation as an Active Process

Some news fixers at first glance appear to represent the act of translation as a very basic, passive task—one from which they actually wish to distance themselves professionally. For instance, an anonymous news assistant working with a US newspaper's bureau in Moscow describes her job in this way: "I mean, in the contract they call it translator-fixer. Traditionally the job was called translator. But it's more than translation—way more" (pers. comm., January 2017). This news assistant implies that she views translation as a very specific task, one that does not account for all the other jobs she must complete on a day-to-day basis.

Another former news assistant with the *LA Times* bureau in Beirut goes even further than this, overtly drawing a distinction between himself and a basic translator:

> I've never been a translator alone, I don't just do that. I mean, the reason why we have such good material is because . . . people assume that I'm just the translator. They'll say things to me that they wouldn't say to the other person. Or, more importantly, you know, let's say that I'm the correspondent and the translator, right, and the interviewee is here, let's say the correspondent has asked a question. Normally, the way it should work is the translator then asks that question, the answer is relayed and then translated, right? . . . Well, I've gone up, and maybe why we've had better luck in terms of the stuff we get, is that once the question is asked, and the answer given, I keep on digging and digging and digging with my own questions, right? (Bulos, pers. comm., June 2015)

In this statement, Bulos directly separates his own role from that of a translator, despite the fact that he regularly translates for the correspondents who work with him. Bulos implies that, by definition, a translator is someone who acts as a passive medium, asking the exact question that the correspondent posed and then "relaying" the answer back to the correspondent. In contrast, Bulos says that he personally goes beyond the work of translating by asking his own questions, "digging and digging and digging" for more information. Bulos suggests that a mere translator does not engage in the "digging" that he believes is more typical of professional journalists.

Yet, at the time this interview was conducted, Bulos also told me that he was not precisely viewed as a "journalist" by his colleagues at the *LA Times* bureau in Beirut. Instead, Bulos said that he was still being paid a news fixer's salary and that he was not reporting stories on his own. He was also not receiving insurance nor any of the other benefits that the staff correspondents received. Though he felt he was doing the work of a journalist, Bulos told me that he was still treated like a fixer, and that this issue certainly tended to surface when he did translation work for the *LA Times* correspondents.

Strikingly, Bulos expressed his dissatisfaction with this arrangement by telling a story about translating for his bureau chief during a trip they had recently taken to Syria:

> I was with Patrick [the bureau chief] in Syria, and I had to basically translate, right? And I mean, this wasn't his fault so much, this was more the fault of—if you interview [someone in Lebanon or Syria], there's a notion when you go in [that] there's the correspondent, you know, the foreigner, of course, and the light man, if you will. And [then there is] the local person who speaks English and Arabic, the brown person, right? And the idea is that the brown person is to be treated like dirt by the interviewee, right? (Pers. comm., June 2015)

Here Bulos suggests that, at least in Syria, the figure of the translator is sometimes racialized and professionally degraded. Because he was translating for "the light man," the interviewee in turn coded Bulos as "the brown man" who also should not be asking any questions of his own. In Bulos's case, the racialized colonial hierarchy that had informed the labor of translation for centuries was imposed upon him from the outside, though not necessarily by the correspondent with whom he was working. Still, Bulos's narrative also seems to suggest that the *LA Times* editors and correspondents subtly allowed that hierarchy to remain intact by relegating Bulos to a position that was lower paid and under-recognized.

Despite the fact that Bulos describes the translation process in very active terms—asking questions of his own and digging for more news material—he still espouses the belief that the labor of translation is traditionally a passive type of labor. This contradiction seems to surface in his narrative because he does not wish to be viewed as a news fixer at all. Instead, as he told me during our interview, Bulos wished to be a proper news correspondent, a goal he later achieved (pers. comm., June 2015). Thus, he separated himself from what he still described as highly active—albeit disregarded and racialized—work.

Another news fixer echoes Bulos's representation of the translator as a racialized and gendered subject. Catalina Hernández, a fixer working in Colombia, tells this story:

> Most people [in Colombia], they see a journalist and they immediately want to go to the journalist and give him their point of view,

especially if he's foreign. So, it was at one point where we had all these guys, and they were all chauvinistic, misogynistic guys, you know, and they didn't want to hear it from me, they wanted to hear it from him [the foreign correspondent]. And I was like "Well yeah, but he doesn't speak Spanish, so you'll have to talk to me." And they all wanted to give their point of view, and they all started talking about anything and everything that concerned them. (Pers. comm., August 2016)

Like Bulos's story, Hernández's narrative underscores the marginalization of the translator figure; the people on the ground do not respect her as much as they respect the journalist, "especially if he's foreign." Yet, in Hernández's case, there is also a gendered quality to the invisibility of the translator—an invisibility that, like Bulos, Hernández refuses to accept. Rather than allowing the "chauvinistic, misogynistic" sources to ignore her altogether, in this situation, Hernández says that she chose to overtly remind them of the language barrier: "He [the foreign journalist] doesn't speak Spanish, so you'll have to talk to me." With this maneuver, Hernández illuminated the active nature of her role as interpreter, emphasizing the fact that these men would not be able to communicate with the journalist without first relying on her linguistic skill.

Unlike Bulos, Hernández does not identify as a journalist but is instead a conservator of works of art, with a master's degree in textiles. Thus, while she represents translation and interpreting as an active and creative process, she does not necessarily portray this labor as inherently journalistic. Other news fixers I have interviewed do not separate the labor of translation from journalistic work at all. For example, Leena Saidi describes her work in this way: "A fixer basically is a reporter in a foreign language" (pers. comm., May 2013). In Saidi's estimation, there is no difference between news fixing and reporting, other than the language itself. She actively helps the correspondent understand both the language and the culture in Lebanon, while also helping the journalist cover the story (pers. comm., May 2013).

Other news fixers are even more explicit about the active nature of translation, highlighting why this skill is so important to the news story:

My niche as a fixer actually, I like to brag about it, is I continue to develop my vocabulary in order for you as a journalist to get the whole thing. Because that makes a massive difference on the story, and I know that, because when I do my [own] stories, I know how much one word can change the whole meaning of the sentence. (Nayel, pers. comm., June 2015)

Here, Nayel illuminates the fact that even the most "literal" act of translation takes a great deal of creativity and intelligence on the part of the news fixer. Nayel says that he is constantly working to develop his vocabulary, learning new English words so that he can translate the nuances of the sources' statements more effectively. Because Nayel also writes some of his own news stories on a freelance basis, he is aware of the communicative power of every single word. For this reason, Nayel suggests that the more he builds his linguistic skill, the more he'll be able to build a linguistic bridge for the journalist.

An anonymous fixer working in Russia also remarks upon the active nature of translating for visiting journalists, emphasizing the different linguistic choices he can make based upon his familiarity with the English language:

> What's interesting is, I prefer to translate, especially simultaneously from Russian into English because I know all these kind of clichés [in English], and then sometimes I just pull them out of my pocket and use them. Whereas, in Russian I tend to overthink things. I want to make it sound prettier than it actually is or make it sound exactly [perfect], because I have such a wider choice [of Russian words]. So, this is why it's hard for me translate. (Pers. comm., January 2017)

This particular fixer highlights the challenge of inhabiting two linguistic worlds at the same time, especially because he has more skill with one language than the other. Though he, as the translator, can understand the complexity of what his clients' sources are saying in his native Russian, when he tries to translate this complexity into English, he has to draw upon a more limited cache of linguistic choices. Each cliché is an active choice that this fixer must make, and each cliché also potentially omits an important layer of meaning. This becomes even more complicated when considering the inevitable untranslatability of certain words and sayings that do not have an equivalent in another language. In these cases, the news fixer has to make an active choice about how to communicate: "I really don't like [translating] the proverbs. You know, like a saying or whatever . . . so you've got to find a good equivalent of that in Russian or in English. So that it all makes sense" (anonymous fixer in Russia, pers. comm., January 2017).

The challenge is not only to clarify these differences for the foreign correspondents. News fixers also have to translate the journalists' words and questions for the people who live in the places the journalists visit. But in order for the foreign correspondents' questions to make sense to the interviewee, news fixers say that they often have to reword the question altogether. In this way, news fixers emphasize the difficulty of separating the act of "literal" translation from broader issues of cultural difference. Namrata Gupta, a news fixer who works with news and documentary crews in India, describes this problem in the following way:

> Sometimes the director would pose a question, which actually, socially or culturally speaking, is not really relevant to the life of the subject. And it doesn't make sense for their life and in their social context. Or the situation doesn't really apply in their lives. So, in that sense, you know, if I'm working as a translator on that particular interview, I'm not simply translating the director's question to the subject and simply translating the subject back to the director. There are times when there are some nuances which the director may not be aware of [in] the subject's life. Some social context, some personal context, in which, because I am a local person who belongs to the same society, perhaps I understand it better. And I am able to help the director understand what it is exactly that the subject is trying to convey or what is it that she is not able to convey. (Pers. comm., June 2016)

At first glance, Gupta's statement might appear to confirm some journalists' and news editors' fears that fixers might mistranslate the correspondents' exchanges with their sources. Certainly, Gupta's production narrative reveals that she does sometimes reshape her clients' questions, as well as the source's answers. Yet, Gupta's narrative also suggests that this "reshaping" is indispensable to the broader act of cross-cultural communication in which she, the source, and her client are engaging. On the one hand, Gupta observes that her client might be so unfamiliar with the source's culture that the literal version of the client's question will make little sense to the source. Thus, Gupta says that she must sometimes reword the question. On the other hand, the source's culture might be so unfamiliar to the client that the literal answer to the client's question might need more explanation. Gupta feels that it is her job to provide this extra information on both sides, specifically so that she can maintain a communicative connection and build a linguistic bridge. Without Gupta's effort at actively reshaping the words and questions she is translating, the conversation might dissolve into disconnection and miscommunication.

Crucially, French fixer Benjamin Zagazag implies that this is not the same thing as mistranslating—or misleading—the client.

My job is not to tell [the client], "You cannot ask this question," because I am not the journalist, you know? I am the fixer. . . . But I really
have to explain then that they have to turn—like, in French, we say,
"to make the corners round." See what I mean? We have to "round the
corners." (Pers. comm., September 2016)

In Zagzag's view, the journalist gets the final say on what types of questions
to ask. Yet, Zagzag also knows that it is important to make the correspondent understand the role that cultural difference plays in the process
of communicating across linguistic and social divides. Interestingly, Zagzag
explains this situation by drawing upon what the anonymous fixer in Russia
would call a "proverb"—a figure of speech that is unique to a particular culture. Zagzag says that in France, it is common to "make the corners round,"
or to soften the approach when asking questions of someone. This specific
cultural attitude toward communication in turn informs the efficacy of the
client's communication with sources on the ground. Because of this, Zagzag
suggests it is imperative that the news fixer takes cultural difference into account when translating the conversation between a foreign correspondent
and a locally based news source.

This is why many fixers say that they tend to focus on translating broader
meanings, rather than literal words. One local producer and fixer who works
across the former Soviet Union says:

The concept of my business is also in me having huge international
production experience as I am both a direct producer and a sort
of translator/interpreter. Almost one hundred percent of all the
disagreements that emerge between professionals from different countries are connected with mere miscommunication occasions, with the
fact that people cannot understand each other. Not necessarily the
exact words, but their meaning. I translate meanings. (Solovkin, pers.
comm., December 2016)

Renato Miller, a fixer working in Mexico, similarly observes that there are certain strategies that can help news fixers "translate meanings":

Localize. Localize. You've got to try to localize. You've got to try to lo-
calize as best as possible. . . . I lived in the States, I lived in Los Angeles,
I lived in Chicago, I traveled around. . . . I own the complete works of
George Carlin. So, I know a lot of slang in English, and I think that

gives me the analytics sometimes to take the slang in Spanish and try
to localize it in English. I mean we don't use slang in journalism, but
you've got to try to communicate the feeling of what the person was
saying. It's not the same to say the sky is blue as the sky is blue. It's not
the same, so you've got to take that and put it on the tape you know so
whoever is going to write it down later on, or the editor of the story,
will have that emotion, or will have that inflection that that person was
using. (Pers. comm., March 2017)

For Miller, "literal" translation is not particularly useful in helping the
client understand the "emotion" or the "inflection" that might have informed
the source's response. To say "the sky is blue" in both languages does not adequately capture the entire meaning of what is being said. Therefore, Miller says
it is important for the fixer to "localize" the translation as much as possible
to help both parties gain a clearer understanding of the larger meaning of the
discussion. Significantly, Miller suggests that to properly localize the translation for both parties, the fixer needs to have some literacy in both cultures.
Miller says that he personally has traveled around the United States, and he
also says that he has long been exposed to US-produced entertainment. This
exposure to "American" culture—on top of his own native familiarity with
the Spanish language—is what Miller says can help him mediate between the
diverse people who live in Mexico and especially the American journalists
who hire him as a fixer.

Rather than acting as a passive medium for the journalist, Miller instead
feels that he acts as an active interpreter, and this is a role that many of my
other interviewees have also described in their production narratives. Still,
playing this active role is not always a simple process. As my interviewees overwhelmingly note, the act of interpreting unfamiliar languages is also fraught
with moments of miscommunication, misunderstanding, and disconnection.
Some of these miscommunications are harmless and easy to overcome. Others
point to much larger cultural disconnections that can be perilous to both the
foreign correspondent and the fixer.

Interpretation and Disconnection

Though Bulos, a former news assistant for the *LA Times* in Beirut, overtly
describes interpretation as a passive task, he also rather paradoxically asserts
that "a fixer can really affect how the story is crafted. Even with my translation,

I could very easily change things around if I wanted to" (pers. comm., June 2015). Because news fixers are aware of the impact their translations can have on the direction of the journalist's story, fixers like Nayel tend to agonize over the perfect word choice, and fixers like the anonymous media employee in Russia wrestle with adequately translating idiomatic expressions. As the anonymous fixer in Mexico argues, some things—like British jokes—are almost impossible to translate (pers. comm., March 2017). This means that the possibility of miscommunication and linguistic disconnection looms large as a potential problem, even at the most "literal" level of translation.

Yet, many of my interviewees suggest that broader cultural disconnections also need to be considered. Another news fixer working in Russia says, "ironically, most of my work is being a cultural interpreter" (pers. comm., January 2017). This fixer seems to conceptualize the work of cultural interpretation as constantly explaining unfamiliar cultural norms to the visiting journalists, as well as to the local people who might be confused by the journalists' behavior. The notion of "cultural interpretation" resonates with the idea of "cultural translation" espoused by scholars Federico Italiano and Michael Rössner: "A concept including all those processes which, by means of de- and re-contextualization, make communication between varied groups—be they linguistically, religiously, socially, generationally, or otherwise defined—and different traditions of discourse possible" (2012, 11). Italiano and Rössner state that cultural translation should be understood as "the performative negotiation of differences between identity constructions" (2012, 12). In other words, translation should be understood as a kind of cultural mediation upon which the possibility of cross-cultural communication depends.

But cultural mediation is rarely a simple process, and the labor of "interpreting" different cultures for the foreign correspondent is no exception. News fixers say that they sometimes struggle to successfully build these communicative bridges, especially when language—at the literal level—is not enough. For instance, a Scottish fixer and producer working in the United States says of her English-speaking clients:

> We speak the same language, yet there is always a communication barrier. I often jump in on meetings to clarify what the "Brits" mean when they are instructing or giving direction to the American crew. I tend to make light-hearted comments, have fun with it. The Scottish accent helps because no one can understand me. (Stirling, pers. comm., September 2016)

In this narrative, Stirling emphasizes the fact that sharing a language does not always guarantee that her clients will be able to communicate without any challenges. Instead, Stirling has to explain "what the 'Brits' mean," drawing upon "light-hearted comments" in order to diffuse the tension and resentment that could easily accompany any moments of miscommunication or disconnection. Strikingly, Stirling says she mobilizes another communicative problem—her Scottish accent—to lighten the mood in these situations. The fact that she is Scottish, and not British or American, places her in a liminal space that helps her act as a safe mediator in moments of communicative failure.

In other cases, the cultural difference is more pronounced, and the news fixer struggles much more to interpret these differences to the client. For instance, an anonymous fixer working in El Salvador recounts this story: "Once I had journalists that came from Denmark, and they really did not understand the culture. I tried to explain to them, things that we cannot do here, or how people would react to some kind of actions, and things like that, right? But they didn't get it" (pers. comm., August 2016). This fixer describes a situation in which her effort at cultural translation—her "performative negotiation of differences between identity constructions" (Italiano and Rössner 2012, 12)—did not ultimately result in the successful construction of a cultural bridge. No matter how hard she tried to explain the crucial differences between the way that people comport themselves in El Salvador and the way they act in Denmark, her clients "didn't get it."

Another anonymous news fixer working in Somalia also flags the very real potential for his foreign clients to misunderstand and misinterpret the broader culture in the region:

> I want these guys [the journalists] . . .to see what the real Somalia means or looks like. . . . They ask for local people, then I organize [for the journalist] to meet with some people in the hotel, so [the journalist] can feel the positiveness of these people [from Somalia]. Because when [the journalist] gets out of the hotel, I don't want them to feel frustrated. They at least learn something of the culture in the hotel, and then when they get out, they feel safe, they feel that these people can be trusted in the journalistic community. (Pers. comm., May 2016)

Here, the news fixer first expresses his desire for his clients to "see what the real Somalia *means*," suggesting that he wants to properly interpret the different cultures of the region for the journalists who visit. Yet, this fixer also knows from experience that foreign journalists tend to "feel frustrated" with these broader cultural differences, pointing to the sense of disconnection that often accompanies miscommunication in the field. Because of this potential for disconnection, this news fixer tries to ease his clients into their encounters with Somali people, just as someone might first teach a student the very basics of a new language. Within the more contained and culturally liminal space of the hotel, the fixer's clients can be exposed to cultural differences in a way that makes them feel safe when they finally leave the hotel.

In order to successfully avoid cultural disconnection, this news fixer must draw upon prior knowledge of his clients' various cultural identifications. He can forecast that his clients might be uncomfortable with the cultures of the region because many of his clients have had this reaction in the past. Yet, news fixers do not always work with clients from one distinct area of the world, making it very difficult to adjust to the various types of difference that could come into play. Nitzan Almog, a fixer working in Israel, notes, "you have to be aware one week that you're working with a crew from Germany, next week, you're working with a crew from Japan, and the next one from Russia. So, you have to keep in mind: different cultures, different expectations, different ways of verbally expressing themselves" (pers. comm., May 2016). Solovkin echoes this problem: "The challenge is that every single client/customer comes with his own background, business traditions, etiquette, even food preference. . . . They are never the same. Americans, European, Chinese, Indians, etcetera, etcetera, etcetera" (pers. comm., December 2016).

Both Almog and Solovkin invoke the complexity of engaging in cultural translation, when their clients' particular identifications might change every week. As Almog notes, each client might have "different ways of verbally expressing themselves," complicating Almog's effort at (1) understanding what his clients are trying to communicate, and (2) interpreting the various cultures of Israel for these different clients. Solovkin emphasizes that this is not merely an issue of linguistic translation; instead, "every single client/customer comes with his own background, business traditions, etiquette, and even food preferences." Navigating these differences can be difficult for news fixers when their clients "are never the same."

Almog and Solovkin both point to the diverse journalists and documentarians who seek their services, illuminating the complexity— and sometimes the *dis*connectedness—of what some scholars have viewed as an increasingly "global" journalism industry. News fixers' production narratives instead paint a picture of an array of different world news markets that are interconnected at some levels but that diverge at other levels. The news fixer is expected to navigate these differences in order to offer a service that is useful to *any* foreign correspondent, hailing from *any* region. As a fixer working in Indonesia suggests, "First they are my client, and in my position, I have to understand [things] about them first, before they c[an] understand me. Before they listen to me, to my recommendations (Samantha, pers. comm., September 2016). By virtue of the work they do, news fixers' identities are in constant motion, a perpetual process of "becoming" (Hall [1990] 2003).

Though news fixers, by definition, are supposed to facilitate the connection of foreign journalists with people on the ground, as well as contributing to the connections between diverse journalists and their increasingly transnational audiences, miscommunications and misunderstandings can frustrate the fixer as much as they can frustrate the client. This is especially the case when the fixer feels that the journalist or documentarian is being culturally insensitive. Maritza Carbajal, a news fixer working in Mexico, tells this story about the disconnection that arose when she interpreted her Anglophone clients as acting insensitively toward Mexican culture:

> Most of my clients are from the States or the UK. And in the beginning when you start fixing, you don't "get" all the cultures very well. Sometimes many things seem to be "bashing" when they're not. . . . And then you realize it's not that [journalists or documentarians] are talking badly about your country. [They are talking] about something that amuses them, surprises them, or shocks them. But that's natural, because I've been in other countries where I found things shocking, but they are not necessarily bad. (Pers. comm., March 2017)

Carbajal describes a situation in which her interpretation of her clients' cultural differences shifted over time. At first, she felt that they were "bashing" her country, something that offended her and hurt her sense of connection with them. Yet, she eventually came to believe that her clients were not degrading her culture as much as they were remarking on the inevitable moments of disconnection: amusement, surprise, or shock that Carbajal has herself experienced when visiting unfamiliar places. Thus, Carbajal says that she has more recently been able to see these moments of cultural disconnection more sympathetically.

Not all stories of cultural insensitivity are so transformative. For example, former Iranian news fixer Nazila Fathi says that some of the foreign correspondents with whom she worked in the 1990s were so uninterested in learning about Iranian culture that their behavior put their Iranian fixers in danger "simply because [the fixers] were accused of not making it clear to the foreign reporter how they had to behave. . . .Iranians were not so sensitive about the stories that people were writing. They were more sensitive if [the journalists] were insulting the culture for some very weird reasons" (pers. comm., July 2017).

For Fathi, this cultural insensitivity raised suspicion among the Iranian people with whom the journalists needed to communicate, and with Iranian officials who targeted fixers after the journalists left the country. Thus, the correspondents' unwillingness to engage with cultural difference led to major disconnections that were dangerous to the fixers who they left behind (ibid.).

In other cases, these moments of disconnection can be dangerous to the journalists themselves, and it is solely because of the news fixers' linguistic and interpretative skills that the correspondents are able to get to safety. For example, Larisa Inic, a fixer working in Serbia, Croatia, and Hungary, tells of the troublesome interactions that she and her clients have had with local police:

> They are following their old orders, and you know, if you are un-lucky to meet someone who [asks the client] "Where are you from?" "Germany." "Germany bombed us." I had [a] situation like that, but then I tried to fix it with not translating every word and trying to ex-plain, peacefully, to the policeman or some official guy who [was] trying to give us some trouble. Because I [didn't] want to fight them, you know, I want[ed] to give my journalist what he want[ed]. (Pers. comm., August 2016)

Through this narrative, Inic tells a story of two kinds of interpretation: (1) the more "literal" linguistic interpretation where she chose not to translate every word the journalist said to the police, and (2) the broader cultural transla-tion in which she engaged in order to make the journalists' presence in the region seem more acceptable to the police. Because these particular clients were German, Inic says that the police were particularly suspicious of them; yet, Inic was able to help her clients overcome this dangerous disconnection by intentionally omitting some of their words from her translation for the police, as well as by "peacefully" explaining their goals to the officials who did not approve of the journalists' presence in the area.

In a similar instance, Gupta recounts this story about a time she was working with a docu-drama crew in India:

> We were filming in the interiors of Rajasthan, and we got into a con-
> flict with the local people. The local people were hostile; they didn't
> want us over there at that point in time. And I, because I am a local
> person, I understand the language that they are talking, [and] I can
> fully and completely understand that the situation is about to get un-
> ruly any time. (Pers. comm., June 2016)

Here, Gupta emphasizes the fact that her knowledge of the language made it possible for her to become aware of something that the crew was missing: the people at the site were becoming "hostile," and it was likely that they might become "unruly." Some foreign correspondents describe this skill as "reading the crowd," a skill they can only deploy if they are familiar with the regional languages (Hasan, pers. comm., January 2013; Gorani, pers. comm., February 2013). In Gupta's situation, the documentarians could not read the crowd, so Gupta had to do it for them. Gupta was able to linguistically connect with the client in order to inform that client about a much larger cultural disconnection—outright hostility that could en-danger the entire crew.

Yet, Gupta's knowledge of what the people at the site were saying did not initially result in her client's swift and efficient understanding of the situation:

> That was one incident in which my producer was not fully supportive.
> And he would not understand why we had to waste our time, and why
> we had to waste our money by abandoning and wrapping up the shoot
> over there at that location. And why we had to move, and he was quite
> adamant. (Pers. comm., June 2016)

Rather than listening carefully to his fixer's advice, this particular producer fought back, refusing to allow Gupta to do the important work of interpreting the reality of the situation. Gupta suggests that this resulted in the crew having to pay off some of the local people in order to be left alone.

Gupta's testimony points to another troubling type of disconnec-tion that can happen in the process of interpreting unfamiliar languages. When the client refuses to listen to the fixer's interpretation, the possi-bility of cross-cultural communication becomes almost nonexistent. In this sense, the labor of interpretation and translation depends heavily on the journalist's or documentarian's willingness to hear and consider what is being communicated. Without this effort at active, ethical listening on the part of the client (Wasserman 2013), the fixer's translation becomes irrelevant. This points all the more to the active and reciprocal nature of translation.

Conclusion

According to contemporary translation and interpretation scholars, "Translation's distinctive ability to offer insight into the language process itself aligns it with ethics and the question of the foreign" (Bermann and Wood 2005, 5). This is because, "in attempts to translate, we become most aware of linguistic and cultural differences, of the historical "hauntings," and of experiential responsibilities that make our languages what they are and that directly affect our attitudes toward the world" (2005, 6). This chapter has investigated both the "linguistic and cultural differences" that specifically impact foreign journalists'—and news fixers'—"attitudes toward the world," attitudes that can in turn affect the viewpoints of increasingly interconnected transnational news audiences. Despite this growing interconnection, the world's diverse journalists and their audiences are still very different from one another, revealing the need for news fixers to engage in both literal and cultural translation. But news fixers suggest that the task of interpreting unfamiliar languages is far from easy.

First of all, news fixers say that they must negotiate the tension between some journalists' tendency to distrust their translators, and the journalists' growing need for interpreters in the era of globalization. While foreign correspondents' dependence on locally based translators results in more work for news fixers, this dependence sits uneasily alongside the clients' discomfort with the possibility of losing control of the story. Since many journalists feel that in news production, translation should be a "literal" process (Bielsa and Bassnett 2009), unaffected by cultural subjectivity (Holland 2017), journalists and their editors worry that the news fixer might intentionally or unintentionally change the meaning of what was said (Palmer and Fontan 2007; Murrell 2015; Palmer 2017). Yet, because they cannot possibly learn all the languages spoken in every place they cover, foreign correspondents and their editors depend heavily on the very skills that they also sometimes distrust.

The fixer's powerful ability to inhabit more than one linguistic world inspires fear on the part of certain clients, but it is also the reason why most of my interviewees represent the labor of interpreting as an active process. Rather than describing themselves as passive channels for the distribution of the journalist's ostensibly coherent message, news fixers instead invoke the caution, expertise, and creativity that they must deploy as they attempt to translate words, sayings, jokes, and broader cultural meanings. These media employees work to build their vocabularies, they try to communicate emotion as well as words, and they sometimes do reword the questions that the journalists ask. But fixers argue that they reword sentences in an effort to facilitate better communication between people from vastly different cultures, rather than to skew the apparent "truth" of the journalist's version of the story.

Translation and interpretation is not always about simple, easy "connection." Sometimes, this work involves a profound sense of disconnection, and is riddled with miscommunication. Sometimes, the news fixer cannot successfully interpret the local traditions for visiting journalists who just "don't get it." Sometimes, the news fixer cannot successfully comprehend the clients' own cultural differences. In more extreme cases, the news fixer may discover that the people on the ground are hostile to the foreign correspondents' presence. In these situations, the news fixer must successfully convince the client of this danger as well.

In the worst cases, foreign correspondents might refuse to listen to their fixers' interpretations of what is happening. These are the moments which perhaps most overtly signal the messy cultural collisions entangled within the labor of "interpreting unfamiliar languages." The labor of translation and interpretation draws special attention to the need for more egalitarian cross-cultural dialogue—not least because "cultural subjectivity" (Holland 2017) does indeed impact the way that this dialogue will proceed. Rather than expecting that cross-cultural dialogue should flow from only one direction and take only one shape, scholars, students, and journalists need to remember that communication is multi-channeled, contingent, and constantly in flux.

It is also imperative to consider the material dangers that some of the world's translators face. When Fathi speaks of journalists' cultural insensitivity in Iran, for example, she in turn speaks of the repercussions that news fixers might face because of that insensitivity (pers. comm., July 2015). When Gupta speaks of the hostility and sudden "unruliness" of certain people at the site, she also speaks of the possibility that she herself could be injured in the field (pers. comm., June 2016). The next chapter of this book explores the production narratives of news fixers who try to keep their clients safe. I hope to show that this labor is haunted by its own shadow—the grave reality that many news fixers themselves get hurt or killed in the process of doing their work.

5

Safeguarding the Journalist

*I feel it's my responsibility, the safety of the journalist is my
responsibility. So, I feel very responsible for the journalist,
not to jeopardize their lives and their safety. This is why
I never think about [whether] they're considering my safety.*

—SUZAN HAIDAMOUS, fixer and news assistant in Beirut

WHEN JOURNALISTS AND editors talk about news fixers, they tend to
represent these media employees as being vital to correspondents' security in the field (Palmer 2017). Hiring news fixers as a basic safety measure
is an established practice in foreign reporting, and it is not uncommon for
correspondents to conceptualize a "good" fixer in terms of safety and security. For instance, Al Jazeera correspondent Hashem Ahelbarra says that his
network's fixers "usually are people who have spent a long period of time with
Al Jazeera, have been tested in terms of integrity, professional journalism,
know-how, all of that stuff. These are really top-notch reporters, especially
in tense war zones because the safety of the people is in their hands" (pers.
comm., April 2013). Ahelbarra is rare in that he goes so far as to describe news
fixers as "top-notch reporters," rather than as unskilled laborers who are hired
in a piecemeal fashion; yet, he directly links fixers' professional "know-how"
to his belief that the safety of Al Jazeera's people is "in [fixers'] hands."

Similarly, BBC correspondent Paul Wood says that when he covered
the Syrian Civil War, he had a "very good fixer" who could easily negotiate
with people from different religious sects and who "saved my bacon a lot of
times" (pers. comm., February 2013). *Wall Street Journal* correspondent and
former Beirut bureau chief Bill Spindle echoes this discourse, touting the
need to find "the right fixer" in "places like Tripoli," which he and his team
"considered quite dangerous" (pers. comm., July 2015). And Spanish journalist and sometimes-fixer Jaime Velazquez says that when he was covering
the Ebola crisis in Sierra Leone, he had a "great" fixer who kept him safe (pers.
comm., September 2016).

In each of these cases, the correspondent suggests that a "good" fixer draws upon regionally specific knowledge in order to keep the foreign journalist safe in dangerous situations. This expectation is so high that it has also been internalized by news fixers, as Suzan Haidamous suggests in the epigraph to this chapter. In Haidamous's view, the fixer often feels a deep sense of personal responsibility for the foreign journalist's well-being. In turn, the correspondent's safety often eclipses the safety of the fixer. This can happen on two different levels. First, news organizations tend to emphasize the safety of their own journalists, while taking far less interest in the safety of the fixers their journalists hire (Palmer 2016, 2017). On another level, news fixers might place more emphasis on their clients' safety, internalizing the logic that their own safety is somehow less important.

Haidamous's statement illuminates the contradiction entangled within the task of "safeguarding the journalist." News fixers' production narratives overwhelmingly suggest that the very act of safeguarding can put the fixer's life in danger, a problem that shadows the growing focus on foreign correspondent's safety in the 21st century (Cottle, Sambrook, and Mosdell 2016; Armoudian 2017; Palmer 2018). This chapter examines this grave contradiction, first investigating news fixers' representations of what is ostensibly their most important task: keeping their clients out of harm's way. I will show that this element of news fixers' labor depends heavily on these media employees' cultural savvy. Indeed, news fixers suggest that they must constantly draw upon shifting types of regionally specific knowledge in order to navigate the various dangers that foreign journalists might encounter—often because they are culturally coded as "foreigners" in the first place. These dangers vary by the region and by the story itself. Some news fixers do not feel that their region is particularly dangerous, especially when compared with proper "war zones" like those found in Syria; yet, even these fixers reveal that every "foreign" story involves a variety of risks that must be navigated.

News fixers feel an intense level of personal responsibility for their clients' well-being. However, this chapter will not stop at an analysis of the news fixers' role in safeguarding the journalist. Instead, this chapter will also offer an analysis of the dangers that news fixers face, dangers that are often difficult for them to overcome. Because news fixers usually live in the places their clients visit, and because they typically have to remain in those places once the client is safely on the plane home, working with foreign journalists can directly affect fixers' long-term well-being. My interviewees say that they can (1) be targeted simply as a byproduct of their client being targeted, (2) be targeted in place of their client, once the foreign journalist has left the region, and

(3) grapple with other risks and strains that are harder to name—emotional trauma, illness, and damaged reputations, just to name a few.

Despite these very real dangers, my interviewees also overwhelmingly assert that news organizations rarely take any systematic level of responsibility for the safety of the fixers who safeguard journalists in the field. While journalists and editors may very occasionally provide fixers with safety equipment, this kind of assistance is never guaranteed. It is also extremely atypical for news organizations to offer their fixers any kind of hazardous environment training. And it is almost unheard of for news organizations to offer benefits such as insurance to their fixers, or to agree upfront on a plan for getting their fixers out of detainment if they are arrested. Though my interviewees say that a handful of the bigger, wealthier news organizations have started examining these policies and responding to these problems, overall, news organizations only address their fixers' safety in a piecemeal fashion.

News fixers' production narratives imply that there is a disturbing double standard that informs news organizations' policies on safety in foreign reporting. Rather paradoxically, many of my interviewees also suggest that they are personally responsible for their own safety, on top of the safety of their clients. Haidamous points to this belief in the epigraph to this chapter. She says that she is typically so worried about the safety of her clients—since safeguarding is, after all, part of her job—that she rarely even thinks about whether her clients are considering her safety. Narratives like Haidamous's suggest how deeply entrenched news outlets' double standards have become, especially when news fixers are internalizing a logic that places them at a serious disadvantage.

While news organizations are increasingly addressing the issue of safety as it applies to staff correspondents (Cottle, Sambrook, and Mosdell 2016; Armoudian 2017; Palmer 2018), my interviewees reveal that these organizations show far less interest in the safety of the locally based fixers on whom they so heavily depend. It is easy to forget that the broader profession of international reporting is built upon a highly embodied foundation. Indeed, critical discussions of the body are rare in many analyses of international processes in general (Youngs 1999; Aldama 2003; Bruff 2013; Cameron, Dickinson, and Smith 2013), and analyses of international reporting are no exception. This is odd, considering the fact that "globalization processes influence the bodies and embodiment of all people" (Casanova and Jafar 2013, x)—most especially the bodies of those whose labor is relegated to the shadows of the world's highly visible and increasingly interconnected array of international news industries. When Arturo Aldama critiques the utopic notion of the "cosmopolitan free market of e-commerce and anonymity" by invoking the laboring, abused bodies upon which global markets are built (2003, 4), he could all too easily be referencing the bodies of the media workers who contribute, at great personal risk, to news organizations' visual and textual narratives about the "world."

The authority of the eyewitness has long depended upon physical presence at the sites under scrutiny (Zelizer 2007), yet this physical presence often means that the body itself must occupy a space of danger. Especially in environments where those in power can inscribe that power onto material bodies, through the "apparatus of violence" (De Certeau, cited in Aldama 2003, 3), foreign correspondents face very real perils in their work. And when foreign correspondents outsource the labor of safeguarding their own bodies, they inevitably place the bodies of their fixers in danger as well. This particular danger shadows the stories of the foreign correspondents whose own endangered bodies are offered as evidence of their individual prowess, dedication, and authority over the story (Palmer 2018).

Keeping Journalists Safe

Despite the fact that they understand security to be a huge part of their job, news fixers have differing opinions on the inherent "dangerousness" of the regions where they work. The perils that news fixers help their clients navigate can vary drastically, depending on the type of story being covered, as well as on the specificities of the region. Some news fixers downplay the "danger" of reporting in the places where they live, focusing more on the concept of "risk." For instance, Swedish fixer and producer Niclas Peyron says:

> Sweden, it's the safest place in the world. Nothing happens. There's never any safety issue, or you know, it doesn't exist. You can park your car on the street with the keys in it. Nothing happens. And the press conferences are organized, and people don't shout, you know, so safety isn't a big issue here. (Pers. comm., September 2016)

With this statement, Peyron situates Sweden as a country where foreign journalists and documentarians do not face many dangers. Yet, Peyron also notes that when visiting clients fail to draw upon the expertise of their fixers, they can run into serious trouble—such as running out of gasoline in the freezing cold. Thus, Peyron's narrative suggests that even in a "safe" country like Sweden, clients who are unfamiliar with the region can find themselves at risk. Peyron implies that this risk can be avoided, if foreign journalists and documentarians take the important step of hiring locally based fixers and producers.

Genny Masterman, a fixer working in Germany, Austria, and sometimes, the UK, also discusses the risks that a client might face, even in these relatively "safe" countries:

> You have to make sure that [the foreign journalists] are safe with the traffic. If someone comes from a country where there is right-hand traffic and then you have left-hand traffic, or the other way around, you have to make sure. It's little things, but you have to make sure they look in the right direction when they're crossing the road. And because they are busy with the cameras and they are thinking about the film, you have to make sure that they cross the road safely. It's just tiny little things. (Pers. comm., September 2016)

Like Peyron, Masterman emphasizes the relative safety of the regions where she works. Yet, she also observes that there are small differences—"tiny little things"—that can have a decisive impact on the client's safety. Obviously, if a client were to get hit by a car, for example, death or injury could result.

Similarly to Masterman and Peyron, Greek news fixer Lamprini Thoma emphasizes the "tiny little things," the risks that can have quite an impact on foreign journalists:

> I had a friend who got lice because she was working with the refugees. That was a small danger, though. I have never faced real danger. It's still a safe country here. And the worst we had was that someone stole a tripod from one of our teams. (Pers. comm., September 2016)

In each of the above statements, Peyron, Masterman, and Thoma all assert that their regions are relatively safe compared with other regions of the world that they might classify as dangerous. Yet, at the same time, each of these news fixers also mentions different risks that their clients face, even in places like Sweden, Germany, and Greece. Their testimonies are important because they illuminate the fact that the task of "safeguarding the journalist" is necessary in almost any region of the world. When the clients are unfamiliar with their surroundings, even the "tiny little" risks can inhibit journalists' ability to get the story and to stay safe in the process.

Some news fixers also downplay the perils of certain regions of the world that have widely been represented as "dangerous" for foreign travelers. Maritza Carbajal, a fixer working in Mexico City, says:

Many of my clients come to me with travel warnings from the United States. They're like, "Oh, but we've been told Mexico City is horribly dangerous, so maybe we should avoid it." . . . I've been to Philadelphia, that's really dangerous as well. I've been scared really badly in Philly. So, I just try to tell them that it's about common sense, it's about not flashing your belongings. It's about being mindful. (Pers. comm., March 2017)

Here, Carbajal emphasizes her belief that Mexico City is no more dangerous than any major city in the United States. Yet, at the same time, she knows that her job is to navigate foreign journalists and documentarians through a space that they have been told is perilous. Thus, Carbajal implies that part of the labor of safeguarding the clients involves putting their mind at ease—helping them understand that there are sensible ways of diminishing the dangers they have heard so much about.

On the other hand, some fixers describe the very distinct perils of working in places that many journalists and documentarians might think of as safe regions. For instance, Chris Knittel, a fixer working in the United States, says that "the difficulties arise from the inherent danger that comes with filming hitmen, gangsters, paranoid drug dealers, smugglers, and the like" (pers. comm., September 2016). For Knittel, covering news and documentary stories in the United States can be every bit as dangerous as covering these stories in regions of the world that have been marked as unsafe by the US Department of State. Since he specializes in a particular type of story, Knittel and his clients tend to engage with some very dangerous people, individuals who might be less interested in adhering to US laws. In this sense, Knittel's production narrative implies that the region itself does not necessarily determine the safety of the client; instead, the level of danger that a client might face also depends on the type of story being covered.

The most obvious type of danger that fixers must help their clients navigate is the peril of covering volatile events, such as militarized demonstrations or active front-line combat. As one anonymous fixer working in the Palestinian West Bank says:

A part of it is always dangerous, because there is always the element of randomness here, and it depends on where you are. If you are at demonstrations and this and that . . . the random effect can hit at any point, where you don't know what is happening. Like you might be standing next to a building that suddenly explodes for some reason. It hasn't happened for quite a long time, but that's the thing about this place, is that you don't know what is going to happen. (Pers. comm., July 2013)

Haidar Adbalhabi, a fixer working in Iraq, tells a story that similarly emphasizes the notion of "randomness," or the contingency of danger, when covering stories about political or military unrest:

> I was there [at the 2015–16 Battle of Ramadi], and the correspondent and the cameraman, and the security advisor from the BBC, all of us [were] on the ground. It's hard, and you hear, from time to time, the snipers' sound from ISIL just going like "pow, pow!" and [the shots are] close to you sometimes, and faraway from you sometimes. (Pers. comm., May 2016)

Like the anonymous fixer working in Palestine, Adbalhabi describes the perils that both fixers and their clients face when they work on stories about social unrest. With these types of news stories, the fixer can give the client advice about where to go and where not to go, as well as advise the visiting correspondent on what type of safety equipment may or may not be most helpful. Yet, there will still be an element of contingency that makes it difficult to forecast the dangers ahead of time. Even a "good" fixer cannot always predict these dangers.

War-zone reporting is not the only type of news or documentary coverage that can put foreign correspondents at risk. Because of this, news fixers suggest that they must safeguard the journalist even when they work far from active front lines. For instance, Namrata Gupta, a fixer working in India, tells of a time when she and her clients

> had somehow managed to arrange a meeting with this particular man who was known to be a pimp. And we had started to have a conversation with him, and we wanted to talk to him about what he had done.... And after some time, our local contact got a phone call saying that ... "Some of these people have figured out that you are from the media, and I think there are now a few goons who are going to come after you; I would really suggest that you drop this interview and do not speak to this man anymore. And I suggest you leave, it's not safe anymore." So, we just had to say goodbye to him and the interview, and really sort of just get into our vans and drive out of the village as soon as possible. (Pers. comm., June 2016)

In Gupta's case, the danger was not linked to an active war zone. Instead, Gupta and her clients found themselves in peril because they had incited the displeasure of some people in the region who did not want their activities broadcasted to the rest of the world. As in war-zone reporting, the danger that Gupta's clients faced was being driven by hostile human subjects; yet, these subjects were operating "underground," in a time of peace. It was Gupta and another "local contact" who were supposed to make this danger intelligible to the foreign clients. Without their knowledge of the situation on the ground, the visiting documentarians could have been injured, or worse.

Sometimes, human subjects are not the driving force behind the danger that foreign correspondents and documentarians face in the field. Michael Kaloki, a fixer working in Kenya, says that a client might be at risk "if you're working in an international park," because they could be "attacked by a wild animal, camping out in the forest, getting bitten by snakes" (pers. comm., June 2016). Both Kaloki and Gupta also note that they have to help the visiting correspondents avoid overheating, as well as the very serious risk of food poisoning:

> It's possible that they may get the "Delhi belly," or fall sick in the first few days because of the food. The food may not suit them, so something as simple as making sure that your team is comfortable, that they are well advised about the weather and what kind of clothes to wear accordingly, and what kind of food to eat and what kind of food to avoid and making sure that they're definitely always drinking safe water, absolutely safe mineral waters. (Gupta, pers. comm., June 2016)

In this statement, Gupta invokes a sentiment that many news fixers seem to share: an intense feeling of responsibility for the well-being of the foreign correspondent or documentarian. Indeed, Gupta suggests that everything from the clients' comfortable clothing to the safety of their food and water is the fixer's responsibility. Since the journalist's body might be acclimated to different bacteria than those in the food and water that he or she encounters in the field, the fixer must actively mediate that difference, finding "safe" food and "safe" water for the correspondent to consume. What is more, since the journalist might be entirely unfamiliar with the precautions needed for functioning in extremely hot or cold climates, the fixer must also mediate that difference, doing the work of educating the client on which precautions are necessary in which environments. And when the foreign correspondent must inhabit actively militarized spaces or travel into spaces where illness runs rampant, the news fixer is expected to pilot the journalist through these situations as well.

The act of safeguarding the journalist is an act of moving back and forth between different lived experiences of risk, and "connecting" the client with the regionally specific knowledge that may help prevent catastrophe. Significantly, this regionally specific knowledge is not necessarily dependent upon the news fixer's status as a so-called native. Plenty of fixers work in regions where they were not born, but they may still possess a deeper level of familiarity with the areas their clients visit. And even those fixers who were born in the regions where they work may not be simplistic "insiders" to the communities the clients wish to engage. Still, these fixers can offer valuable insight that the clients themselves do not possess. For example, Mexican fixer Maritza Carbajal says:

> There are places where I don't go without security. . . . It's going to be like that, [and] you have to give me a security guard who was born and raised in the community. Because the security guard will go outside to his friend and say, "You know this big production company is coming, everybody should behave. Nobody's touching them." (Carbajal, pers. comm., March 2017)

Carbajal's statement points to the very direct sort of cultural mediation that occurs when someone who is an "insider" can speak on behalf of the news team. This insider status is not a given, simply because Carbajal identifies herself as Mexican. Instead, she finds it necessary to hire security people who are from the specific community that the news or documentary team will be visiting. Thus, in Carbajal's case, being "from Mexico" does not necessarily equal "being an insider," pointing again to the culturally liminal position that news fixers occupy. Yet, Carbajal is familiar enough with the community to know that she must outsource the task of safeguarding to someone who reads as even more of a cultural insider than Carbajal does.

The key is that the news fixer understands and negotiates the more overtly "foreign" status of the visiting correspondent, a status that, by definition, can place the correspondent in danger. For Samuel Okocha, a fixer working in Nigeria, this foreign status is sometimes explicitly racialized: "When [the people on the ground] see a white guy, they think this guy has lots of money. You know if you can fly all the way from Europe to Lagos, of course you have some money. . . . So, they want a share of that money" (pers. comm., May

2016). In other words, Okocha suggests, the whiteness of the foreign journalist is associated with the more privileged side of global capitalism—with
the mobility and wealth that is so often represented in advertising and in
Hollywood movies. By virtue of the fact that some foreign journalists are
culturally coded as "white," they are also culturally coded as "wealthy." This
places them in an immediate position of vulnerability, according to Okocha.

Abd Nova, a former fixer based in Lebanon, asserts that foreign
correspondents need to rely on their fixers' advice in these situations rather
than thinking that they can outsmart the racial and cultural codes that operate
in places like Syria: "Coming back from [there] is not as easy as you think. He
[the foreign correspondent] wants to go into Syria. I said... 'you know you're
blond with blue eyes and you speak Arabic . . . even if you wanted to pretend,
you're going to a Muslim area, you want to pretend you're Muslim—you can't
do that'" (pers. comm., June 2015). Nova's statement overtly critiques the notion that foreign correspondents can "pass" as cultural "others," flatly rejecting
the feasibility of this idea by saying, "you can't do that." For Nova, it is not
enough that the foreign correspondent speaks Arabic—there are too many
other cultural codes in place, and these codes cannot be deployed by cultural
outsiders as easily as they might think.

Nova's statement not only references this mistaken assumption on the
part of some foreign correspondents in Syria; it also retrospectively critiques
the antics of correspondents like John Simpson and Yvonne Ridley, both
of whom dressed in burkas in order to "safely" move through Afghanistan
in 2001 (Tomlin 2001; Morgan 2001). These white, Anglo correspondents
were widely discussed in the Anglophone news industry discourse during
the early days of the war in Afghanistan, especially because they had tried
to "pass" as racial and cultural "others" in order to get the story. While this
apparently worked for John Simpson—at least during the 2001 conflict in
Afghanistan—Ridley was captured in the very burka that she thought would
hide her whiteness and her Westernness (Morgan 2001). This points to the
difficulty of simply wearing cultural difference like a costume, a difficulty
with which locally based news fixers are all too familiar. While cultural identity can, on some levels, be intentionally performed, it is also imposed from
the outside, leading to the constant negotiation (Sporturno 2014) that defines
the news fixer's work.

Fixers' production narratives suggest that they have a much more
nuanced view of the complexity of cultural difference than do some foreign
correspondents. This is part of why fixers view cultural mediation as such an
integral part of their job. But my interviewees also intimate that the work

of safeguarding the journalist cannot happen without proper communication, and this communication is a two-way street. On the one hand, the fixer must clearly inform the client of the potential danger. On the other hand, the client must trust the fixer and listen to this important media employee's advice. Without this second part of the equation, the effort at safeguarding can easily fail. Ginnette Riquelme, a Chilean fixer and photographer working in Mexico City, perhaps puts it best when she says: "The point is . . . these people trust you. You say you have to leave, [then] you have to leave" (pers. comm., March 2017). Oren Rosenfeld, a fixer and local producer working in Israel, also emphasizes the importance of trust, saying, "I call the shots, I call everything, because it's my life on the line as well. Nobody tells me what to do; I have to tell them what to do" (pers. comm., May 2016).

In many cases, this trust is easily given. For instance, Ray Homer, a former ABC correspondent during the Lebanese civil war in the late 20th century, says that during the war, ABC's local fixers and drivers

> saved our lives, you know. When we would go out, even here in Beirut, we would go out with drivers. We'd be driving down the road with a Lebanese driver, driving the car. He'd say, "This doesn't look right. Going down this road, it doesn't look right. It doesn't feel right. Something's wrong here." [Then] we're not going to go. That's fine. Whatever you say. (Pers. comm., June 2015)

Homer suggests that during the civil war in Lebanon, he and his crew understood the importance of trusting their fixers, knowing full well that this trust might save their lives. Many news fixers also say that they have worked with journalists like Homer, who listen carefully to their advice in dangerous situations.

Yet, sometimes, foreign journalists do not listen to their fixers' advice. Mostafa Sheshtawy, a fixer working in Egypt during the post-Mubarak unrest, tells of an Italian photographer who failed to take his warnings seriously: "I told her, 'Don't go to that street. That street is always full of secret police, and they're wearing civilian clothes, and they will arrest you in a second.' Now, that's exactly what happened" (pers. comm., July 2015). Sheshtawy says that this photographer had previously been working in Turkey, where the risks were different than they were in Egypt. According to Sheshtawy, the photographer thought that because she knew the ropes of working in Turkey, she also thought she knew how to handle Egypt's risks. But as Sheshtawy reveals, the risks inherent to working in one region cannot easily be mapped onto another region. Thus, Sheshtawy suggests that it would have been better if this pho-tojournalist had listened to the fixer she had hired to help her navigate the unique challenges of covering the unrest in Egypt.

There are correspondents who learn from moments like these. Abigail Hauslohner, a correspondent for the *Washington Post,* recounts a time when she was covering the 2011 conflict in Libya, and she didn't listen to her driver:

> I had to jump in a rebel truck. Our driver had actually refused to go up that far with us. So, we were basically beholden to the rebels, which is a bad place to put yourself in. . . . The rockets were just hitting this whole road. . . . A French freelancer—either French or French Canadian, I'm not sure—who was up there with us—ended up getting hit by an RPG. . . . And that was, I think, a really harrowing experience where I was angry at myself for having been so stupid as to be in that position. And you know, we could have easily been that guy or worse. It was one of those really stupid journalist moments where you're like, "OK, that could have been my last day, and I'm extremely lucky, because that was stupid." (Pers. comm., February 2013)

Here, Hauslohner describes a "harrowing" experience in which she decided to part ways with her driver—who, tellingly, was not interested in going further himself. Crucially, Hauslohner states that she now sees this particular decision as a "stupid" one, because she realizes that she could easily have been killed by going to an area where even her driver refused to go. Thus, Hauslohner's tes-timony reveals that foreign correspondents can learn from the mistake of not listening to their drivers and fixers—as long as these correspondents survive the mistake in the first place.

Some journalists appear to be less thoughtful about the tension that can arise between the journalists' desire to keep going and the fixers' focus on safeguarding. An anonymous photojournalist working in Istanbul tells of a time when he was covering the Syrian refugee crisis, and his fixer convinced him to leave a certain area because it was too dangerous: "But apparently I was wrong because we could have done a better story there. I mean, he pushed me for nothing. . . [He said,] 'OK, let's leave, it's dangerous,' but it wasn't dangerous" (July 2015). In this particular journalist's opinion, his fixer was not properly safeguarding him at all—instead, he was being overly cautious. Freelance Finnish correspondent Iida Tikka tells a similar story where she felt her driver was the "type" who preferred to operate only in safer areas—as op-posed to other drivers who prefer to seek danger (pers. comm., January 2017).

News fixers are aware of this attitude on the part of some correspondents, as an anonymous fixer working in Palestine observes: "I'm on journalism Facebook pages, and I see journalists talking about these things . . . some feel like their fixer doesn't want them to do something or the fixer feels like they are just white idiots that want to go and put themselves in danger and be martyrs. I can see how the interaction can be sour" (pers. comm., July 2013).

This potentially "sour" interaction points to the broader instability of the world's increasingly interconnected news markets, where foreign correspondents often feel the need to place themselves at greater and greater risk to help their news organizations get the stories that numerous other organizations around the world might also be chasing (Cottle, Sambrook, and Mosdell 2016; Armoudian 2017; Palmer 2018). Yet, it is not only the foreign correspondents who risk their material bodies in the process of helping their news outlets maintain a competitive edge in a saturated 21st-century media environment. The all but invisible bodies of their news fixers are also at risk. This is why fixers like Luna Safwan recount the "many disagreements" that fixers and correspondents have when "they would want to go in further, and I would be afraid sometimes" (Safwan, pers. comm., June 2015). According to news fixers' production narratives, there is sometimes good reason to be afraid.

Keeping the Fixers Safe

When discussing the dangers that news fixers face in the field, foreign correspondents, editors, and industry commentators often invoke the notion of inevitability. My own previous research has shown that this is particularly true of the discourse on news fixers that surfaces in Anglophone news industry trade magazines (Palmer 2017). Some of the journalists and editors I interviewed also reveal this tendency. Jeff Neumann, a freelancer working in Beirut, bluntly says that "drivers and fixers always get killed" (pers. comm., June 2015), a statement that highlights the regularity of these incidents but also suggests their ostensible inevitability. CNN war correspondent Michael Holmes almost seems to weave these incidents into the broader fabric of life in a war zone, saying, "I've seen a lot of hacked up bodies, and smelled a lot of dead people. Including in the case of our translator and driver, seeing them basically killed in front of us" (pers. comm., January 2013). And Ray Homer describes a situation in Iraq—where two of the ABC bureau's Iraqi staff were killed—in these terms: "There could be enemies everywhere. You just didn't know. I mean, and there was so much upheaval and chaos" (pers. comm., June 2015).

Each of the above correspondents has undeniably been affected by the disasters that befell their news fixers and drivers in the field. Holmes saw his translator and driver killed before his very eyes, and Homer had grown quite close with the Iraqi staff members who were shot in Baghdad. Yet, each of these correspondents also implies that this kind of incident is inevitable. For Holmes, the encounter with "hacked up" dead bodies is an integral element of working in a war zone; the bodies of his fixer and driver appear to be no exception. Similarly, Homer suggests that the very nature of Iraq—the "upheaval and chaos"—explained the deaths of his colleagues. And when Neumann asserts that "drivers and fixers always get killed," he draws upon the same rhetoric that surfaces in the Anglophone news industry's trade discourse (Palmer 2017): rhetoric that rather obliquely notes the commonality of these incidents without raising questions about why these incidents occur or how they could be prevented.

News fixers also tend to describe moments of danger that they face in their work. However, fixers' production narratives suggest that there are actually some very specific reasons why these incidents happen: (1) fixers are targeted because their clients are targeted (because they are accompanying their clients through dangerous areas), or (2) fixers are targeted *in place of* foreign journalists who have already left the field. On one level, news fixers find themselves at risk simply because they work with journalists who actively seek to cover dangerous stories, such as those that focus on militarized conflict. For instance, Ukrainian fixer Anna Nekrasova tells this story about the most dangerous moment of her work in Ukraine:

> When we crossed the street on the day where people were shot down by the police. . . . I was scared. I was scared, I remember at that moment. . . .We ran there, we saw injured people, we heard different sounds of guns. . . . The only thing you are thinking about is to be in a safe place. . . . That was probably my worst experience of fixing there. (Pers. comm., August 2016)

In this statement, Nekrasova vacillates between using the pronoun "we"—to describe her position as a media employee who accompanies the correspondent in the field—and using the pronoun "I"—mostly when she is recounting the way she individually felt in that particular moment. As a fixer working with a client, Nekrasova was part of a "we," who "saw injured people," who "heard different sounds of guns," and who "crossed the street" into a violent area. As an individual, however, Nekrasova was "scared" and thinking of how to get to "a safe place." Significantly, she does not describe her own endangerment as inevitable. Instead, her narrative suggests that she was endangered because she was accompanying a war correspondent into a hostile environment. While the "randomness" of risk is certainly a part of the warzone, as other fixers argue, Nekrasova does not appear to assume that her physical endangerment is unavoidable.

Some fixers overtly flag the fact that they are more at risk because they are working with *foreign* correspondents: with journalists who are culturally coded as outsiders by the people in the field. Though many of my interviewees have cited this "foreignness" as a major source of vulnerability for the client, some of them also observe that their very association with this foreignness places the fixer in more danger. For example, Sharad Adhikaree tells of a time when he was working with foreign journalists during the 2005 Maoist rebellion, about 150 kilometers northeast of Kathmandu:

[Maoists] are quite hostile to Indians and to some Americans. [And] I was with them, with Americans. So that's why [the Maoist rebels] thought, "Maybe you are spying." We had just crossed a suspension bridge to enter a certain area, but they said, "Okay," and two armed guys, carrying guns, they came, and they said, "Okay, we want to talk to you." And they took us to a small village, and they started interrogating us. "Why have you come here? Who gave you the permission? Can you talk to us?" . . . . And the next day they let us go farther, but one of the [Maoist] guys, he was always with us. (Pers. comm., August 2016)

Adhikaree's narrative suggests that because he was specifically working with American journalists, the Maoist rebels detained the journalists and Adhikaree. According to Adhikaree, the rebels directly associated him with the US correspondents, and this association made them believe that Adhikaree and his clients were spies. There is nothing new in the assumption that a news fixer might be a spy; interpreters and translators have been accused of spying for centuries (Kanya-Forstner 1994; Castillo and Schweitzer 2001; Hamilton 2009; Amich 2013). This is largely because of their culturally liminal positions, because of their ability to inhabit two or more linguistic, social, and political worlds at once. As Adhikaree suggests, there are some groups or individuals who do not appreciate such liminality. When they see a news fixer working with a foreigner who has been culturally coded as the "enemy," the news fixer can be read this way as well.

Not only can fixers be associated with foreign "enemies"; they can also be associated with foreign cash cows. Rami Aysha, a fixer and freelance reporter working in Beirut and Syria, says that over the years since the Syrian Civil War began, Syrian rebels have increasingly started seeing journalists "as a dollar sign" (pers. comm., June 2015). "And what infuses this risk of seeing you as a dollar sign," says Aysha, "is actually when you are with a foreigner." In this statement, Aysha points to the blurred line between the foreign correspondent and the locally based fixer. Though the foreigner is the one who Syrian militants might associate with wealth, the fixer (the "you," in Aysha's statement) will also be "seen as a dollar sign."

This is despite the fact that journalists and editors in the industry do not tend to view fixers as being the "same" as journalists. Indeed, correspondents and their editors tend to expect that the fixer takes care of the journalist and not the other way around. Aysha says that he was once kidnapped in Syria, alongside a Danish journalist with whom he was working. According to Aysha, he and the Danish journalist were both eventually able to get free, but the experience hurt Aysha's reputation as a local fixer and reporter (pers. comm., June 2015). Because other journalists in the area believed it was Aysha's responsibility to protect the Danish journalist, Aysha says that many correspondents in Beirut began to whisper that he wasn't good at "risk assessment." This rhetoric seemed to forget that Aysha had faced a great deal of personal danger when he and his colleague were kidnapped.

Aysha's narrative suggests a double standard in the practice of international news reporting, where fixers and other locally based media employees are held so responsible for foreign journalists' safety that they are even blamed when their own lives have been placed at risk. The burgeoning "safety culture" (Palmer 2018) that has become such a central part of the industry of foreign news reporting seems to categorize news fixers as a safety precaution for the foreign journalist, rather than focusing on how fixers themselves could be better protected. At its most vulnerable, embodied level, the precariousness of fixers' labor is hidden from view, written into the industrial discourse as something either inevitable or as something less relevant than the safety of the foreign journalist.

Even though the foreign correspondents' safety gets the most attention, the journalist usually has the luxury of leaving an unsafe region and moving on to the next one, while locally based news fixers do not always enjoy the same level of global mobility. Because they must so often stay behind when the journalist leaves, news fixers' production narratives suggest that fixers are also often targeted *in place of* foreign correspondents. For example, an anonymous fixer working in Somalia says:

> I have been threatened so many times. I can say millions of times, countless times by these bad guys—in Al-Shabaab. . . . You have to move to different neighborhoods, to different locations in the same city. For example, if I am staying where I am staying now, then I have to move in the next day or the next couple of weeks to a new location. Because it is too risky for me to stay in the same place, as these guys will always try to hunt down and assassinate me because of the work I am doing. Because I have worked with so many international people. (Pers. comm., May 2016)

Similarly, Chris Knittel, a producer and fixer working in the United States, says:

> Once the cameras and crew are gone, you must deal with any aftermath or perceived problem that may arise after the [documentary] film airs. If a gang member thinks that the editing team didn't alter his voice enough, you may have an entire blood set gunning for your head. Unlike a director and producer who flies in to film a story and then disappears, you must continue to live amongst your subjects. Relationships continue whether they are up or down, and you are always connected to the story that "lives outside the frame." (Pers. comm., September 2016)

Both of these fixers imply that locally based media employees tend to be targeted in place of foreign journalists who have already left the region. The anonymous fixer from Somalia says that he has directly experienced the problem of being the one who is left behind, perpetually changing his address to escape the wrath of local militant groups who disapprove of his work. And though Knittel works in the ostensibly "safer" and "freer" context of the United States, even he asserts that fixers "are always connected to the story that 'lives outside the frame'" (pers. comm., September 2016). This continual connection to the story can be so dangerous that it can cause the fixer to "have an entire blood set gunning for your head."

The above statements attest to some of the most extreme dangers that fixers face in the process of doing their work. Yet, there are subtler risks that fixers must navigate as well. Some of my interviewees describe the major health problems they have experienced after long, draining stints in the field. Others underscore the difficulty in maintaining close relationships with their families and the difficulty in building new relationships. Still others highlight the emotional toll that international reporting can take on them—a toll that ranges from the challenge of "keep[ing] a certain amount of distance" when covering "some really very awful stories," (Masterman, pers. comm., September 2016), to full-blown post-traumatic stress disorder. These issues can impact news fixers who cover combat, as well as fixers who work in ostensibly safer environments; and, as Knittel suggests, it is not easy for the fixer to find respite when he or she is "locally" based and, thus, is "always connected to the story that 'lives outside the frame'" (Knittel, pers. comm., September 2016).

This continued connection to the story that foreign journalists can leave behind is perhaps the major difference between the risks that fixers endure and the perils that foreign correspondents so famously face in the field. The other major difference is the level of support (or lack thereof) that fixers receive from the news organizations that hire them. Staff correspondents who work for a certain organization increasingly tend to receive free hazardous environment training, proper safety equipment, insurance, assistance if they have been kidnapped, and psychotherapy, if needed (Cottle, Sambrook, and Mosdell 2016; Armoudian 2017; Palmer 2018).

FIGURE 5.1 Journalists and news fixers alike can find themselves in situations where they need safety equipment pictured here. Free for commercial use, information here at https:// www.maxpixel.net/Human-Journalist-Press-Attack-Gas-Mask-Violence-2339771.

However, news fixers display a fairly unified perspective on whether news organizations tend to offer these benefits to them, as media employees working in the same environments as the staff correspondents. "No, absolutely not," says Fathi (pers. comm., July 2015). "Nope," says Carbajal. And Gupta also responds quite definitively of her experiences working in India:

> No, no, no, no, no, no. It's just the salary that you earn, your per day fees that you make, but on top of that in terms of insurance or any kind of benefits, any kind of safety procedures in place that ensure your well-being in case something happens—I have yet to come across something which is formal and official which takes care of that for you. (Pers. comm., June 2016)

News fixers' production narratives overwhelmingly paint a picture of a system in which their labor is not protected in the same way as the labor of the staff correspondents who often become famous for braving the perils of the field. Though some news fixers speak of piecemeal situations in which individual journalists may try to help them, they also suggest that news organizations' general lack of interest in their safety is a deeply entrenched, *systemic* problem. Since news fixers' labor is "underground" labor—since it is usually freelance, temporary, and hidden from public view—the long-standing tradition has been to pay fixers in cash and to expect that their fee will also cover any major injuries or health issues they may sustain as a result of their work. What is more, since news organizations conceptualize fixers as *part of* the security infrastructure that they build for their staff correspondents (Palmer 2017), they do not, in turn, build a security infrastructure for the fixers.

As Ingrid Le Van, a fixer working in Brazil, puts it, "there's this sort of underlying, unwritten rule, that it's part of the mix as a fixer, [that] you should know where the danger is, and it's part of your role to know if [a story] is feasible or not. And the risk is sort of factored in" (pers. comm., August 2016). Though the general idea is that "the risk is sort of factored in" to the fixers' fee, the question remains whether the fee truly covers the full extent of the risk that some fixers face. Moe Ali Nayel, a fixer working in Beirut, has a decisive opinion on whether the fixer's daily rate is enough to cover medical bills:

> Of course not. Of course not. I was beaten up once in the car while doing a story, and the journalist was a friend too, honestly, and she

couldn't do anything. She was working for a broadcast television channel. They had a large budget, but all they could offer me was a CAT scan and that's it. And they reimbursed me for it once they paid me after all. And I knew she couldn't do anything else apart from that, because literally I don't exist. . . . I don't exist in this equation. (Pers. comm., June 2015)

Nayel was lucky in the sense that the broadcast network bothered to cover the CAT scan, even though this organization did not cover the other medical bills involved in his recovery from being physically attacked on the job. Significantly, Nayel says that nothing else could be done "because literally I don't exist." In other words, Nayel's labor as a fixer is located so deeply underground that, in this case, there was no identifiable policy that would lead the news organization to fully account for his well-being.

Most news fixers say that benefits like medical insurance are firmly out of their grasp. In fact, the only fixers I interviewed who are regularly covered by insurance are those who own or work at large production companies. In those cases, the owners of the production companies typically insure the fixers who are assigned to visiting clients (Almog, pers. comm., May 2016; Stirling, pers. comm., September 2016; Anonymous, pers. comm., March 2017). Other than in these instances, receiving insurance is very rare, even for news assistants who work for big name news bureaus. The tradition is to offer a larger salary and full benefits to the foreign correspondents based at the bureau; yet, the news assistants receive a much lower salary with no health benefits at all. "To be honest," Haidamous observes, "we're asked sometimes to get like [flak] jackets, that's all. . . . they ask us, 'Do you have one? You don't? OK, it's better that we get one for you.' But not more than that." (pers. comm., June 2015). Even though this news assistant for the *Washington Post* bureau in Beirut feels more responsible for the correspondents' safety than her own, all that the bureau seems to be able to offer her in return is a flak jacket.

For fixers like Abeer Ayyoub, who work on the much more typical freelance basis, even the flak jacket is hardly a guarantee:

That's not obligatory and the fixer cannot ask for it. But I had a flak jacket of my own, and then at the beginning of the war, the organization that owns it, they took it back from me. And I felt super endangered, and now I'm trying to buy my own flak jacket as a freelancer and as a stringer on my own. No one can provide me with this very expensive flak jacket. I was employed by the Human Rights Watch in 2010, and they gave it to me and then I stopped working with them and I had to give it back. (Pers. comm., September 2014)

Ayyoub's narrative suggests that she was actually forced to relinquish her flak jacket at a time when she might have needed it the most—"at the beginning of the war" in Gaza. Ever since then, Ayyoub says she has struggled to obtain a flak jacket of her own, which can cost around USD$1,000—a prohibitive expense for freelance fixers working in poorer parts of the world.

In response to stories like Ayyoub's, some news editors say that while news organizations have not traditionally taken an institutionalized approach to protecting locally based media employees, journalists and other news executives have been able to help in other ways—namely by evacuating particular fixers and stringers from the regions where they work (Bennett, pers. comm., February 2015; Hoffman, pers. comm., February 2015; Homer, pers. comm., June 2015). For instance, Homer asserts that

> there wasn't a formal insurance system in Iraq [during the Second Gulf War], but the American networks have had a history of taking care of local employees. They did this in Vietnam. They evacuated many, many, many of their people in the days of the Vietnam War. And, in fact, I've worked with some of the guys who were Vietnamese, who were Vietnamese cameramen working for ABC in Vietnam during the war and now live in America, are American citizens, and are still doing the same job as cameramen. (Pers. comm., June 2015)

Though these types of efforts are admirable, they signal a more individualized approach to taking care of locally based media employees rather than a systematic approach. And while evacuation can sometimes be a major boon, from the fixers' perspective it can also be tricky. In order to be evacuated, the news fixer must uproot from his or her home and essentially live as an exile in a foreign region. On top of this daunting emotional transition, the bureaucracy of evacuating can also be challenging, as an anonymous fixer based in Moscow observes. This fixer feels that most of his clients would try to relocate him if he got into trouble working in Russia; yet, he would have to deal with the process of getting permission to work in the United States or the United Kingdom, as well as establishing legal residency (pers. comm.,

January 2017). This is no easy task, especially if the news organization does not offer full legal assistance to the fixer being evacuated.

The individualized approach to protecting news fixers is something that a number of my interviewees have mentioned—both the fixers and the journalists I have interviewed. While many journalists feel an emotional bond with their fixers, and while many of them do what they can to help their fixers in the field, the correspondents and even the bureau chiefs often do not have the ultimate say in what can be done to help their locally based colleagues—pointing again to the need for a more systematic approach to the problem of news fixers' safety. Velazquez describes things this way:

> You're a foreign journalist, and [your editors] send you to the Ebola outbreak in Liberia and Sierra Leone. And, of course, your network is giving you some boots and gloves and hand sanitizer, and many things that you may need to stay safe while reporting. But then you arrive there, and you find that your fixer, the guy that is actually going to take you to those dangerous places, doesn't have boots and doesn't have gloves. And normally you try, when you are in those kinds of situations, you buy some boots for him, and then you buy sanitizer for him, and then you buy gloves for him. And you do it with your own money, because you're not going to ask your network for boots for your fixer. You can, but I don't know what the administrative people are going to say. (Pers. comm., Sep 2016)

Velazquez's statement points first to the very real concern that some foreign journalists do feel for their fixers—a concern so great that they might take it upon themselves to pay for the fixers' safety equipment. Yet, this statement also points to a systematic problem, one that can hardly be solved at the individual, personal level. News organizations do not appear to have very many policies that account for news fixers' safety. Because of this, a journalist who buys a fixers' equipment may not get reimbursed, making it more difficult for reporters—most especially freelance correspondents—to individually care for their fixers. This conundrum illuminates the deep structural constraints that limit the protection of news fixers in the field. Since these media employees' labor is conceptualized as the temporary and fluid work that is outsourced at a lower cost, news institutions rarely have the proper mechanisms in place to account for fixers' safety.

Though some journalists, editors, and news fixers do say that these problems have (very recently) started improving (Owen, pers. comm., February 2015; Velazquez, pers. comm., September 2016; Riquelme, pers. comm., March 2017)—especially as far as the bigger, better-funded news outlets like the BBC are concerned (Ayyoub, pers. comm., September 2014; Rosenfeld pers. comm., May 2016)—other fixers suggest that there is far more work to be done. For instance, Kenyan news fixer Michael Kaloki says:

> I find when you work with big organizations, especially large stations, some of them do offer [temporary insurance and safety equipment]. But you usually need to ask in advance to understand what it is they will offer or not. And the other thing I find also is sometimes when you ask, the producers are not too knowledgeable about it. . . . Because a number of producers I've spoken to about this issue have had to refer to their bosses to figure out exactly what they may be able to offer to their fixers in regard to health and safety. (Pers. comm., June 2016)

Kaloki suggests that there is still not enough institutional policy in place to guarantee that the field producers and journalists will actually even know what they are allowed to offer news fixers. And though fixers like Rosenfeld assert that the BBC has become one of the main exceptions to this trend (pers. comm., May 2016), other fixers suggest that many news companies still have not systematized any significant set of standards for protecting fixers in the field.

Oddly, some news fixers rather paradoxically assert that they are unconcerned about this state of affairs. These fixers might cite the relative safety of their region—be it the frozen Swedish countryside (Peyron, pers. comm., September 2016) or the refugee camps in Lebanon (Nova, pers. comm. June 2015). Others might invoke their self-sufficiency in the field, their love of adventure (Samad, pers. comm., August 2015) or their belief that they were "built for this type of work" (Knittel, pers. comm., September 2016). Still others might reflect upon the ostensible "inevitability" of the danger in their regions, a danger so inevitable that they are no longer afraid of it (anonymous Palestinian fixer, pers. comm., July 2013; Miller, pers. comm., March 2017). In each of these cases, the news fixers' production narratives illuminate the very real risks for which these fixers are not well-protected; yet, these media employees also appear to have internalized the attitudes that situate fixers as part of the security infrastructure rather than as employees in need of security themselves.

But other news fixers are more overtly critical of this double standard. Nayel says that the safety of the fixer is one of the biggest problems in the business (pers. comm., June 2015), while Adhikaree baldly states: "Fixers are in the most danger . . . we have to think about the security of fixers" (pers. comm., August 2016). Leena Saidi, a well-known news fixer in Beirut, goes so far as to say that "if a company uses a fixer on a regular basis, then I think they're just as responsible for making sure that fixer has [received hazardous environment] training. It's the right thing" (Pers. comm., May 2013). And Immanuel Muasya, a fixer working in Kenya, says:

> I think there should be maybe like a contract that you sign, [saying] that if anything happens in the next two months, the next two, three months, or when the story breaks, these guys [the news organizations] are responsible for your safety. But I think that is also going to be a long discussion, because people will tell you, "You knew what you were getting into before you started the job." (Pers. comm., May 2016)

Muasya invokes the rhetoric of individual responsibility that permeates the international news industry more broadly (Palmer 2018), rhetoric that many fixers have internalized. News fixers' production narratives overwhelmingly suggest that these media employees are expected to take care of the foreign correspondents who hire them. Yet, this focus on the correspondents' safety rarely translates into a reciprocal focus on the fixers' well-being, especially at the institutional level. Though the task of "safeguarding the journalist" can put the fixer in grave danger, news organizations have yet to systematically take responsibility for the news fixers' safety in the field. News fixers' production narratives reveal that the risks informing their already hidden labor also remain "underground," while the vital cultural mediation in which fixers engage continues to be inadequately protected.

Conclusion

"Safeguarding the journalist" is perhaps the most important task in the news fixer's repertoire. Yet, it is also the task that most profoundly illuminates the embodied nature of fixers' underground labor. When foreign correspondents succumb to dangers in the field, they are often portrayed as heroes (Palmer 2018)—a phenomenon that is not particularly unique in the history of Western capitalism. As Edward Slavishak argues, dangerous labor has long been celebrated as a sign of masculine prowess, especially in the United States.

What is more, the laborers most at risk have long internalized this celebratory attitude toward the dangers they face as they toil for big businesses (2010). But in the case of news fixers, the risks these particular employees face are often hidden from public view or at least under-discussed in comparison to the risks faced by foreign correspondents. Even so, news fixers' bodies are constantly in danger as they do their work, partly because, without their bodies, they could not do their work at all.

Lisa Jean Moore and Mary Kosut argue that "the body is our first introduction to the performance of the self and identity—our expression of agency while at the same time its structural location in stratified worlds that limit that very agency" (2010, 2). This is at least partly because our "flesh is inscribed with meaning both from ourselves, with our consent, and by others against our will" (2010, 2). Even those news fixers who do not work in war zones must draw upon a variety of embodied cultural performances in order to complete their tasks, while also negotiating the cultural identifications imposed upon them externally. The task of safeguarding the journalist is one of many instances in which this proves to be true, but it is perhaps the task that best highlights the fact that cultural mediation is rooted in the body— and the body can fall prey to illness, strain, injury, or death as a result of engaging in this mediation.

Fixers' narratives imply that they feel personally responsible for their clients' safety and well-being. Some news fixers even think of their clients as "family" (Samad, pers. comm., August 2015), while others take great professional pride in receiving compliments on the security they provided after the fact (Haidamous, pers. comm., June 2015). Some news fixers also reveal the tendency to feel as though they are personally responsible for their own safety—especially because, as "local" media employees, they are ostensibly better equipped to take care of themselves.

Yet, other news fixers raise questions about this double standard, telling stories that illuminate the marked lack of regard that news organizations show for the well-being of the fixers their correspondents hire in the field. Though these stories suggest that individual journalists and bureau chiefs sometimes become emotionally bonded to their fixers and do what they can to help them, these stories also imply that the problem of news fixers' safety cannot sufficiently be solved at the individual level. Instead, there needs to be a deep structural change in the profession of international news reporting, where news fixers' safety would be systematically addressed—both in policy and in practice.

This type of change is extraordinarily difficult to enforce across the diverse and competing news markets that are increasingly interconnected, yet still very different from each other. As Joel Simon, executive director of the Committee to Protect Journalists asserts, disparate news organizations have disparate financial resources, as well as distinct professional cultures (pers. comm., April 2015). These factors play a huge role in the type of responsibility that news outlets might take for the various people they employ in the field, be they freelance correspondents, stringers, drivers, or fixers. Simon seems to feel that it is currently most pragmatic for the major international news outlets to take more responsibility for their various employees' safety, invoking the notion of a delicate "information ecosystem" that must be carefully protected:

> If you are an international news organization, you need to have the broadest possible vision and understanding for this information ecosystem and recognize that you have a responsibility not only for the individual that you employ or have contracted, but for all the different pieces that allow that person to function. And as those elements become further removed, then the responsibility diminishes. But, the duty of care obviously extends to anyone that this person might employ to assist with news gathering, and certainly that's clear. And then, as you move further away from that person, the responsibility is less, but still exists. (Pers. comm., April 2015)

While Simon points to the very real unevenness of approaches that various news organizations might take when addressing the problem of safety in the field, he does suggest that the wealthier, "big brand" outlets should think more critically about "all of the pieces" involved in the "information ecosystem." This book has argued that news fixers comprise a crucial—yet hidden—layer of this ecosystem, something that their production narratives reveal. Yet, Simon's statement also grapples with the question of professional proximity, implying that the "further" a given element of this ecosystem is located from the news organization itself, the lower the level of responsibility on the part of the news outlet.

The question is, how "faraway" are news fixers from the news organizations that hire them, especially if they serve as important elements of this "information ecosystem"? Other activist organizations see fixers as central enough to deserve their own safety funds. For instance, John Owen, chairman of the UK-based Frontline Club, says that his organization has a fund dedicated to helping "local fixers and news gatherers" (pers. comm., February 2015). On top of this growing attention from activist groups, many of my interviewees say that certain news organizations, such as the BBC, are becoming much better about protecting locally based media employees. Even so, these important steps have yet to be undertaken in any significantly systematic fashion. News fixers' perspectives on this problem are clear: there is much, much more work to be done on the issue of protecting the locally based media employees who often risk their lives to engage in the dynamic and essential labor of cultural mediation.

For this reason, news fixers' safety is of grave relevance, not only to news organizations but also to scholars and students. There is a profound need for scholars to more carefully consider the embodied risks that fixers face in their work. Since a number of scholars have already shown an interest in the labor of international reporting and in the question of how to achieve a truly "global" media ethics (Couldry 2013; Ward and Wasserman 2010; Ward 2013; Wasserman 2011; Rao 2011), it makes sense that these scholars should also take an interest in the precariousness of news fixers' labor. For one thing, fixers' work reveals the inevitably material aspects of global media ethics, the hard truth that ethical (or unethical) behavior in international journalism can directly impact the bodies and psyches of the people who engage in this practice. While the well-being of foreign correspondents has received increased attention from scholars and news industry practitioners, the plight of news fixers has barely been discussed at all—especially from the fixers' perspectives. Because of this, scholars need to actively engage in more egalitarian cross-cultural dialogue, listening more closely to the stories of risk that define the underground labor of international reporting.

6

Conclusion

RELINQUISHING THE STORY: WHERE DOES THE LABOR END?

*As far as I'm concerned, it's [the clients'] story. I mean
I came up with the story, but they are paying me to help
them... It's their story, and I'm helping them do it, and I'm
getting paid to do it.*

—Anonymous fixer in Palestine

*We [fixers and local journalists] are double-challenged; we
want to get the experience, we want to learn from [foreign
correspondents]. But we also want to make something of
our own.*

—LUNA SAFWAN, former fixer working in Beirut

BECAUSE THE NEWS fixer's labor is so often tied to a specific news or documentary project, and because the fixer is ultimately "not the journalist"
(Anderson, pers. comm., June 2015), at some point the work of news fixing
must come to a definitive end. It would be easy to say that after the fixer engages
in each of the important tasks that this book has described—conceptualizing
the story, navigating the logistics, networking with sources, interpreting unfamiliar languages, and safeguarding the journalist—the fixer then concludes
this work by simply handing over the final product to the correspondent or
documentarian. Yet, the act of relinquishing the story is not merely a bookend
to the fixer's work. It is not the punctuation to the purportedly linear narrative of what the news fixer's job involves. Instead, "relinquishing the story" is
something that the fixer must do throughout the process of completing all the
other tasks. In other words, the fixer is expected to relinquish the story at the
very beginning of the assignment as well as at the assignment's end.

Since the meaning of the term "story" changes throughout the foreign
correspondent's time in the field, the precise thing that must be relinquished

also changes. For instance, the act of "conceptualizing the story" requires that fixers walk a fine line between making suggestions on what Herbert Gans calls the "selection" and the "suitability" of the topic the journalist will cover (1979) and "taking over" a creative process that ultimately belongs to the foreign correspondent (Thoma, pers. comm., September 2016). In a similar vein, the work of navigating the logistics of the story involves a constant negotiation between the fixer's regionally specific knowledge of material conditions on the ground and the journalist's agenda. At this phase in the assignment, the "story" is something that must be successfully pursued, and it is up to the fixer to privilege the correspondents' agenda on how this pursuit should happen.

The same goes for the process of networking with sources. A good news source is one of the most important elements of the international news story. Because of this, the fixer is expected to respond to the journalist's need for a compelling interview, despite the fact that the client sometimes abuses the fixer's contacts or fails to consider the dignity of the source. In these cases, relinquishing the story refers to the fixer's effort at securing the best interviews, even when the client is showing cultural insensitivity. And when the fixer helps the client interpret unfamiliar languages, he or she is expected to ask another person's questions from another person's perspective. Finally, when the fixer works to safeguard the journalist, the journalist's safety regularly trumps the fixer's own. Relinquishing the story can mean many things, but, in each case, it requires a certain level of self-sacrifice on the part of the news fixer, as well as a certain level of self-erasure.

The concluding chapter to this book will first investigate why the act of relinquishing the story *matters*—for better or for worse. This section will explore news fixers' narratives about their investment or disinvestment in the stories that they have helped create. Fixers' production narratives suggest that some news fixers actively encourage and participate in their own erasure from the story, either because they are not aspiring journalists, because they are getting paid to help their clients, or because they prefer not to take on the same level of responsibility that correspondents must shoulder. Even so, other fixers "want to make something of our own," as Luna Safwan asserts in the epigraph to this conclusion (pers. comm., June 2015). For these media employees, it is essential that they feel involved in the story, and they seem to value the opportunity to construct stories by themselves.

Teasing out this ambivalence, the conclusion will also critically analyze the issues of compensation and giving credit—issues that ostensibly mark the end of the fixer's place in the story. Since the news fixer is paid to help the journalist, as the anonymous fixer working in Palestine attests in her epigraph to this chapter, it supposedly makes sense that the story "belongs" to the journalist, and not the fixer. Yet, other news fixers do not seem to agree with this stance, instead portraying the issue of compensation as a complex moment of cross-cultural exchange—a moment in which news fixers can either be shown appreciation for their contributions OR a moment in which they can be exploited by the news organizations that hire them. For the client, paying the fixer might end the fixer's labor, and it even might end the working relationship. But for the fixer, the issue of compensation illuminates the fixer's liminality in an international journalism profession that is already informed by a great deal of uncertainty.

The problem of giving credit is also a hot topic for news fixers. Most of my interviewees suggest that they do not tend to receive bylines or other forms of attribution for their contributions to the final product. Some news fixers seem indifferent to this phenomenon, while others find it to be highly problematic. Again, news fixers' ambivalence toward the act of relinquishing the story surfaces here, with certain fixers saying they have never even checked to see if they are credited, and with others asserting that they work too hard to be so completely erased. The news fixers who want to work as professional journalists especially see this as a stumbling block for their professional mobility. They wonder how they can build portfolios when their professional experience is invisible. Yet, even those fixers who do not identify as journalists sometimes seem to think that their contributions are substantial enough to merit more public appreciation.

The question of how to properly compensate and credit news fixers inspires marked ambivalence from fixers themselves. I will take fixers' ambivalence seriously in this conclusion, arguing that in the process of paying more attention to fixers' narratives on the act of relinquishing the story, scholars, students, and journalists can learn much more about the nuances of international reporting. The locally based guides who help international journalists cover the news are far more than "native informants," "forever foreclosed" within the space of the postcolonial media text (Spivak 1999), although that theoretical concept does productively gesture at the deep dependence of postcolonial texts upon these informants who have been erased from textual and sociopsychological representation. International correspondents indeed depend heavily on news fixers to write their final stories. But news fixers are active human subjects who either make a claim for their influence on the news story itself or who shrug their shoulders at their erasure and continue building relationships—and entire careers—around the concept of their own invisibility.

Investing (or Disinvesting) in Ownership of the Story

Some news fixers say that they are not particularly invested in taking full ownership of the story. For these media employees, relinquishing the story itself is a welcome relief from responsibility and the stress that might go with it. Leena Saidi, a fixer and former journalist working in Beirut, explains why she made the shift from journalist to fixer:

> I wanted more of a life, because I have two daughters that are now twenty-one and eighteen. I just wanted to be with them when they were in their teenage years, as they were growing up. I'd left them quite a lot when they were younger. . . . And I thought that fixing is ideal because you don't take the story on. Well, you take it as you know it, but you don't have to sit down and write it. You go out, you fix, you come back, it's done. You don't have to go and write it. But you've almost reported it. (Pers. comm., May 2013)

For Saidi, ownership of the story meant working longer hours—time that she could be spending with her daughters. On top of that, ownership of the story meant that she had to "sit down and write it," an extra layer of work that she was happy to hand over to someone else, once she realized her daughters were growing up without her. In Saidi's case, relinquishing the story was easy. It was a conscious choice to step back from the part of reporting that she found to be the most time-consuming. At the same time, Saidi felt that in fixing, "you've almost reported it"—in other words, the fixer "almost" does the work that Saidi herself used to gain so much satisfaction from doing. That distinction of "almost" was enough for Saidi to feel good about her work while ultimately avoiding the heavy responsibility of writing.

Haidar Adbalhabi, a fixer working in Iraq, also emphasizes the stress that comes with "owning" the story:

> [When you] work as a fixer, you don't get that responsibility. I mean like [when you are] working as a journalist, a local journalist. Because you know that anything you are editing . . . you will be responsible for it. I mean [any] things [that] an Iraqi PM or any political guy [might say], and you have to be honest, and you have to put every single word he said exactly. And you cannot change or say something he didn't say. (Pers. comm., May 2016)

In this statement, Adbalhabi seems to suggest that local journalists in Iraq bear a special burden when it comes to accuracy, a double-edged sword that can get those journalists in trouble with the Iraqi government. In contrast, Adbalhabi says that news fixers in Iraq do not carry that same burden, because they are not the ones writing the stories about the Iraqi government. Thus, in the act of relinquishing the story, Adbalhabi implies that the fixer can also ensure his or her own safety, at least where the reports themselves are concerned. Adbalhabi echoes the logic of some news fixers who work in extremely dangerous regions, and who often prefer to be erased from the final product in order to stay anonymous. This is certainly one striking reason why news fixers might feel disinvested in ownership of the story.

For other news fixers, relinquishing the story is ideal because it helps them to feel more "relaxed" in the process of doing their work. Russian fixer and videographer Valentin Savenkov uses this word when he describes the difference between playing the double role of fixer and cameraman on the one hand or simply acting as fixer on the other hand: "When I am only the fixer, I almost relaxed" (pers. comm., January 2017). Though Russian fixer and TV journalist Ksenia Yakovleva does admit that "I always have my own idea of how [stories could be reported], maybe because I work in a newsroom," she also says that "what I like about producing and fixing is that, at the end of the day I don't have to worry about it. . . . For me it's all about relax[ing], translat[ing], and that's the reporters' job to find those things they want, those ideas, how to use them" (pers. comm., January 2017).

Both Savenkov and Yakovleva note that they possess a great deal of media expertise. Savenkov was a filmmaker before the fall of the Soviet Union, and he switched to video shooting and fixing almost as soon as the Soviet Union dissolved (pers. comm., January 2017). Yakovleva works for a well-known television news network based in Moscow. Both of these fixers are also media professionals, and this expertise does indeed inform their ability—and sometimes, their impulse—to intervene in how the story is being constructed. But they both remark that when, as news fixers, they relinquish the story, they can enjoy the lower level of responsibility that comes with that act of relinquishment. Especially in Yakovleva's case, the lack of worry that accompanies the correspondents' responsibilities can help her focus on her important tasks.

Other news fixers do not feel particularly invested in taking ownership of the story because they do not identify as journalists, and they do not necessarily enjoy writing the story. For instance, Abd Nova, a former fixer who previously worked in Lebanon, says, "I never thought I would ever work as a journalist's fixer or researcher. And sometimes I was offered [the chance] to write, but I just hate writing politics" (pers. comm., June 2015). Nova says that before he was forced to flee Syria during the civil war, he went to medical school. He had hoped to be a doctor one day. Instead, he ended up "fixing" for journalists covering the Syrian refugee crisis in Lebanon, simply to pay the bills. For this reason, Nova says he never felt much concern about whether he could claim the story as his own. From his perspective, "fixing" was just about helping where he could and getting paid to give that help.

Significantly, Nova separates the work of "helping" from the act of writing the story, suggesting that the fixers' assistance is different from the more creative, skilled labor in which the correspondent engages. This attitude also surfaces in the accounts of some editors and journalists. For instance, David Hoffman, former managing editor of the *Washington Post,* says that Iraqi fixers and stringers were not paid as much as staff correspondents during and directly after the Second Gulf War because "they were just doing a different level of work" (pers. comm., February 2015). In turn, freelance correspondent Josh Wood says that, "for the most part," the fixers he hires are "just trying to make some money" (pers. comm., June 2015). And freelance correspondent Sulome Anderson takes overt ownership of the stories she tells, saying that the fixer is "not the journalist. I'm the journalist. . . . I do the work myself. . . . I have the story, I ask the questions. It's not like he's doing my job for me" (pers. comm., June 2015).

While some journalists and editors do make the same distinction that Nova makes, emphasizing this separation between those who have ownership of the story and those who do not, others see things differently. For example, Mike Garrod, creator of the World Fixer website, says, "a lot of people on our site are photographers, producers, very successful producers, very successful journalists. We've got guys there that have got thirty years of foreign correspondence work behind them" (pers. comm., August 2015). In turn, Alasdair Baverstock, a freelancer working in Mexico, says that the fixers he hires "are generally journalists themselves. The best fixer will not [be] someone who generally thinks of themself as a fixer" (pers. comm., March 2017). And Anderson notes that many fixers in Lebanon are also aspiring journalists: "They want to write or report and, God bless them, that they should. And the shitty thing about local journalists is that they are not treated the same. They're not given the same weight (pers. comm., June 2015).

Anderson highlights a sentiment that also surfaces in the production narratives of the news fixers who most decisively do feel invested in taking at least some ownership of the stories they help create. For these fixers, being treated collegially and being "involved" in the story is enough to make them feel as though their contribution matters. For instance, a former fixer and news assistant working in Russia says that some of the correspondents with whom she previously worked "were very nice people, very professional, [and] I found they were relying on me, my knowledge, my expertise, and I felt more like a colleague with whom reporters were cooperating in their project" (Anonymous, pers. comm., January 2017). Yet, this same fixer says that

> in some cases, there are journalists who kind of just give you instructions and, yes, they asked me for things to contribute, like to find ideas, find people, call people—even take some calls, translate them. But there's always some distant hierarchy. They kind of give you orders, and they work the project. So, you feel like you're just kind of following instructions, but you are not so much involved in the actual project. (Pers. comm., Jan 2017)

In this news fixer's view, journalists' efforts at maintaining the "hierarchy" between fixer and correspondent plays a distinct role in making her feel as though she is not "involved in the actual project." This lack of involvement then makes her feel less ownership of the story—perhaps the very thing that the correspondents were aiming for as they bolstered these hierarchies in the first place. But this act of distancing the fixer from the story does not go unnoticed.

Safwan emphasizes this same sense of investment, describing her work as a former staff fixer/news assistant for Lebanon's English-language news outlet, NOW Lebanon:

> I never felt that I'm actually just a fixer or someone who translates. I was in the story; I was involved in the story. I used to help in writing the story. Which was very fundamental for me, because, sometimes being a [fixer] makes you feel isolated from the story. You just translate the quotations, you develop the contacts, and then, they do the job, or they do the work. (Pers. comm., June 2015)

As Safwan's statement suggests, there is often a moment, toward the end of the assignment, when news assistants and fixers hand off the job to the correspondent—and while fixers draw upon various descriptions of this ostensibly different work that correspondents might do, they often associate it with the act of writing the story. This is why Safwan suggests that the invitation to help write the story makes her feel more involved. Safwan's stance is, in some ways, quite different from Nova's; he prefers not to help write the story, but like Safwan, he also associates writing with a higher level of labor, with work that seems to point to greater investment in (and ownership of) the story.

Some news assistants and fixers are very clear about the fact that they value writing their own stories above fixing. Nabih Bulos, a former news assistant for *the LA Times* bureau in Beirut, falls into this category: "There are some people who want to be fixers and they do it well, and that's fine, you know, that's perfectly respectful, and you probably make more money, in truth. But, the fact of the matter is, I don't see the point in fixing for someone when I could just as easily write the story myself" (pers. comm., June 2015). For Bulos, writing the story himself is tantamount to moving out of the realm of "fixing" and into the realm of reporting. He personally feels less invested in a story that he has not helped write, despite the fact that he could potentially make more money as a fixer than as a journalist. Thus, for Bulos, relinquishing the task of writing of the story is the very thing that makes him care less about the story in general.

On the other side of things, Jaime Velazquez appears to be much more enthusiastic about handing off the writing to someone else and taking the higher amount of money. This Spanish fixer and journalist working in South Africa says that fixing "is like starting to be your own reporter, and then you don't have to finish it. And then you get paid more than you get paid doing it for your Spanish newspaper or TV or whatever. So, for me, one hundred and fifty euros was really, really OK. And then I had my French colleagues telling me, 'No, you should have asked for two hundred'" (pers. comm., September 2016). In Velazquez's view, there is great value in "not having to finish" the story—in relinquishing the moment of "finishing" to someone else.

This value is especially striking for Velazquez when he considers the amount of money he can make as a fixer. The issue of compensation is a messy one, however, and although news fixers' production narratives do reveal a general sense of satisfaction with their rate of pay, not all fixers feel that "getting paid" for their services is more valuable than feeling a sense of ownership of the story. Alongside this issue, the process of compensation is complicated by the very cultural differences that fixers are hired to help their clients navigate.

Getting Paid for the Work

In the introduction to this book, I said that news fixers generally seem satisfied with the amount of money they make, despite the fact that the pay rate can vary drastically by region. For instance, a news fixer in Ghana may accept a minimum of USD$50 a day, while a news fixer in Moscow might expect USD$200 a day, and a fixer in the United States might be more accustomed to receiving anywhere from USD$400–$700 a day. Yet, other factors also come into play. The more experienced a news fixer is, the more he or she might charge the client. The rate can in turn be impacted by the perceived "dangerousness" of the assignment or the number of tasks the fixer might have to complete in a set amount of time. Finally, news fixers tend to charge the poorer freelance journalists less money, while big brand television crews might be charged much more.

Though the amount of payment can vary a great deal—and occasionally, news fixers do complain about this discrepancy—the majority of my interviewees say that they make good money as news fixers. Some fixers also say that the actual process of compensation goes smoothly. Sometimes, fixers receive a great deal of praise and appreciation for their hard work (Haidamous, pers. comm., June 2015; Duarte, pers. comm., August 2016), and, in certain cases, a fixer might even receive more money than was originally negotiated (Nekrasova, pers. comm., August 2016). There are fixers who also remark that they cannot imagine the news outlets failing to pay them for their work. This is most especially because news fixers tend to be highly networked with each other and can quickly taint the reputation of a news organization that does not hold up its end of the bargain.

Despite these good experiences with compensation, other news fixers say that their experiences have not been quite so positive. One challenge that fixers face is that clients from different cultural backgrounds might handle compensation differently. For example, Lamprini Thoma, a fixer working in Greece, says that the mode of payment

> depends on the company. There are some people who just pay you—the Australians are like that—they pay you the same day, at the end of the day, every day. I think it's something cultural, you know? Different organizations, like the BBC or *Time* magazine, they have you on contract. So, you know, it depends on who you're working with and what's the tradition in their country. (Pers. comm., September 2016)

Significantly, Thoma directly associates her clients' different modes of compensation with their cultural differences. Thoma observes that clients from one country might pay her at the end of every day, while others might work out a contract that they honor later in the process. Crucially, Thoma says that her clients pay her according to "the tradition in their country" rather than necessarily adhering to the traditions of compensation in Thoma's region of the world. As far as the issue of compensation is concerned, Thoma has to accommodate her clients' traditions rather than making them pay her according to her cultural traditions. In this regard, Thoma must act as a kind of cultural mediator even when her work is ostensibly done, stepping out of one compensatory tradition and into another, in order to finalize her labor and relinquish the story.

Navigating the question of compensation is not always easy for news fixers, especially when their cultural mores might discourage the overt discussion of money. Kosho Sato, a fixer working in Japan, says that "most Japanese [people], they have a hard time asking [about] the paying money stuff. So right after the job I ask [my clients] to pay me. Sometimes I ask [for a] written contract, or sometimes I have them give me half the money first and the rest of the money later" (pers. comm., August 2016). Interestingly, Sato suggests that his cultural tradition makes it difficult to overtly discuss money; yet he personally combats the impulse not to address payment by addressing it very directly. Like Thoma, Sato notes that he might be compensated in a number of different ways. Not only does he have to navigate the different approaches to paying the news fixer for the work—he implies that he also has to combat his own cultural traditions just to take charge of the process.

Sometimes, the clients' preferred mode of payment can be a problem for the news fixer because of cultural and political differences. For instance, Savenkov says that it can be quite difficult for a fixer in Russia if foreign journalists pay by money transfer because of Russian banks' policies regarding foreign currencies:

> I know many people who worked with foreigners accept cash only . . . very many people accept only cash because they have no US dollar account. So, it's political, in Russia. There is some specific [protocol] in sending money to Russia. You cannot transfer money from your account to my account directly. You must use a so-called correspondent bank. This may be an American bank, a big American bank that collects all the [money] transfers and then transfers them to my bank. And maybe accountants in the USA, in England, in Australia, they don't understand it. (Pers. comm., January 2017)

Savenkov says that in these cases where accountants in the United States, England, or Australia do not understand how transfers are handled in Russia, they might halt the payment, which leaves the fixer without the money that he or she needs. In these cases, the broader interconnection of news markets around the world does not necessarily point to total seamlessness in the complex labor of international reporting, nor does it simplistically point to the fast and easy flow of capital in the age of globalization.

What is more, cultural difference—and the intense disconnections that can come as a result—can disturb the process of compensation for the fixer in a very diffuse way, making it difficult for the fixer to truly let go of the assignment and move on to the next one. Since fixers often try to make these "lump sums" stretch across the weeks or months when they secure no assignments, and since they sometimes have to pay for initial fixing expenses with their own money, the failure to get paid in a timely manner can truly hurt their ability to drop one story and go on to a new one.

Velazquez addresses this issue in his discussion of the challenges of fixing in some parts of Africa, where the financial system may operate more informally than in the clients' home regions:

> Some fixers, they had to pay the hotel room for example, and they never got the money back. . . . That can happen, not because of the journalists, but because of the company. If you didn't do things in the proper way. Sometimes for example, you need an invoice, and when you go to some places, especially in Africa, you go to Mozambique or whatever, and you finally get a room, they [the concierges] are going to take a piece of paper and they are going to write you a note, saying, "One room, twenty, fifty dollars." And that is not a proper invoice. . . . And always you have the foreign journalist who has been working with you saying, "I'm so sorry, I'm so sorry, I'm really embarrassed because of this, because of what happened, but the administration people are not going to accept that invoice." (Pers. comm., September 2016)

Like Savenkov, Velazquez highlights a cultural difference that plays out more at the institutional level than at the individual level. While the foreign journalist may be sorry and embarrassed that the news fixer cannot get reimbursed for the hotel room, the administrative systems typical of larger corporations in the United States and Britain can override the feelings of individual journalists and fixers. Administrators at large news organizations based in the West are used to dealing with a very specific proof of payment—proof that may not be the cultural norm in some of the places where fixers like

Velazquez work. Because of these cultural differences at the systemic level, news fixers can struggle to be fully compensated for their labor.

Though Savenkov and Velazquez highlight the systemic nature of this problem, cultural differences on the question of payment can also trickle down to affect individual interactions between fixers and their clients. Immanuel Muasya, a fixer working in Kenya, says: "You get producers you are working with, and you go, and you ask them for maybe money for fuel, and they start being so grumpy, and they'll be like, 'Why do we need the money for fuel?' or 'Are you sure we need this and that?' And it becomes so hard—when I'm working with guys who are like that, it becomes so hard to do anything" (pers. comm., May 2016). Things can get especially difficult for Muasya when he also has to make a number of payments before the clients arrive in order to take care of the logistical issues that he is hired to help journalists navigate:

> Before the team comes, I have to pay for some stuff. I have to pay for maybe half the money for the car, for the driver to be settled, without worrying about money. I need to pay people for a couple of days before these guys can get Kenyan currency, stuff like that. Sometimes I need to pay for licenses before these guys come. And sometimes, by the time they get here, your account is messed up, you can't get any more money. So even for yourself, buying yourself food, it becomes a problem. (Pers. comm., May 2016)

Yet, Muasya observes that some journalists and producers do not want to pay for his food on the job, even when he has no money left to pay for it himself: "Sometimes you get guys who come and they're like, 'We're not going to spend money on your lunch, we don't have any money for that.' And at the end of the day they'll sit somewhere in a hotel, and they'll have a really hefty meal" (pers. comm., May 2016).

Muasya's production narrative suggests that particular clients undervalue his work at the level of financial compensation, constantly trying to "save" money by shorting him when he needs to be reimbursed. Muasya has a philosophy on why this might be: "The problem is, most of these people, when they come to Kenya, or they come to Africa, they have this view that everyone in Kenya is poor, and everyone is trying to get some money off you" (pers. comm., May 2016.). Significantly, one of the journalists I interviewed echoed this very sentiment, claiming that fixers "are always asking for money. All the time. And you can't really calculate your budget because it happens all the time. Are you willing to pay him? I don't know if we really need to pay him.

And in Somalia, our fixer was like just squeezing the money out of us every time because—well, you know. At the time, there were very, very few white Caucasians [in the area]" (Balamutenko, pers. comm., January 2017).

It is important to note that this particular journalist not only echoes Muasya's description of the logic on paying news fixers, but he also couches this logic in explicitly racialized terms. According to this journalist, his fixer was "squeezing the money out of us" at least partly because the journalist and his team were white correspondents from Russia. Arguably, this news crew's preconceived notions about their whiteness and about the blackness of their fixer directly affected the way they understood the fixers' request for help paying the expenses in the field.

Of course, this is the testimony of only one journalist. Most correspondents do not appear to explicitly draw upon racial stereotypes to explain their attitudes toward paying news fixers. Yet, it is fairly common for journalists to assert that fixers are expensive. What is more, some correspondents and editors go so far to argue that fixers make good money for the regions where they're working. David Hoffman, former managing editor of the *Washington Post*, certainly makes this argument in his justification of why the paper's Iraqi staff were paid less than the foreign staff during and directly after the Second Gulf War (pers. comm., February 2015). Alasdair Baverstock, a freelancer working in Mexico, also makes this argument, asserting, "a Mexican journalist, if you're working on a local paper, you'll earn less than minimum wage generally, maybe four thousand pesos a month. So, for them [fixers], a day of fixing is a lot better than a day of reporting" (pers. comm., March 2017).

Still, not all fixers agree that this is a fair logic or that they are paid well for where they are located. Colombian fixer Catalina Hernández baldly states that most news organizations "are cheap," though she feels she has personally worked with a few individual journalists who have tried to make up for this (pers. comm., August 2016). Similarly, Ingrid le Van, a fixer working in Brazil, says:

> Because of this frequent perception of, "Oh, [Brazil] is a developing country and they're poor," people [clients] just assume that things are cheap here. And I've traveled to many places around the world, and I can tell you it's definitely not cheap to live in Rio. I've been living here for a quite a few years now, and my daily expenses—whether it's rent, food, transport, anything—I would compare to any European country. . . . So people think that, "Oh, I'm coming to Rio, I'm going to pay [the fixer] fifty dollars and be done with it." But you know, the

standard of living here is very high, and I don't find it fair to charge that little. Not because I'm being greedy, but because the living is expensive here. (Pers. comm., August 2016)

Like Muasya, Le Van notes that journalists tend to make some problematic assumptions about how much her services are really worth—all based on their perception of how "wealthy" or "developed" Brazil purportedly might be. Yet, as Le Van suggests, it is difficult to live on the amount that many journalists initially try to pay her, especially because as a fixer she is paid by the assignment and has to make that money last until the next story comes along. In order for Le Van to relinquish one story and eventually move to the next, she has to be properly compensated.

In the most extreme cases, clients might leave the region without paying their fixer, or they might renege on the amount that was originally negotiated. Hwaida Saad, a news assistant who used to work as a freelance fixer in Beirut, says that when she was freelancing, a client once decided to pay her less than agreed. The correspondent paid her for only 12 or 13 days of work, when they had agreed upon 15 days of work: "So it happens. But, in the beginning, because I wanted to get more contacts, I didn't argue much" (pers. comm., June 2015). A few other fixers I interviewed say that at least once they had a client who did not bother to pay them at all (Haidamous, pers. comm., June 2015; Nayel, pers. comm., June 2015; Lioumi, pers. comm., September 2016). In these rarer cases, my interviewees suggest that the relationship between the fixers and their clients became neglectful and abusive, pointing to the total devaluation of the fixers' labor.

Typically, news fixers' production narratives do not suggest this level of disregard on the part of their clients. Still, the various compensatory issues outlined in this conclusion can complicate the fixers' ability to relinquish the story. Fixers might struggle to lay one assignment to rest and move on to a new one when they have no money to pay their own bills. They might also struggle to get started on the next story if their new clients expect them to pay for initial expenses out of pocket, with the vague promise of reimbursement somewhere down the line. Without having been quickly and fairly compensated for the previous assignment, it can be difficult for news fixers to shoulder the preliminary costs of the next assignment.

But alongside these concrete material concerns, the issue of compensation also illuminates another problem with the expectation that the fixer swiftly relinquishes the story, as soon as the correspondent has decided it is time. The very notion of "relinquishing" the story depends on the news fixer's status as someone who is "not the journalist" (Anderson, pers. comm., June 2015), and thus, as someone who does not own the story on a personal or professional level. Consequently, some correspondents and news editors invoke the fixer's compensation as a justification for ignoring the fixer's thoughts on how the story is told, how the journalist wants the fixer to function in the field, or how much credit the fixer should be given for the final product. The idea seems to be that fixers are fixers because of the money—because they get paid to "help" but not to report.

For instance, Baverstock bluntly says that the news fixer should not try to question the journalists' version of the story because they're getting paid for a service, and that service is to do things the journalists' way: "If the fixer knows exactly the story you're trying to tell, they have no reason to—because they're getting paid, they're working for you—they have no reason to try and hinder that" (pers. comm., March 2017). Other correspondents and editors feel that they're paying for a different service: namely, the ability to trust that the news fixer will "have their back" in the field. For example, Bill Spindle, a former *Wall Street Journal* bureau chief and security manager says, "we, from very early on, tried to hire regular people to work with us. They were not free-lance, they were on a contract. And so, we were paying them regularly. And then that way, we trusted them" (pers. comm., July 2015). Spindle is referring to the figure of the news assistant, who "regularly" works with the same news bureau. But it is interesting to note that Spindle equates the concept of steady, contracted pay with the idea that the *WSJ* staff could more easily trust the assistants they hired.

Another anonymous field producer who formerly worked for Al Jazeera echoes Spindle's notion that news organizations have to pay fixers for their trust, asserting: "I always pay the people what is due, as much as I can get away with. Even if I get the money out of my own. . . . Whatever I need, to try to keep people loyal to you in a war zone" (pers. comm., April 2013). It is important to note that this producer does not say she tries to pay fixers their due because it is the collegial or ethical solution. Instead, she implies that good compensation is a way of buying the fixers' loyalty, of ensuring that they will support the correspondent in a volatile environment.

Other correspondents and news editors may not go as far as those discussed above, but they might focus on the notion that fixers are unskilled laborers—that they are "just trying to make some money" (Wood, pers. comm., June 2015), "to make some money on the side," (Matar, pers. comm., June 2015), or that they're able to capitalize on explosive news events to make some "easy money" (Tikka, pers. comm., January 2017). In these cases, correspondents and news editors emphasize (1) their belief that news fixers are well paid, and (2) their belief that news fixers are not actually journalists (Anderson, pers. comm., June 2015). These two beliefs subtly blend together in this type of discourse, serving as justification for the fixer's lack of professional or personal ownership of the story.

Yet, while certain news fixers indeed care primarily about the money, others value their work for different reasons. Nayel says that some though some fixers "don't care if the story was done accurately, if facts are good," and that some fixers might even "make up facts in order to get the story done and get paid for it," Nayel also says that he personally "won't make [the facts] up for you. I'll tell you, I'll still do the story. I need more time. And if it probably won't be possible, I'll tell you, 'look, we can't set up this story. It's not going to happen'" (pers. comm., June 2015). Here, Nayel invokes the uncomfortable necessity of sometimes telling the correspondent "no," an issue that this book has discussed in earlier chapters. For Nayel, a news fixer who cares about the integrity of the story will say "no," even if that means he will not immediately be able "to get the story done and get paid for it." Nayel will not simply manufacture a flawed story and hand it over to the journalist, just so that he can get a paycheck—complicating the discourse that situates news fixers as nonjournalists who are only looking for easy money.

The notion of easy money also does not inspire Rami Aysha, a journalist who, like Nayel, has periodically worked as a fixer in Lebanon. Aysha tells the story of a correspondent who had already treated him rather poorly on the job—who had, in fact, abandoned him several times in the middle of a dangerous situation. At a certain point, Aysha and the correspondent found themselves in a combat zone that Aysha felt was not safe, leading him to eventually leave the correspondent to fend for himself:

> Later on, he followed me, and he complained. He was like, "Why did you leave me?" I was like, "You forgot that you left me three times already? So, you are allowed to leave me, [but] I am not allowed to leave you." And then he said, "But I will pay you money." And I was like, "Yeah, but my life is more important than your money." (Pers. comm., June 2015)

In this narrative, Aysha highlights an instance in which a client tried to use the promise of compensation to justify his rather skewed expectations: he could abandon his fixer at whim, but his fixer could not leave a dangerous situation if the correspondent wanted to stay. Aysha's narrative staunchly clarifies his own thoughts on that logic: "My life is more important than your money." With this declaration, Aysha's story profoundly contests the sentiment that fixers care primarily about their compensation, complicating that particular justification for drawing a stark boundary between fixer and correspondent.

In a less extreme example, a former Beijing news assistant for CBS and NPR says that, during his time in China, he cared more about upward professional mobility than money:

> The thing about NPR is that once you work for a certain amount of time as an assistant, they will actually promote you to associate producer. . . . I mean, technically, you're not that different from a news assistant, the work you do. But the title is all that counts, because then you can say, "I worked at NPR as an associate producer." . . . They give you a raise, a slight raise, but not very high. (Yizhou Xu, pers. comm., January 2016)

Xu's statement implies that when he was working as a news assistant, he was much more interested in the potential ability to tout his experience as an associate producer for NPR, than in the "slight raise" that accompanied this shift in title. For Xu, "getting paid" was not the issue. Instead, he welcomed the chance to move upward through the ranks and eventually be viewed as a professional journalist rather than an unskilled laborer looking for easy money.

This notion of upward professional mobility resonates even more when considering another mechanism through which news fixers are typically encouraged to relinquish the story: the issue of getting credit for their work. Nazila Fathi, who worked as a fixer in Iran during the 1990s, describes the problem this way: "We [fixers] did most of the work, we put ourselves at great risk, and we were the invisible people behind the stories. Nobody knew it. I mean, there were just the big names, on top of stories that were being nominated for the Pulitzer" (pers. comm., July 2015). Fathi highlights a controversial issue that often comes at the end of the news fixer's assignment: whether the fixer will receive visible, professional credit.

Getting Credit for the Work

Before analyzing news organizations' policies on giving news fixers credit, it is important to mention some of the other factors that might determine whether fixers receive a byline. For one thing, some fixers overtly ask not to be credited because they do not wish to be associated with any particular type of assignment. An anonymous fixer working in Moscow says, "You never know how the credit may work, because once I did a documentary for *National Geographic*, at one of the few times I actually got the credit. And for five or six years after that, I was getting requests do to more prison stories, just because I was on the credits [of that story]" (pers. comm., January 2017). For this particular fixer, it is better not to be credited at all. This way, he will not end up getting "typecast" as a fixer who only works on certain types of stories.

Alongside situations like this one, some locally based media employees—not only fixers, but also stringers and camera people—overtly ask to remain anonymous, for fear of persecution. This is especially the case when the fixers are working with news organizations whose cultural perspectives might anger the wrong people and lead the locally based media employee to be harmed. Similarly, some government officials do not like to see the names of their locally based journalists listed in foreign news reports. Fathi notes that while she was working as a fixer in Iran in the 1990s,

> the Iranian authorities did not like to see the names of fixers on the stories. I don't know why, what the problem was, but it was something that we had to fight for. They were not giving us credentials, and they kept warning us that they didn't want our names on the stories, so it was a dual battle to fight with Iranians to get credentials. Otherwise, I mean, if you don't, if you didn't have a press card in Iran, and your name appeared on the story, or if there was even an attribution, you could get into a serious problem. (Pers. comm., July 2015)

Fathi's statement underscores the fact that the opposition to giving fixers visible credit for their work can sometimes come from other areas, rather than from the news organizations themselves. Yet, Fathi also says that when she first started working as an Iran-based fixer for the *New York Times*, "[they] had this rule that fixers couldn't get bylines at all." Hence, the "dual-battle" Fathi invokes in her earlier discussion.

More than 20 years after Fathi worked as a fixer in Iran, there are now some news fixers who say that they do receive some form of attribution, at least occasionally. Carlos Duarte, a fixer working in Guatemala, says that he always gets credit for his work (pers. comm., August 2016), while Benjamin Zagzag, a fixer working in France, says that he was credited at least once (pers. comm., September 2016). Ginnette Riquelme, a Chilean fixer and photographer working in Mexico City, says that this varies by news organization; she has personally seen PBS credit their fixers at the end of their TV reports (pers. comm., March 2017). And Thoma feels that the issue of getting credit varies more by the nationality of the news organization: "Swedish journalists always do that. . . . And German journalists too. They do that, yes, they refer to us. . . . No Australians, French, American, Irish, British, no" (pers. comm., Sep 2016).

Things become even more complicated for news assistants who work regularly with major news bureaus. Though Hwaida Saad, a news assistant with the *New York Times* bureau in Beirut, says that as a freelancer she rarely received credit, she does say that the *New York Times* will at least list her as a "contributor" to the story—and occasionally, she will even get a proper byline (pers. comm., June 2015). An anonymous news assistant formerly working at the Moscow bureau for a major US newspaper says that she also received a contributor's credit, which means that her name would appear unobtrusively at the bottom of the story she helped report. Suzan Haidamous, a news assistant for the *Washington Post's* Beirut bureau says that she tends to get the contributor's credit as well, but that proper bylines listed at the beginning of the news report are scarcer: "Many, I'm talking like many [correspondents] don't even ask, 'Do you want your name to be published?'" (pers. comm., June 2015).

Here, Haidamous implies that the correspondent working on the story has a great deal of power over whether the news assistant gets a byline at all, something that Paulina Villegas, a news assistant for the *New York Times* bureau in Mexico City, also notes (pers. comm., March 2017). These statements both suggest another sort of double standard in the international reporting industry, where the correspondent—by virtue of the title he or she holds—is automatically assumed to possess so much ownership of the story that he or she can then decide whether the fixer or news assistant can claim any level of ownership at all. This is no small thing. The contributor's credit is far less visible on the page than the correspondent's byline, which means that many readers might not notice it at all. The difference between a "contributor's" credit and a byline can be substantial for a news assistant who feels invested in the story or for a news assistant who seeks upward professional mobility.

For instance, Nabih Bulos, a former news assistant for the *Los Angeles Times* bureau in Beirut, says: "It serves no purpose for me to have a contributing [credit], you know, to be like 'OK, blah, blah,' and [I] contributed something. I mean, that's nice and all. But, the fact of the matter is, I'm busting my ass off all day" (pers. comm., June 2015). Bulos says that his ultimate goal was to be a correspondent and not a news assistant—a goal he later achieved. Because of this, the contributing credit "serve[d] no purpose," and it also did not reflect the huge amount of work he feels he invested in the story. Unfortunately, Bulos implies, news assistants' work is not always valued in the same way that correspondents' work is valued.

Villegas says that an elaborate amount of haggling can go into the distinction between "how much" work a news assistant did or did not do—a distinction that also determines whether the news assistant will receive a contributor's listing or a proper byline:

> It kind of goes based on a case by case basis, I guess. Most of the time, it kind of depends on how much work I put into it . . . not in terms of like a specific number, but yes, the amount of reporting, interviews I did, and if I did "in the field" reporting. Most of the time I do get a byline if I'm traveling. But not always. I thought that was kind of a rule, but I discovered it's not. Sometimes it's not. It's weird. (Pers. comm., March 2017)

Villegas's statement points to the unpredictability of how her work will be valued by a particular correspondent. As she says, there is no "specific number" by which to determine her level of contribution to the story, and there are also no hard and fast rules. Instead, it appears that the correspondent (or in some cases, the bureau chief) will value Villegas's level of work according to their feelings on the matter at the time.

Still, news assistants are undeniably lucky to get contributor's credits, compared with what many freelance fixers have experienced. Sharad Adhikaree remarks: "I have never been given any bylines or any credits. . . . I talked to some of [my clients] initially, but they said this is the situational policy. Unless they state that they are using a freelancer or something, they cannot give [me credit]." For Adhikaree, the prospect of getting paid for his contribution is simply not enough: "OK, they pay to use my work. I mean, this is not fair, sometimes it's still not fair, because some journalists, they come, [and] they have not done enough research" (pers. comm., August 2016).

With this assertion, Adhikaree invokes a problem raised earlier in this book: news fixers' perception that foreign correspondents are sometimes unprepared for the assignment they are parachuting in to cover. Significantly, Adhikaree directly links this problem with the controversial issue of the fixer receiving a byline. Adhikaree seems to be suggesting that if a correspondent comes to Nepal without having completed the proper level of research, then it is unfair for that correspondent to take full credit for the story. If Adhikaree must work overtime to fill in all the blanks in the journalists' knowledge, then how can the journalist truly claim sole ownership of the story?

Unlike Adhikaree, other news fixers say that they do not care about whether they get a byline. For instance, Genny Masterman, a fixer working in Germany and Australia, says that "sometimes my name is in it, and sometimes it's not, but I just always have a look. I know I've worked on the project, and that's enough for me (pers. comm., Sep 2016). Masterman says that it is enough for her to personally know that she contributed to a story; yet, she also says that she "always ha[s] a look," to see whether she has received any sort of visible, professional credit. This suggests a bit of ambivalence on Masterman's part. Larisa Inic, a fixer working in eastern Europe, also reveals this ambivalence: "I don't mind if they give me a credit or not. It would be nice, it would be nice. But they give me references, so it's also cool" (pers. comm., Aug 2016). Inic implies that professional references are just as important to her as receiving credit, because through those references she can get more work as a news fixer. Yet, she also says, "it would be nice" to be directly credited with her involvement in the story.

Other news fixers are far less ambivalent on the subject. Renato Miller, a fixer working in Mexico, says that he feels he should be credited "because I was there. I'm also a very important piece of the machinery that made it happen. Yeah. You should be credited. . . . It doesn't matter if it's a wedding or if it's a firefight in Tijuana. Everybody who was there should be credited. Of course. It's only fair" (pers. comm., March 2017). Like Adhikaree, Miller invokes the notion of "fairness," suggesting that if he personally played a role in producing the final product, then he should receive visible, professional credit for his work. Another anonymous fixer and local producer working in Mexico emphasizes the fact that the fixer sometimes has to work harder than the correspondent does: "I've also had situations where you're the guy on the ground, and you get to do most of the kind of muscle, and let's say, dirty work for projects. . . . They [the correspondents] come [to Mexico], and then you stay [behind when they leave], and then, people, you know, they win prizes for your work" (pers. comm., March 2017).

Like Fathi, this particular news fixer and producer observes that fixers put an incredible—and sometimes perilous—amount of energy into a story, only to watch other people win prizes without ever crediting the fixers who helped them. Catalina Hernández, a fixer working in Colombia, says that this failure to give appropriate credit is a problem because "if it wasn't for [the fixer's work], they wouldn't be able to write their story, right?" (pers. comm., August 2016). Significantly, Hernández invokes international correspondents' deep level of dependency on the news fixers who remain invisible to news audiences: "I looked at the articles these guys wrote, and they sent me copies, but I was like, 'Oh, I would have liked for my name to have been in the bottom of the article, like "fixer, translator, thank you to—.' But that didn't happen" (pers. comm., August 2016).

Velazquez suggests that this dependency continues to be relegated to the shadows: "In the end, you are just a fixer, so you are not part of the report, your name is not there. It doesn't matter if you managed to discover where—I don't know—Saddam Hussein was hiding, because your name is not going to be anywhere. That is sometimes the really disappointing side of the fixing job. Because you really do a lot of work, and it's nowhere to be seen afterwards" (pers. comm., September 2016). If, by definition, the fixer is expected to relinquish the story, then it seems that news organizations can continue to justify their erasure of fixers' labor from the final news product. Even if, as Velazquez suggests, the news fixer breaks a major news story, that fixer would still not receive credit, because he or she is "just a fixer"—a hired hand, paid to help as much as needed and then expected to disappear.

It is in the act of relinquishing the story, then, that the "underground" quality of news fixers' work perhaps becomes most obvious. As with many types of labor in the era of global capital, this work is vital to the functioning of the world's various international news industries. Yet, by refusing to regularly and systematically give credit to news fixers for their work, these industries tend to give the impression that their correspondents are the sole laborers in the field. Even so, news fixers' production narratives paint a picture of an increasingly interconnected set of world news markets that deeply depend upon the fixers' role as cultural mediators. If news organizations truly must rely on locally based media workers to help them conceptualize the story, navigate the logistics of the assignment, network with sources, interpret unfamiliar languages, and keep their correspondents out of harm's way, then it is difficult to understand how these organizations could also expect fixers to relinquish ownership of the final product. At the very least, it seems ethical that news organizations would make news fixers' involvement much more transparent to news audiences by giving them a byline. But at the present moment, news fixers' production narratives illuminate the fact that their complicated, precarious, and vital labor remains largely underground.

Looking Ahead

News fixers' stories show that these media workers are skilled at looking ahead. From the moment their clients first contact them, to the ambivalent moment of relinquishing the story, fixers are thinking about the bigger picture: will this particular story idea be feasible to pursue, how will they address the logistics, which of their contacts should be involved, where will language barriers pose a problem, and how will they keep the client safe? Alongside each of these concerns, news fixers are always thinking about their next assignment: How can they keep their network of contacts happy, so as to use these sources again in the future, and how can they keep their clients happy enough to give them recommendations down the line? It appears that the most successful fixers live with one foot in the present and with one foot planted firmly in the future.

Yet, in order to provide the necessary level of sociopolitical context to the foreign correspondents who hire them, fixers suggest that they must also have a clear understanding of the past—most specifically, of the histories of the regions where they live and work. These histories inform the lived experiences of the people who foreign correspondents feature in their stories. Thus, "context" can be incredibly important to a news fixer, whether or not that fixer ultimately decides to argue for a certain political perspective. For instance, Nitzan Almog, a fixer working in Israel, says that there are some clients "that show a certain face of Israel, and you can't interfere with that, because they came to do a story from their point of view" (pers. comm., May 2016). At the same time, Almog says:

> I think it's important, valuable at the end, when they [the clients] leave, that I helped them to understand both sides. Because I belong to the "left" side. I'm for coexistence and peace and all that, but on the other hand, when people start talking very badly about Israel, that kind of annoys me. . . . I care for Israel, but I always try to see the agony on the [Palestinian] side and the problems on the other side. Because that's the only way the peace will come. (Pers. comm., May 2016.)

Almog indicates that while he may not try to impact the angle of his client's story, he does hope that he can at least help his clients see things from more than one perspective at the end of the assignment. What is more, he implies that he feels a personal investment in this, rather than a simplistically professional investment. Helping people to "see" the various sides to the story of his region is something that he believes might contribute to eventual peace in the region.

Another anonymous fixer working in Palestine also alludes to the importance of context, when she says: "The challenge—all the time—[is] just to find something and be true to the story. Because I've noticed that some journalists just write really cheesy stories. Stories that are easy to do, filled with stereotypes. For me, I don't want to be that person" (pers. comm., July 2013). According to this news fixer, "being true to the story" of her region of the world is tantamount to avoiding stereotypes and refusing to do the stories that are "easy to do." As many of my interviewees have argued, fixers can potentially help journalists tell more nuanced stories by providing them with the context that they could not easily discover on their own. Considering this context, often from someone else's perspective, is not "easy to do"—but it is necessary, according to the anonymous fixer from Palestine, if one hopes to "be true to the story."

This book has tried to "be true" to the stories that news fixers tell about their work—the stories that are sometimes hidden from the general public's ears. Though it is clear that fixers' narratives are told from very particular perspectives, I argue that it is time for these perspectives to be heard. All too often, scholars focus on the perspectives of the foreign correspondents who travel to unfamiliar regions instead of on the viewpoints of the people who help them complete their challenging assignments. This focus on the foreign correspondent has led to a rich scholarly literature on the profession of international reporting, a literature that contributes to scholars', students', and the general public's knowledge of an important cross-cultural practice. Even so, there are multiple layers to this practice, and the myth of the intrepid foreign reporter needs to be complicated. Without foreign correspondents' fixers, the profession of international reporting could not exist. And without heeding news fixers' perspectives on their precarious labor, scholars, journalists, and the general public will never fully understand the cultural complexity of international reporting as a professional practice and a public service.

For this reason, this book has first argued that scholars and journalists have much to gain from listening to news fixers' perspectives on the work they do. Academics and students based in the Anglophone West are accustomed to hearing the perspectives of foreign correspondents—usually of correspondents who work for major, English-language news outlets, although sometimes also of correspondents who work for organizations based in Western Europe. Especially for scholars who value the notion of journalistic objectivity, the perspectives of news fixers might be rather difficult to accept. Though many fixers value journalistic objectivity, they might also have very different understandings of what is (or is not) happening in a particular part of the world, understandings that might compete directly with journalists' concept of the "truth." Rather than writing fixers' different understandings off as bias, it might be more productive for the listener to take a step back and consider even those viewpoints that are most disruptive to the status quo.

News fixers are well-equipped to present scholars, students, and journalists with various examples of the impact that sociocultural difference continues to have on international reporting, even in the ostensibly "converged" age of globalization. This is because news fixers are, by definition, mediators of sociocultural difference. The second argument advanced in this book has emphasized the news fixer's role as cultural mediator, asserting that fixers' production narratives overwhelmingly portray their labor as culturally performative rather than merely logistical. What this means is that news fixers represent their work as an active and creative effort at mediating between different (and sometimes competing) lived experiences of race, ethnicity, gender, sexuality, religion, politics, community, and nation.

As someone who must acquaint him- or herself with a multitude of cultural identifications, the news fixer is never simplistically "local" to a specific region. What is more, the fixer's labor reveals that foreign correspondents are culturally particular rather than being abstractly global. Even those correspondents who work for the largest and wealthiest international news organizations in the world are still particular in their lived experiences and in their viewpoints. Fixers' production narratives illuminate this fact, as well as illuminating the identificatory collisions inherent to international news reporting—however seamless and far-reaching the practice of news reporting is argued to have become (Berglez 2013; Löffelholz and Weaver 2008).

The people who do the work of news "fixing" differ from each other a great deal, and they also differ from each of the disparate clients with whom they work. Even so, their stories of cultural mediation share some common themes. Especially when they describe their most valuable services, fixers tend to list the same five responsibilities: conceptualizing the story, navigating the logistics, networking with sources, interpreting unfamiliar languages, and safeguarding the journalist. News fixers represent each of these tasks as active and creative processes of cultural mediation, as a process of "assum[ing] various identities in different contexts of interaction" and engaging in "constant negotiation" with difference (Sporturno 2014, 123). While each task is an active effort at connection—at bridging cultural divides in order to help the journalist successfully tell the story—the labor of cultural mediation is inevitably also fraught with moments of disconnection and miscommunication. Thus, I have analyzed news fixers' examples of communicative failure as well as success in hopes of learning more about the unevenness and messiness that informs the practice of international reporting.

This messiness and unevenness can have a profound impact on news fixers as professionals, especially since their production narratives suggest that fixers comprise an underground economy. The third and final argument advanced in this book interrogates the hidden nature of news fixers' work as well as raising questions about news organizations' tendency to undervalue fixers' labor. Not only do news fixers address this devaluation of the work they do; this devaluation also sometimes surfaces in the interviews I conducted with journalists and editors, as well as in the journalism industry discourse (Palmer 2017). While correspondents might come to feel quite attached to particular news fixers, and while they might thank them verbally, or in behind-the-scenes trade articles, it is still rare for journalists to systematically give news fixers written, professional credit for their involvement in the story. This is due to the fact that fixers are often viewed as part of the journalistic infrastructure—as freelance laborers who provide a paid service but who ultimately are not journalists.

Though news organizations routinely outsource the indispensable labor of cultural mediation to news fixers, and though fixers might help with everything from determining what the story is to how the story will be filmed or written, fixers seem to suggest that journalists and editors still draw a line between themselves—the "skilled," creative labor—and fixers—the "unskilled," logistical labor. Indeed, it is this very line that is used to justify the expectation that fixers eventually relinquish the story altogether, either at the writing stage, the stage where bylines are determined, or, more abstractly, in terms of claiming any sort of personal or professional ownership of the product of their labor. For this reason, I argue that news fixers represent their work as unfolding "underground," though it is, in many ways, the backbone of the international reporting profession.

Should this labor remain "underground?" Some fixers do not seem concerned about the answer to this question, and their perspectives also matter. There are fixers who value the experiences that their work brings, and they respect the line that has been drawn between themselves and their clients. At the same time, other fixers feel that they deserve far more recognition for the work they do. Their perspectives matter as well. This book contends that, at the very least, scholars and journalists need to gain a clearer understanding of news fixers' perspectives on their role in international reporting. By listening to the stories that news fixers tell, we can learn much, much more about the cultural differences that continue to complicate the vital practice of international news reporting in the contemporary age.

Research Methods

In the process of conducting the research for this book, I drew upon qualitative methods that were informed by the insights found in feminist philosophy, postcolonial theory, and critical media ethics. The feminist theorist Sandra Harding has famously made a distinction between the concept of method, "techniques for gathering evidence," and methodology, "a theory and analysis of how research should proceed" (1987, 2). Following Harding, I would like to discuss both my method and my methodology in this appendix. Harding asserts that these concepts need to be reexamined epistemologically, with a reevaluation of how researchers come to "know" something in the first place (1987). This is a question I have perpetually tried to ask myself throughout the process of writing this book. How have we, as scholars, come to "know" what the practice of international reporting entails? How have we come to "know" what "the story" is and who gets to tell that story?

Intersectional feminist and postcolonial research methodologies tend to interrogate the primacy of "Western" research practices:

> From an indigenous perspective, Western research is more than just research that is located in a positivist tradition. It is research which brings to bear, on any study of indigenous peoples, a cultural orientation, a set of values, a different conceptualization of such things as time, space and subjectivity, different and competing theories of knowledge, highly specialized forms of language, and structures of power. (Tuhiwai Smith 2014, 58)

Because of the privileged position of Western research in the academic world—a research tradition in which I have also been trained—feminist and postcolonial theorists emphasize a few important methodological concepts that inform their research methods. One of these concepts is self-reflexivity, where the researcher must consider his or her own social positioning, as well as his or her own role in knowledge production (Alcoff 2014). The other concept is that of collaboration in knowledge production, where the researcher actively works with the human subjects being studied, in order to better understand the ways in which they make meaning of their own worlds (Buch and Staller 2014).

The notion of seeking sociocultural context looms large in feminist and postcolonial discussions of methodology, as does the idea of engaging with sociocultural difference (rather than trying to explain it away, in the interest of "generalizability"). These concepts are also not unfamiliar to critical media ethicists. For instance, the work of Herman Wasserman and Shakuntala Rao underscores the importance of cultural context, suggesting that there can be no "global" media ethics that exists outside of history, politics, and culture (2008; 2011; 2015). Wasserman's 2013 discussion of "ethical listening" also serves as an example of this type of methodology, in that it interrogates the hegemony of Western research traditions that assume their own universal appeal.

I have drawn heavily on the theories found in the field of critical media ethics as I have devised my methods for this research. I have also found it necessary to draw upon some of the media theories that see media practices and institutions as being informed by social privilege and power. According to Norman Fairclough, the mass media function within an ideologically inflected "social system" and contribute to the construction, rather than the mere reflection of, that system (1995, 12). This is an argument that resonates for my discussion of the international news industries' "underground" economy. Similarly, I value the work of the humanist media scholar John Caldwell, who argues that the producers of various media form their own cultures through the work that they do, and that engaging with their production narratives can help media scholars to better understand the political, economic, and sociocultural milieu in which those media institutions interact (2008).

With these critical methodologies in mind, I have primarily drawn upon the qualitative method of semi-structured, in-depth interviewing for this book. As Sharlene Hesse-Biber suggests, "A semi-structured interview is conducted with a specific interview guide—a list of written questions that I need to cover within a particular interview"—but it is not bound only to these questions, nor is it worried about the order in which these questions occur (2014, 186–187). Such an approach leaves room for spontaneity and collaboration within the interviewing process. Indeed, when I conducted my interviews, my interviewees would often "turn the tables" and begin interviewing me. I was open to this throughout the interviewing process, willing to share my stories in the same way I hoped that each interviewee would also share some of their stories.

Before I go into more detail about the interviews I conducted, I would like to engage in the same self-reflexivity that feminist and postcolonial theorists recommend. I am a white, cis-gendered woman who is also a US citizen by birth. Though I previously (and rather briefly) worked as a domestically based television news producer, and thus have some small level of "insider's" knowledge on that particular branch of US journalism as a field, I am now an associate professor of media and communications studies at a major public research university in the United States. In short, I have been trained from within the very scholarly tradition that feminist and postcolonialist standpoint theory critiques, and I am also "located" within what many would view as a privileged sociocultural position.

In the process of conducting my interviews, I did sometimes find myself speaking with a person who did not possess the same level of education that I possess or with someone who might never be able to enjoy the same international mobility that I can enjoy, due to my socioeconomic privilege and my status as a US citizen. In these cases, I tried to maintain an awareness of this inegalitarian social positioning without inadvertently victimizing the interviewee or restaging my privilege. However, the more we dived into the interview itself, the more I realized that although some of my interviewees might be coded as "less privileged" in some respects, these individuals did not think of themselves in this way. They thought of themselves as active agents in their own lives, something that it is crucial for even the most well-meaning critical scholars to remember.

Alongside that insight, I also found the concept of "privilege" to be quite slippery in general. I interviewed people who had traveled all over the world and some who had gone to graduate school. Some of my interviewees even possessed multiple national citizenships or lived in societies where (unlike in the United States) health care and other important public services were covered by the government. Thus, my purportedly "privileged" position often shifted. No matter who I was interviewing, I saw that my interviewees viewed their sociocultural backgrounds and lived experiences as being simply different from my own. Through the process of thinking self-reflexively, I was also constantly reminded that the "locally based" people I was studying could (and should) not be easily "homogenized," "romanticized," or even "victimized" (Wasserman 2011). Instead, they brought a vast level of competing knowledges and experiences to the table, very directly collaborating with me as I tried to understand the stories they told about their work as news fixers.

Overall, I interviewed 75 people who identified as "fixers"—either because they were currently doing that work or because they had formerly worked in that capacity. My interviewees have worked in 39 different countries (see figure A.1). Forty-seven of them identified as male, and 28 identified as female. No one openly identified with any other gender, a phenomenon that deserves its own future study. The vast majority of the interviewees said they had completed at least some university-level education, and many, though not all of them, specifically studied journalism at a university. Others studied everything from music, to medicine, to art. Some of these interviewees said that they hold dual national citizenships, and some have grown up outside the nations in which they hold citizenship. Some of my interviewees were technically in exile or identified as refugees. Others had the privilege of traveling to a particular location, "falling in love" with it, and staying there indefinitely.

I recruited my interviewees in three ways: (1) Through websites like the now-defunct Lightstalkers and the relatively new HackPack and World Fixer, where fixers

Appendix 1 Geographical Sample*

Nations Where Interviewees Work	Number of Interviewees Who Work There*
Lebanon	9
Israel	3
Palestine	3
Turkey	1
Pakistan	1
Egypt	1
Iran	1
Iraq	2
China	1
Indonesia	1
India	1
Nepal	1
Japan	2
Kenya	2
Somalia	1
Nigeria	1
Ghana	1
South Africa	1
El Salvador	1
Colombia	1
Brazil	1
Guatemala	1
Mexico	8
Serbia	2
Croatia	2
Hungary	1
Bosnia and Herzegovina	1
Ukraine	2
Russia	16
Sweden	1
Greece	2
France	2
Belgium	1
Italy	1
Spain	1
Austria	1
Germany	1
United Kingdom	1
United States	2

*Some of my interviewees say that they work in multiple countries, explaining why the number of interviewees listed in this table is higher than 75.

can publicly advertise their services, (2) by more broadly searching for news fixers' websites or social media profiles online, and (3) through connections I made with other interviewees who trusted me enough to share their contacts. The World Fixer website is structured so that visitors to each profile can see whether the fixer in question has been "verified" as having actually engaged in the prior work they listed on their page. I tried to make a point of (1) only interviewing those individuals who had been verified on World Fixer, or (2) only interviewing the contacts of other fixers who had been verified on World Fixer. The Lightstalkers and Hackpack websites did not have a "verification" function at the time I used them to search for interviewees. I only interviewed one person posting on Lightstalkers—Abd Nova—as the website went offline shortly after I used it. In the case of my interviewees who had posted on Hackpack, I made sure to ask detailed questions and seek detailed answers. I also noticed that these individuals often referred to each other as colleagues or competitors. In this way, I tried to ensure that my interviewees were who they claimed to be.

I also tried to interview a large number of people from a wide variety of regions and professional backgrounds, so that I could more confidently identify and make an argument for the common themes that surface among news fixers as a group of professionals. My goal was to gain an array of perspectives from people working in various geographical regions of the world. I would like to point out that I was leery of focusing solely on the category of "nation," since news fixers (as well as other people) cannot be simplistically aligned with nation-states in the age of globalization. With this goal in mind, I searched for fixers by broader geographical region, seeking a multifaceted (though not necessarily exhaustive) set of perspectives. Still, I did find that websites like World Fixer ultimately organized fixers' profiles by country, pointing to the continued (and rather paradoxical) relevance of the nation-state in the globalized era.

I was also searching for people who worked specifically with journalists or with documentary teams. This particular criterion did rule out a number of potential interviewees, since some fixers only worked with entertainment or advertising media. This criterion also led me to geographical regions of the world more heavily saturated with journalists needing fixers in the first place, revealing again the power of competition and marketability in the world's increasingly interconnected news industries. I noticed a similar logic when I drew upon the contacts of fixers whom I had already interviewed; most of their contacts were located in the same regions where they also worked.

Due to the temporal, spatial, and financial limitations inherent to any multisite, international study, I conducted a large number of my interviews on Skype, WhatsApp, or on the phone. A small selection of my interviews also had to be conducted by email, although that was not ideal. The interviews conducted by phone, Skype, or WhatsApp ranged anywhere from approximately 20–60 minutes. However, I was also aware of the field of ethnography's call for researchers to travel "to the environments or natural settings where social life occurs," (Buch and Staller 2014, 108), and so I journeyed in person to Beirut, Moscow, and Mexico City to conduct face-to-face interviews.

I worked in Beirut from May 27 to June 21, 2015. I visited Moscow January 4–13, 2017, and Mexico City March 15–23, 2017. I chose to visit these specific places because they serve as three very different but internationally significant news hubs, where I was sure to be able to locate and interview a diverse array of news fixers. I also interviewed one former fixer in person when I was conducting research on war reporters in Doha from April 2–11, 2013. Similarly, I interviewed one fixer in person while conducting research on war reporters in Istanbul from July 1–11, 2015.

In these environments, I especially relied on networking with a few preliminary contacts I made ahead of time to get more locally based fixers to speak with me. The interviews I conducted in person tended to last longer than my remote interviews, usually running somewhere between 40 and 90 minutes. It should be noted that I worked with my university's research ethics office (IRB) to ensure the protection of my interviewees. If someone asked me to remain anonymous, then I did not include any identifying information on that person in this book. My IRB protocols discouraged my taking videos or photos of the people I interviewed, which is why none of them appear in this book's photos.

With each of my interviewees, I loosely structured our conversation around topics that emerged from the following research questions:

1. How do fixers understand and value the work they do?
2. In what ways do fixers feel that cultural differences (e.g., race, ethnicity, class, gender, nationality, religion) inform news fixers' labor?
3. What do fixers think about questions of security and risk in the field?
4. How are fixers compensated for their labor, and how do they feel about this?

Sometimes, my interviewees would spend a great deal of time responding to these research questions, while at other times they steered the discussion in different directions that were also fruitful. I made a point of letting this happen rather than trying to maintain control of the conversation.

This approach allowed me to identify emergent themes that were important to the people being interviewed, themes that informed the larger narratives fixers were constructing about their work. I analyzed my interview transcripts with the goal of letting these stories speak on their own terms, rather than attempting to impose too many predetermined categories upon the data. In order to more thoroughly analyze what turned out to be a vast volume of data, I used the MAXQDA software for qualitative data analysis. This software helped me code my material in a more flexible manner, discovering the themes that emerged as I went along.

Finally, in this research I also drew upon interviews conducted with 60 foreign correspondents, news editors, and news executives to provide my readers with these perspectives as well. Though the goal of this book was to focus on news fixers' own perspectives on their work, I found it useful to place fixers' perspectives alongside the sometimes very different, and sometimes very similar, viewpoints of the people who

Appendix 2 News Fixers Interviewed*

1. Anonymous fixer working in Palestine # 1, July 2013
2. Anonymous fixer working In Palestine # 2, July 2013
3. Abeer Ayyoub, fixer working in Gaza, September 2014
4. Leena Saidi, fixer working in Beirut, May 2013
5. Moe Ali Nayel, fixer working in Beirut, June 2015
6. Luna Safwan, former NOW Lebanon news assistant, June 2015
7. Abd Nova, fixer formerly working in Beirut, June 2015
8. Anna Lekas Miller, fixer and freelance foreign correspondent working in Beirut, June 2015
9. Suzan Haidamous, news assistant for *Washington Post* Beirut bureau, June 2015
10. Rami Aysha, fixer working in Beirut, June 2015
11. Hwaida Saad, news assistant for *New York Times* Beirut bureau, June 2015
12. Nabih Bulos, former news assistant and current correspondent for *LA Times* Beirut bureau, June 2015
13. Anonymous fixer and photographer working in Turkey, July 2015
14. Salman Siddiqui, former AFP stringer and freelancer working in Pakistan, April 2013
15. Mostafa Sheshtawy, fixer formerly working in Egypt, July 2015
16. Nazila Fathi, former freelance fixer and contract correspondent for *New York Times* in Iran, July 2015.
17. Samad, fixer working in Iraq, August 2015
18. Yizhou Xu, former CBS and NPR news assistant in Beijing, January 2016
19. Haidar Adbalhabi, fixer working in Iraq, May 2016
20. Oren Rosenfeld, fixer and producer working in Israel, May 2016
21. Immanuel Muasya, fixer working in Kenya, May 2016
22. Anonymous fixer working in Somalia, May 2016
23. Samuel Okocha, fixer working in Nigeria, May 2016
24. Vedomey Komi Mawufemo, fixer working in Ghana, May 2016 (interview by email)
25. Nitzan Almog, fixer and producer working in Israel, May 2016
26. Michael Kaloki, fixer working in Kenya, June 2016
27. Noam Shalev, fixer and producer working in Israel, June 2016 (interview by email)
28. Gloria Samantha, fixer working in Indonesia, June 2016
29. Namrata Gupta, fixer working in India, June 2016
30. Anonymous fixer working in El Salvador, August 2016
31. Catalina Hernández, fixer working in Colombia, August 2016
32. Ingrid Le Van, fixer working in Brazil, August 2016
33. Carlos Duarte, fixer working in Guatemala, August 2016
34. Daniel Saneo, fixer working in Serbia and Croatia, August 2016
35. Anonymous fixer working in Japan, August 2016

36. Sharad Chirag Adhikaree, fixer working in Nepal, August 2016
37. Kosho Sato, fixer working in Japan, August 2016
38. Larisa Inic, fixer working in Hungary, Serbia, and Croatia, August 2016
39. Dzmitry Halko, fixer working in Ukraine, August 2016 (interview by email)
40. Anna Nekrasova, fixer working in Ukraine, August 2016
41. Niclas Peyron, fixer working in Sweden, September 2016
42. Lamprini Thoma, fixer working in Greece, September 2016
43. Genny Masterman, fixer working in Germany and Austria, September 2016
44. Anonymous fixer working in Italy, September 2016 (interview by email)
45. Jaime Velazquez, fixer and correspondent working in South Africa, September 2016
46. Benjamin Zagzag, fixer working in France, September 2016
47. Irene Lioumi, fixer working in Greece, September 2016
48. Chris Knittel, fixer and producer working in the United States, September 2016 (interview by email)
49. Elizabeth Stirling, fixer and producer working in the United States, September 2016 (interview by email)
50. Elie Petit, fixer working in France, September 2016 (interview by email)
51. Anonymous fixer working in Moscow, January 2017
52. Evgeni Balamutenko, fixer and TV correspondent working in Moscow, January 2017
53. Alyona Pimanova, local producer and head of a Russian production company, Munro Productions, January 2017
54. Daniel Smith, local producer and head of a Russian production company, Munro Productions, January 2017
55. Artem Galustyan, fixer and correspondent working in Moscow, January 2017
56. Anonymous former news assistant for Moscow bureau of major US newspaper, January 2017
57. Alexander Bratersky, fixer working in Moscow, January 2017
58. Ksenia Yakovleva, fixer and television news producer working in Moscow, January 2017
59. Vasiliy Kolotilov, fixer working in Moscow, January 2017
60. Konstantin Salomatin, fixer working in Moscow, January 2017
61. Valentin Savenkov, fixer and videographer working in Moscow, January 2017
62. Anonymous fixer working in Moscow, January 2017
63. Diana Kultchitskaya, former fixer working in Moscow, January 2017
64. Anonymous fixer and documentarian working in Moscow, January 2017
65. Taras Rynza, fixer and videographer working in Moscow, January 2017
66. Stanislav Solovkin, fixer and producer working across former Soviet Union, December 2016 (interview by email)

67. Ginnette Riquelme, fixer and photojournalist working in Mexico City, March 2017
68. Alasdair Baverstock, fixer and freelance correspondent working in Mexico City, March 2017
69. Paulina Villegas, news assistant for *New York Times* Mexico City bureau, March 2017
70. Irina Minaeva, fixer working in Mexico City, March 2017
71. Ulises Escamilla Haro, fixer working in Mexico City, March 2017
72. Renato Miller, fixer working in Mexico City, March 2017
73. Prometeo Lucero, fixer and photojournalist working in Mexico City, March 2017
74. Anonymous local producer and head of a production company in Mexico City, March 2017
75. Maritza Carbajal, fixer working in Mexico City, March 2017

---

*Some of my interviewees asked to remain anonymous. Their names and other identifying information do not appear in this book.

hire them. This brought more complexity to the topics discussed in this book, providing readers with a few possible viewpoints from which to understand the phenomena in question.

My interviews with correspondents and news executives were also semi-structured, focusing mainly on questions of how journalists hire fixers, what those fixers do, whether they receive protection, and how much they get paid. Many of these interviews were conducted on Skype, WhatsApp, or by phone, although some were conducted in person during my aforementioned site visits. Some of these interviews with journalists and news executives were conducted specifically with the goal of talking about news fixers, and a very few of the interviewees that fell within this category also doubled as interviewees in the "fixer" category. In other words, these individuals said that they have worked as both correspondents and fixers. This is something that I have tried to clarify in the text of this book. Some of my other interviews with journalists and executives were actually conducted for an earlier research project, with different research goals in mind. In these cases, I went back through my "old" transcripts to see what these journalists and news executives had said about fixers. To my surprise, I found that they had said a great deal. Their stories deserve a place in this book as well.

Appendix 3 Correspondents and News Executives Interviewed

1. Joel Simon, Committee to Protect Journalists executive director, April 2015
2. Ray Homer, former ABC Baghdad bureau chief and Transterra Media content officer, June 2015
3. Roger Matar, CEO of Newsgate production house, June 2015
4. Ayman Mhanna, SKeyes Media executive director, June 2015 (interview by email)
5. Philip Bennett, former *Washington Post* managing editor, February 2015
6. John Owen, former head of CBC Television News, and chairman of the Frontline Club, February 2015
7. Bill Spindle, former Middle East bureau chief and current energy writer for *Wall Street Journal*, July 2015
8. David Hoffman, former *Washington Post* foreign editor, February 2015
9. Mike Garrod, Founder of World Fixer website, August 2015
10. William Schmidt, former *New York Times* deputy managing editor, March 2015
11. Susan Chira, former *New York Times* foreign news editor, November 2016
12. Alyona Pimanova, local producer and head of a Russian production company, January 2017
13. Daniel Smith local producer and head of a Russian production company, Munro Productions January 2017
14. Anonymous local producer and head of a Mexican production company, Munro, Productions, March 2017
15. Alasdair Baverstock, fixer and freelance correspondent working in Mexico City, March 2017
16. Sandra Patargo, Article 19 Protection and Defence Program, March 2017
17. Artem Galustyan, fixer and correspondent working in Moscow, January 2017
18. Nikolay Korzhov, Russian freelance correspondent in China, January 2017
19. Iida Tikka, Finnish freelance correspondent in Moscow, January 2017
20. Evgeni Balamutenko, fixer and TV correspondent working in Moscow, January 2017
21. Jaime Velazquez, fixer and correspondent in South Africa, September 2016
22. Taghreed El-Khodary, former stringer for the *New York Times,* April 2015
23. Anonymous correspondent for a major US newspaper in Istanbul, July 2015
24. Anonymous photojournalist and fixer in Turkey, July 2015
25. Anna Lekas Miller, fixer and freelance foreign correspondent working in Beirut, June 2015
26. Yusuf Sayman, freelance photojournalist in Turkey, July 2015
27. Samya Kullab, former correspondent for Lebanon *Daily Star*, current senior correspondent at Iraq Oil Report, June 2015
28. Simon McGregor-Wood, former ABC news correspondent, current correspondent for TRT World

29. Sulome Anderson, freelance correspondent in Beirut, June 2015
30. Nour Malas, *Wall Street Journal* correspondent in Beirut, June 2015
31. Jeff Neumann, freelance correspondent in Beirut, June 2015
32. Josh Wood, freelance correspondent in Beirut, June 2015
33. Kareem Shaheen, *Guardian* correspondent in Beirut, June 2015
34. Liz Sly, *Washington Post* bureau chief in Beirut, June 2015
35. Lourdes Garcia-Navarro, former correspondent and current on-air host for NPR, July 2014
36. Marquita Pool-Eckert, former CBS correspondent, February 2015
37. Dalia Khamissy, former AP photo editor in Beirut, June 2015
38. Abigail Hauslohner, *Washington Post* correspondent, February 2013
39. Andrew Mills, former freelance correspondent in Beirut, April 2013
40. Anonymous Al Jazeera field producer, April 2013
41. Shawn Baldwin, freelance photojournalist, February 2013
42. Ben Gittleson, former freelance correspondent, current assignment editor at ABC news, February 2013
43. Hala Gorani, CNN correspondent and anchor, February 2013
44. Michael Holmes, CNN correspondent and anchor, January 2013
45. Angus Hines, ABC field producer, February 2013
46. Caroline Wyatt, BBC correspondent, May 2013
47. Hashem Ahelbarra, Al Jazeera English correspondent, April 2013
48. Holly Pickett, freelance correspondent, July 2013
49. Kate Adie, BBC correspondent, June 2013
50. Lama Hasan, ABC correspondent, January 2013
51. Jonathan Miller, ITN correspondent, May 2013
52. Alexander Marquardt, ABC correspondent, January 2013
53. Noreen Jameel, former field producer for Al Jazeera, current consultant at VICE Media, February 2013
54. Rachel Beth Anderson, former freelance correspondent and current filmmaker, January 2013
55. Rosie Garthwaite, former freelance correspondent, current film producer February 2013
56. Paul Wood, BBC correspondent, February 2013
57. Zeina Khodr, Al Jazeera English correspondent, January 2013
58. Anonymous CBS correspondent in Syria, December 2012
59. Anonymous CNN camera woman, December 2012
60. Anonymous former NBC correspondent, June 2012

References

Alcoff, Linda. 2014. "The Problem of Speaking for Others." In *Just Methods: An Interdisciplinary Feminist Reader*, ed. Alison M. Jaggar. Oxfordshire: Taylor and Francis. Kindle edition, 484–495.

Aldama, Arturo. 2003. *Violence and the Body: Race, Gender, and the State*. Bloomington: Indiana UP.

Allan, Stuart, and Barbie Zelizer. 2004. *Reporting War: Journalism in Wartime*. New York: Routledge.

Amich, María Gómez. 2013. "The Vital Role of Conflict Interpreters." *Nawa Journal of Language and Communication* 7, no. 2: n.p.

Appelbaum, Richard P., and William Robinson, eds. 2005. *Critical Globalization Studies*. New York: Taylor and Francis.

Armoudian, Maria. 2017. *Reporting from the Danger Zone: Frontline Journalists, Their Jobs, and an Increasingly Perilous Future*. New York: Routledge.

Banks, Miranda, Bridget Conor, and Vicki Mayer. 2016. *Production Studies, The Sequel: Cultural Studies of Global Media Industries*. New York: Routledge.

Bassnett, Susan. 2014. *Translation Studies*. 4th ed. New York: Routledge.

Berglez, Peter. 2013. *Global Journalism: Theory and Practice*. New York: Peter Lang.

Bermann, Sandra, and Michael Wood, eds. 2005. *Nation, Language, and the Ethics of Translation*. Princeton, NJ: Princeton UP.

Bhabha, Homi. [1988]. 2006. "Cultural Diversity and Cultural Differences." In *Post-Colonial Studies: A Reader*, ed. Bill Ashcroft et al. New York: Routledge, 155–157.

Bhabha, Homi. 1994. *The Location of Culture*. New York: Routledge.

Bielsa, Esperança, and Susan Bassnett. 2009. *Translation in Global News*. New York and London: Routledge.

Boczkowski, Pablo J. 2010. *News at Work: Imitation in an Age of Information Abundance*. Chicago: U of Chicago P.

Boyd-Barrett, Oliver. 1980. *The International News Agencies*. Ann Arbor: U of Michigan P.

Boyd-Barrett, Oliver, and Terhi Rantanen, eds. 1998. *The Globalization of News*. Thousand Oaks, CA: Sage.

Broussard, Jinx Coleman. 2013. *African American Foreign Correspondents: A History*. Baton Rouge: Louisania State UP.

Bruff, Ian. 2013. "The Body in Capitalist Conditions of Existence: A Foundational Materialist Approach." In *Body/State: Gender in a Global/Local World,* ed. Angus Cameron, Jen Dickinson, and Nicola Smith. Surrey, UK: Ashgate, 74–90.

Buch, Elana D., and Karen M. Staller. 2014. "What Is Feminist Ethnography?" In *Feminist Research Practice: A Primer*, ed. Sharlene Hesse-Biber. Thousand Oaks, CA: Sage. Kindle edition, 107–144.

Bunce, Mel. 2010. "'This Place Used to Be a White British Boys' Club': Reporting Dynamics and Cultural Clash at an International News Bureau in Nairobi." *The Round Table* 99, no. 410: 515–528.

Bunce, Mel. 2011. "The New Foreign Correspondent at Work: Local-National 'Stringers' and the Global News Coverage of Darfur." 1–36. http://openaccess.city.ac.uk/3600/1/The_new_foreign_correspondent_at_work.pdf

Burbank, Jane, and Frederick Cooper. 2014. "Imperial Trajectories." In *Thinking Globally: A Global Studies Reader*, ed. Mark Juergensmeyer. Berkeley: U of California P, 36–40.

Caldwell, John Thornton. 2008. *Production Culture: Industrial Reflexivity and Critical Practice in Film and Television*. Durham, NC. Duke UP.

Cameron, Angus, Jen Dickinson, and Nicola Smith, eds. 2013. *Body/State: Gender in a Global/Local World*. Surrey, UK: Ashgate.

Carlson, Matt. 2017. *Journalistic Authority: Legitimating News in the Digital Era*. New York: Columbia UP.

Carlson, Matt, and Seth C. Lewis, eds. 2015. *Boundaries of Journalism: Professionalism, Practices and Participation*. New York: Routledge.

Casanova, Erynn Masi de, and Afshan Jafar, eds. 2013. *Bodies Without Borders*. New York: Palgrave MacMillan.

Castillo, Susan, and Ivy Schweitzer. 2001. *The Literatures of Colonial America: An Anthology*. Hoboken, NJ. Wiley.

Chakrabarty, Dipesh. 2004. "Where Is the Now?" *Critical Inquiry* 30, no. 2: 458–462.

Chatterjee, Partha. 2005. "The Nation in Heterogeneous Time." *Futures* 37: 925–942.

Cisneros, Sandra. 1991. *Woman Hollering Creek, and Other Stories*. New York: Vintage.

Cohen, Erik. 1985. "The Tourist Guide: The Origins, Structure and Dynamics of a Role." *Annals of Tourism Research* 12, no. 1: 5–29.

Cottle, Simon, Richard Sambrook, and Nick Mosdell. 2016. *Reporting Dangerously: Journalist Killings, Intimidation and Security*. New York: Springer.

Couldry, Nick. 2013. "Why Media Ethics Still Matters." In *Global Media Ethics: Problems and Perspectives*, ed. S. J. Ward. Chichester: Wiley-Blackwell, 13–28.

Cronin, Michael. 2003. *Translation and Globalization*. New York: Routledge.

Cronin, Michael. 2017. "Translation and Globalization." In *The Routledge Handbook of Translation Studies*, ed. Carmen Millán and Francesca Bartrina. New York: Routledge, 491–502.

Crystal, David. 2012. *English as a Global Language*. Cambridge: Cambridge UP.

Darian-Smith, Eve, and Philip McCarty. 2017. *The Global Turn: Theories, Research Design and Methods for Global Studies*. Berkeley: U of California P.

Dell'Orto, Giovanna. 2016. *AP Foreign Correspondents in Action: World War II to the Present*. New York: Cambridge UP.

Fairclough, Norman. 1995. *Media Discourse*. London and New York: Bloomsbury Academic.

Fernández-Ocampo, Anxo. 2014. "Engravings of Interpreters in the Photographic Era." In *Framing the Interpreter: Towards a Visual Perspective*, ed. Anxo Fernández-Ocampo and Michaela Wolf. New York: Routledge, 27–36.

Gans, Herbert J. 1979. *Deciding What's News: A Study of CBS Evening News, NBC Nightly News, Newsweek, and Time*. Evanston, IL: Northwestern UP.

Griffiths, Gareth. [1994] 2006. "The Myth of Authenticity." In *Post-Colonial Studies: A Reader*, ed. Bill Ashcroft et al. New York: Routledge, 165–168.

Hall, Stuart. [1990] 2003. "Cultural Identity and Diaspora." In *Theorizing Diaspora: A Reader*, ed. Jana Evans Braziel and Anita Mannur. Malden, MA: Blackwell, 233–246.

Hall, Stuart, Chas Critcher, Tony Jefferson, John Clarke, and Brian Roberts. [1978] 2013. *Policing the Crisis: Mugging, the State and Law and Order*. 2nd ed. New York: Palgrave Macmillan.

Hallin, Daniel C. 1986. *The Uncensored War: The Media and Vietnam*. Berkeley: U of California P.

Hamilton, Alastair. 2009. "Michel d'Asquier, Imperial Interpreter and Bibliophile." *Journal of the Warburg and Courtauld Institutes* 72: 237–241.

Hamilton, John Maxwell. 2011. *Journalism's Roving Eye: A History of American Foreign Reporting*. Baton Rouge: Louisiana State UP.

Hamilton, John Maxwell, and Eric Jenner. 2004. "Redefining Foreign Correspondence." *Journalism* 5, no. 3: 301–321.

Hannerz, Ulf. 2004. *Foreign News: Exploring the World of Foreign Correspondents*. Chicago: U of Chicago P.

Harding, Sandra G. 1987. *Feminism and Methodology: Social Science Issues*. Bloomington: Indiana UP.

Hardt, Hanno. 1990. "Newsworkers, Technology, and Journalism History." *Critical Studies in Media Communication* 7, no. 4: 346–365.

Hardt, Hanno, and Bonnie Brennen, eds. 1995. *Newsworkers: Toward a History of the Rank and File*. Minneapolis: U of Minnesota P.

Herman, Edward, and Robert McChesney. 2001. *Global Media: The New Missionaries of Global Capitalism*. London: Continuum.

Hesse-Biber, Sharlene. 2014. "Feminist Approaches to In-Depth Interviewing." In *Feminist Research Practice: A Primer*, ed. Sharlene Hesse-Biber. Thousand Oaks, CA. Sage. Kindle edition, 182–232.

Holland, Robert. 2017. "News Translation." In *The Routledge Handbook of Translation Studies*, 2nd ed., ed. Carmen Millán and Francesca Bartrina. New York: Routledge, 332–346.

Holloway, J. Christopher. 1981. "The Guided Tour: A Sociological Approach." *Annals of Tourism Research* 8, no. 3: 377–402.

Italiano, Federico and Michael Rössner, eds. 2012. "Translatio/n: Narration, Media, and the Staging of Differences." Bielefeld, Germany: Transcript.

Juergensmeyer, Mark, ed. 2014. *Thinking Globally: A Global Studies Reader*. Berkeley: U of California P.

Kanya-Forstner, A. S. 1994. "French Missions to the Central Sudan in the 1890s: The Role of Algerian Agents and Interpreters." *Paideuma* 40: 15–35.

Karttunen, Frances. 2000. "Interpreters Snatched from the Shore: The Successful and the Others." In *The Language Encounter in the Americas, 1492–1800*, ed. Edward G. Gray and Norman Fiering. New York and Oxford: Berghan Books, 215–229.

Kellner, Douglas. 1992. *The Persian Gulf TV War*. Boulder, CO: Westview Press, 1992.

Kellner, Douglas. 2003. *From 9/11 to Terror War: The Dangers of the Bush Legacy*. Lanham, MD: Rowman and Littlefield.

Knightley, Phillip. 2004. *The First Casualty: The War Correspondent as Hero and Myth-Maker from the Crimea to Iraq*. Baltimore: John Hopkins UP.

Krishnaswamy, Revathi. 2008. "Postcolonial and Globalization Studies: Connections, Conflicts, Complicities" In *The Postcolonial and the Global*, ed. Revathi Krishnaswamy and John C. Hawley. Minneapolis: U Minnesota P, 2–21.

Langford, Rachael. 2014. "Framing and Masking." In *Framing the Interpreter: Towards a Visual Perspective*, ed. Anxo Fernández-Ocampo and Michaela Wolf. New York: Routledge, 39–50.

Lefebvre, Henri. 1992. *The Production of Space*. Hoboken, NJ: Wiley.

Löffelholz, Martin, and David Weaver. 2008. *Global Journalism Research: Theories, Methods, Findings, Future*. Ann Arbor: U Michigan P.

Luna, José Carlos de la Puente. 2014. "The Many Tongues of the King: Indigenous Language Interpreters and the Making of the Spanish Empire." *Colonial Latin American Review* 23, no. 2: 143–170.

Lung, Rachel. 2011. *Interpreters in Early Imperial China*. Amsterdam/Philadelphia: John Benjamins.

Mairs, Rachel, and Maya Muratov. 2015. *Archaeologists, Tourists, Interpreters: Exploring Egypt and the Near East in the Late 19th-Early 20th Centuries*. London: Bloomsbury.

Massey, Doreen. 1994. *Space, Place, and Gender*. Cambridge, UK: Polity.

Matheson, Donald, and Stuart Allan. 2009. *Digital War Reporting*. Cambridge: Polity.

McClintock, Anne. 1995. *Imperial Leather: Race, Gender, and Sexuality in the Colonial Contest*. New York: Routledge.

McLeary, Paul. 2006. "The Stringers." *Columbia Journalism Review* 44 (March/April): 20–22.

Miller, Toby. 2007. *Cultural Citizenship: Cosmopolitanism, Consumerism, and Television in a Neoliberal Age*. Philadelphia: Temple UP.

Mitra, Saumava. 2017. "Adoptability and Acceptability of Peace Journalism Among Afghan Photojournalists: Lessons for Peace Journalism Training in Conflict-Affected Countries." *Journal of the Association for Journalism Education, UK* 6, no. 2: 17–27.

Moeller, Susan. 2009. *Packaging Terrorism: Co-Opting the News for Politics and Profit*. Hoboken, NJ: John Wiley and Sons.

Moore, Lisa Jean, and Mary Kosut, eds. 2010. *The Body Reader: Essential Social and Cultural Readings,* New York: New York UP.

Moraga, Cherríe. 1983. *Loving in the War Years*. Boston: South End Press.

Morgan, Jean. 2001. "Rivals Launch Backlash Against 'Foolhardy' Ridley." *Press Gazette*, October 10. Http://Www.Pressgazette.Co.Uk/Node/21092.

Murrell, Colleen. 2010. "Baghdad Bureaux: An Exploration of the Interconnected World of Fixers and Correspondents at the BBC and CNN." *Media, War & Conflict* 3, no. 2: 125–137.

Murrell, Colleen. 2013. "International Fixers: Cultural Interpreters or 'People Like Us'?" *Ethical Space* 10, nos. 2/3: 72–79.

Murrell, Colleen. 2015. *Foreign Correspondents and International Newsgathering: The Role of Fixers*. New York: Routledge.

Nayar, Pramod, ed. 2016. *Postcolonial Studies: An Anthology*. Malden, MA: Blackwell.

Nerone, John, and Kevin G. Barnhurst. 2003. "US Newspaper Types, the Newsroom, and the Division of Labor, 1750–2000." *Journalism Studies* 4, no. 4: 435–449.

OED Online. 2007. "Logistic, Adj. and N." Oxford UP. http://www.oed.com/view/Entry/109812.

Palmer, Jerry. 2007. "Interpreting and Translation for Western Media in Iraq." *Translating and Interpreting Conflict* 28: 13–28.

Palmer, Jerry, and Victoria Fontan. 2007. "'Our Ears and Our Eyes': Journalists and Fixers in Iraq." *Journalism* 8, no. 1: 5–24.

Palmer, Lindsay. 2016. "'Being the Bridge': News Fixers' Perspectives on Cultural Difference in Reporting the 'War on Terror.'" *Journalism*, June. https://doi.org/10.1177/1464884916657515.

Palmer, Lindsay. 2017. "Lost in Translation." *Journalism Studies* 19, no. 9: 1331–1338. https://doi.org/10.1080/1461670X.2016.1271284.

Palmer, Lindsay. 2018. *Becoming the Story: War Correspondents Since 9/11*. Urbana: U of Illinois P.

Palmer, Lindsay, and Jad Melki. 2018. "Shape Shifting in the Conflict Zone." *Journalism Studies* 19, no. 1: 126–142.

Paterson, Chris. 2010. "The Hidden Role of Television News Agencies: 'Going Live' on 24- Hour News Channels." In *The Rise of 24-Hour News Television: Global Perspectives,* ed. Stephen Cushion and Justin Lewis. New York: Peter Lang, 99–112.

Paterson, Chris. 2014. *War Reporters Under Threat: The United States and Media Freedom*. London: Pluto.

Paterson, Chris A., and Annabelle Sreberny. 2004. *International News in the 21st Century*. Washington, DC: Georgetown UP.

Paterson, Chris, Kenneth Andresen, and Hoxha Abit. 2011. "The Manufacture of an International News Event: The Day Kosovo Was Born." *Journalism* 13, no. 1: 103–120.

Pedelty, Mark. 1995. *War Stories: The Culture of Foreign Correspondents*. New York: Routledge.

Pennycook, Alastair. 2017. *The Cultural Politics of English as an International Language*. Oxfordshire, UK: Taylor and Francis.

Powers, Matthew. 2018. *NGOs as Newsmakers: The Changing Landscape of International News*. New York: Columbia UP.

Pratt, Mary Louise. [1992] 2008. *Imperial Eyes: Travel Writing and Transculturation*. 2nd ed. New York: Routledge.

Rao, Shakuntala. 2011. "The 'Local' in Global Media Ethics." *Journalism Studies* 12, no. 6: 780–790.

Rao, Shakuntala, and Herman Wasserman. 2015. *Media Ethics and Justice in the Age of Globalization*. Basingstoke, UK: Palgrave MacMillan.

Ricchiardi, Sherry. 2006. "Out of Reach." *American Journalism Review* 28 (April/ May): 28–35.

Robertson, Roland. [1995] 2006. "Glocalization." In *The Postcolonial Studies Reader*, 2nd ed., ed. Bill Ashcroft, Gareth Griffiths, and Helen Tiffin. London and New York: Routledge, 477–480.

Robinson, William. 2005. "What Is a Critical Globalization Studies? Intellectual Labor and Global Society." In *Critical Globalization Studies*, ed. Richard P. Appelbaum and William Robinson. New York: Taylor and Francis, 11–18.

Roland, Ruth. 1999. *Interpreters as Diplomats: A Diplomatic History of the Role of Interpreters in World Politics*. Ottawa: U of Ottawa P.

Said, Edward. 1978. *Orientalism*. New York: Pantheon Books.

Salazar, Noel B. 2006. "Touristifying Tanzania: Local Guides, Global Discourse." *Annals of Tourism Research* 33, no. 3: 833–852.

Sambrook, Richard. 2010. "Are Foreign Correspondents Redundant?" Reuters Institute for the Study of Journalism. http://reutersinstitute.politics.ox.ac.uk/our-research/ are-foreign-correspondents-redundant.

Seo, Soomin. 2016. "Marginal Majority at the Postcolonial News Agency: Foreign Journalistic Hires at the Associated Press." *Journalism Studies* 17, no. 1: 39–56.

Sharma, Sarah. 2014. *In the Meantime: Temporality and Cultural Politics*. Durham and London: Duke UP.

Shome, Raka, and Radha Hegde. 2002. "Postcolonial Approaches to Communication: Charting the Terrain, Engaging the Intersections." *Communication Theory*, 12, no. 3: 249–270.

Slavishak, Edward. 2010. "Made by the Work: A Century of Laboring Bodies in the United States." In *The Body Reader: Essential Social and Cultural Readings,* ed. Lisa Jean Moore and Mary Kosut. New York: New York UP, 147–163.

Smith, Linda Tuhiwai. 2014. "Research Through Imperial Eyes." In *Just Methods: An Interdisciplinary Feminist Reader,* ed. Alison M. Jaggar. Oxford and New York: Taylor and Francis. Kindle edition, 57–67.

Spivak, Gayatri Chakravorty. 1999. *A Critique of Postcolonial Reason: Toward a Vanishing History of the Present.* Cambridge: Harvard UP.

Spoturno, María Laura. "Revisiting Malinche: A Study of Her Role as an Interpreter." In *Translators, Interpreters, and Cultural Negotiators: Mediating and Communicating Power from the Middle Ages to the Modern Era,* ed. Federico M. Federici and Dario Tessicini. New York: Palgrave Macmillan, 121–135.

Tessicini, Dario. 2014. "Introduction: Translators, Interpreters, and Cultural Negotiation." In *Translators, Interpreters, and Cultural Negotiators: Mediating and Communicating Power from the Middle Ages to the Modern Era,* ed. Federico M. Federici and Dario Tessicini. New York: Palgrave Macmillan, 1–9.

Thussu, Daya Kishan. 2007. "The 'Murdochization' of News? The Case of Star TV in India." *Media, Culture & Society* 29, no. 4: 593–611.

Thussu, Daya Kishan, and Des Freedman. 2003. *War and the Media: Reporting Conflict 24/7.* Thousand Oaks, CA: Sage.

Tomlin, Julie. 2001. "BBC Crew's Trek to Make Kabul Rendezvous." *Press Gazette,* November 14. http://Www.Pressgazette.Co.Uk/Node/21153.

Tuchman, Gaye. 1980. *Making News: A Study in the Construction of Reality.* New York: First Free Press.

Tumber, Howard, and Frank Webster. 2006. *Journalists Under Fire: Information War and Journalistic Practices.* Thousand Oaks, CA: Sage.

Tymoczko, Maria, ed. 2010. *Translation, Resistance, Activism.* Amherst: U of Massachusetts P.

Usher, Nikki. 2014. *Making News at The New York Times.* Ann Arbor: U of Michigan P.

Usher, Nikki. 2016. *Interactive Journalism: Hackers, Data, and Code.* Urbana: U of Illinois P.

Venuti, Lawrence. 1998. *The Scandals of Translation: Towards an Ethics of Difference.* New York: Routledge.

Ward, Stephen J. A., ed. 2013. *Global Media Ethics: Problems and Perspectives.* Hoboken, NJ: John Wiley and Sons.

Ward, Stephen J. A., and Herman Wasserman, eds. 2010. *Media Ethics Beyond Borders: A Global Perspective.* New York: Routledge.

Wasserman, Herman. 2011. "Towards a Global Journalism Ethics via Local Narratives." *Journalism Studies* 12, no. 6: 791–803.

Wasserman, Herman. 2013. "Journalism in a New Democracy: The Ethics of Listening." *Communicatio: South African Journal for Communication Theory and Research* 39, no. 1: 67–84.

Wasserman, Herman, and Shakuntala Rao. 2008. "The Globalization of Journalism Ethics." *Journalism* 9, no. 2: 163–181.

Williams, Kevin. 2011. *International Journalism*. Thousand Oaks, CA: Sage.

Wright, Kate. 2018. *Who's Reporting Africa Now? Non-Governmental Organizations, Journalists, and Multi-Media*. London: Peter Lang.

Youngs, Gillian. 1999. *Political Economy, Power, and the Body: Global Perspectives*. Basingstoke, Hampshire: Palgrave MacMillan.

Zelizer, Barbie. 2007. "On 'Having Been There': 'Eyewitnessing' as a Journalistic Key Word." *Critical Studies in Media Communication* 24, no 5: 408–428.

Zelizer, Barbie, and Stuart Allan. 2002. *Journalism After 9/11*. New York and London: Routledge.

Index